Law Rela[...] Financial [...]

Graham Roberts

The Chartered Institute of Bankers
Emmanuel House
4–9 Burgate Lane Canterbury Kent CT1 2XJ
United Kingdom

CIB Publishing is the imprint of the Chartered Institute of Bankers, a non-profit making registered charity, and are distributed exclusively by Bankers Books Limited which is a wholly owned subsidiary of the Chartered Institute of Bankers.

ISBN 0–85297–491–4

To C.C. for helping me discover the energy to
write this book

Graham Roberts is Director of Banking Programmes at London Guildhall University and a Senior Visiting Fellow at Queen Mary and Westfield College. After practising at the Bar, he joined the academic world in order to specialise in banking law. He has many years experience of lecturing and examining in this subject and has written for banking and legal journals. He is the author of the *Law Relating to International Banking*.

Contents

Table of Cases

Table of Statutes

Preface

There is an enormous amount of law which can be relevant to banking. Even taking the term in its traditional sense this is so and as banking expands into financial services generally so the scope widens further. Any textbook on the subject thus has to be selective both in deciding what topics to include and in determining the relative emphases granted to the chosen topics.

The parameters of this book are that it is devoted entirely to the law of England and Wales. This necessarily includes some European law but no law from other jurisdictions is included and no international law is included. Regulation of banking and of financial services is also excluded because the law awaits a fundamental change in this area with the inception of the Financial Services Authority. This book therefore aims to cover the law relating to the private relationships which banks establish with their domestic customers, including business customers.

One of the interesting aspects of the law that is within the scope of this book is its history. It emerged from nineteenth century contract law cases which established a pro-customer culture, perhaps because the customer was typically middle class in those days when workers were paid in cash and had no need of a bank account. As banking expanded through the population in the twentieth century, banks started to introduce express terms into their contracts with customers which naturally leant towards the interests of the banks. This development in consumer contracts, which was reflected in all industries, was met by the introduction of consumer protection legislation which tilted the pendulum once more. Interestingly, this consumer protection legislation also benefited business customers in many cases. In the last decade the self-regulation trend has emerged along with the advent of alternative forums for the resolution of disputes such as the Office of the Banking Ombudsman. These trends recognise the attractions of flexible Codes of Practice and of a forum which removes the litigation cost risk which deters a litigant facing the financial might of a large corporation.

One of the effects of this latest development is that few cases are coming before the courts so there is little opportunity for judicial interpretation of current legal issues, another is that the non-legal Codes of Practice are beginning to assume as much importance as the law in some areas of banking. It follows that the views taken on both the law and on the Codes by the Office of the Banking Ombudsman are of some significance. In this book I have therefore attempted to set out these matters alongside the law when they impact on a given topic, in order to give the reader a full picture of the legal and extra-legal rules applicable to the topic.

I was delighted to have the opportunity to discuss some of the issues with Michael Reddy, Chris Eadie and Hugh Williams of the Office of the Banking Ombudsman. I thank them and I also thank Susan Ward and her legal team at APACS for the benefit of their knowledge. I am also grateful to Alastair Rutherford-Warren and to Walter Hall and Mohamed Khan. The Banking Code which appears in Appendix Three remains the joint copyright of the British Bankers Association, the Buildings Societies Association and APACS. The Mortgage Code which appears in Appendix Two remains the copyright of the Council of Mortgage Lenders. I would like to acknowledge the profound contribution of Andrew Laidlaw to the first two editions of the original incarnation of this book and the considerable care taken over the production of the present edition by Finola McLaughlin of the Chartered Institute of Bankers. Finally I would like to thank Agnes, Jesse and John for their moral support.

In the text, wherever a case was heard before an appeal court, the letters CA, HL or PC indicate the court concerned. The law is as stated at 1 September 1998.

Graham Roberts
London

1   The banker-customer relationship

1.1 INTRODUCTION

The banker-customer relationship has long been held to be based on a contract between the parties.[1] The English common law of contract permits the parties to reach any bargain they please with only a limited degree of interference but in recognition of the extent of inequality of bargaining power in the market place, statutory provisions have gradually been introduced[2] which can override the terms of any agreed contract in order to protect the interests of a party with weak bargaining power who enters into a contract with a party of greater power. Such protection is in particular brought in for the benefit of a party who is considered to be a 'consumer' when dealing with a party who is carrying on a business. More recently a further development has been the introduction of self-regulatory provisions[3] which grant consumers certain rights which exist outside of the law and which are enforceable through alternative forums such as the Office of the Banking Ombudsman.

The contract which arises from a banker-customer relationship can take a number of forms but it can usefully be considered in three separate categories:

(a) contracts between banks and large corporate customers of roughly equal bargaining power;

[1]*Joachimson v Swiss Bank Corporation [1921] 3KB 110.*
[2]*Commencing with the Unfair Contract Terms Act 1977.*
[3]*The Code of Banking Practice (First Edition) was introduced in 1991. See G. Roberts (1995) 8 JIBFL 385. The Mortgage Code was introduced in 1997. See A. Rutherford-Warren (1998) 5 JIBFL 192.*

(b) contracts between banks and smaller corporate or unincorporated business customers;

(c) contracts between banks and consumer customers.

The statutory and self-regulatory provisions to be discussed below refer to these categories. A bank in a banker-customer contract should note that:

(i)   it is never able to exclude liability for another's death or personal injury resulting from negligence[4];

(ii) it can only exclude liability for other loss arising from negligence if it is reasonable to do so[5]. A major factor in determining whether it is reasonable to do so is the balance of bargaining power between the parties[6] thus in category (a) relationships above, it is much more possible to exclude liability for this type of loss;

(iii) when it deals with the customer on its written standard terms of business, it cannot exclude or restrict its liability for its breach of contract, nor can it claim to be able to render a performance substantially different from that which was reasonably expected of it.[7] These restrictions apply to all contracts with consumers whether on standard terms of business or not.[8] This rule thus applies to all category (c) relationships and to most category (b) relationships;

(iv) in contracts with consumers which are not individually negotiated, any term which, contrary to the requirement of good faith, causes a significant imbalance in the parties' rights and obligations to the consumer's detriment is not binding on the consumer;[9]

[4]*Unfair Contract Terms Act 1977, section 2(1).*

[5]*Section 2(2).*

[6]*Schedule 2.*

[7]*Section 3.*

[8]*Section 3(1)*

[9]*Unfair Terms in Consumer Contracts Regulations 1994. This rule does not, however, apply to the main subject matter of the contract nor to the adequacy of the price for the services supplied. It would appear to follow from this that the interest rate charged for a loan is not capable of being rendered unenforceable as unfair on the consumer.*

(v)   in all contracts, an implied term is included which requires the bank to carry out its service to the customer with reasonable care and skill.[10] Any attempt to exclude the effect of this term will be subject to the Unfair Contract Terms Act and, in the case of contracts with consumers, to the Unfair Terms in Consumer Contracts Regulations;

(vi) in all contracts with 'personal customers', there is a requirement that all written terms and conditions will be fair in substance.[11] This rule applies only to category (c) relationships and is directly enforceable only through the Office of the Banking Ombudsman. Some banks do not belong to the Banking Ombudsman scheme.

The recent history of proposals for change to the banker-customer relationship begins with the commissioning by the then Conservative government of the Review of Banking Services Law and Practice in 1987. This Review Committee reported in 1989[12] with a great number of proposals for legislative change and a Code of Practice was also proposed. In March 1990 the Government published a White Paper entitled 'Banking Services: Law and Practice'.[13] Only a small number of minor legislative changes survived from those recommended by the Review Committee and these related mostly to cheques, to electronic funds transfers and to payment cards. Fewer still of these have been enacted, the main examples include statutory recognition of the 'account payee' crossing on cheques and the permitting of truncation of cheques. The White Paper did, however, adopt the notion of a non-statutory statement of best practice and in December 1991 a Code of Practice entitled 'Good Banking' was published jointly by the British Bankers Association, the Building Societies Association and the Association for Payment Clearing Services. The governing principles of the Code were stated to include:

---

[10]*Supply of Goods and Services Act 1982 section 13.*
[11]*The Banking Code, Third Edition.*
[12]*Known as the 'Jack Report', 1989, Cm622.*
[13]*Cm 1026.*

(a) banks will act fairly and reasonably in all their dealings with their customers,

(b) banks will help customers understand how their accounts operate and seek to give them a good understanding of banking services,

(c) to maintain confidence in the security and integrity of banking and card payment systems.

The Third Edition of the Code, published in 1997, sets out a more comprehensive list in requiring banks to (amongst others):

(a) act fairly and reasonably in all their dealings with the customer;

(b) give information on services and products in plain language;

(c) help the customer to choose a product or service to fit his needs;

(d) help the customer understand the financial implications of products such as mortgages and savings products;

(e) have safe, secure and reliable banking systems;

(f) correct errors and handle complaints speedily;

(g) consider cases of financial difficulty sympathetically and positively.[14]

The Code addresses a number of specific areas of banking practice, the law relating to which is dealt with in this book, for example, opening an account, the incorporation of express terms and conditions in the banker-customer relationship, the levying of charges, the duty of confidentiality, bankers' references, and various matters concerning the use of plastic cards. The provisions of the Code on these matters are dealt with in the relevant parts of the following text. The Code is also set out in full in Appendix 3. The Mortgage Code was introduced in 1997 and a Second Edition was published in April 1998. It contains similar 'Key Commitments' to the Banking Code. Its most significant provisions relate to advice–giving by lenders and intermediaries as to which mortgage to choose and which ancillary insurance products are chosen. It is set out in full in Appendix 2.

It must be noted, however, that the Codes do not constitute law as such. Breach of them by a bank entitles the customer to make a

[14]*The Banking Code Key Commitments, section 1.1.*

complaint to his bank and failing satisfaction then to the Office of the Banking Ombudsman,[15] assuming the bank concerned is a member of the scheme. The Banking Ombudsman is empowered to hear complaints relating to the provision of banking services by a bank to an individual.[16] Thus customers can complain in respect of the service offered to them by their banks but 'banking services' is so defined as also to permit a guarantor of an individual's debt to make a complaint against the beneficiary bank as can the payee of a cheque backed by a cheque guarantee card against the paying bank, a true owner of a cheque erroneously paid into an account of a collecting bank against that collecting bank and a requestor of a banker's reference against the bank which provided the reference.[17] The Ombudsman's Terms of Reference define 'individual' to include not only sole traders but also partnerships and even small companies.[18]

The Ombudsman may make an award in the complainant's favour up to a maximum sum of £100,000 based upon what is appropriate to compensate the customer for loss or damage or inconvenience suffered by him by reason of the acts or omissions of the bank.[19] The Ombudsman is not restrained by judicial rules on the assessment of damages. He should have regard to what is fair in all the circumstances as well as any applicable rule of law, general principles of good banking practice and any relevant code of practice and he may deem any maladministration or other inequitable treatment by a bank as constituting a breach of that bank's obligation to the complainant.[20] In practice, the Ombudsman will also consider a complaint which is statute-barred on the basis that the complainant became aware of the grounds for complaint after the cause of action

---

[15]*Or in the case of a building society to the Office of the Building Societies Ombudsman. The Banking Ombudsman scheme was established in 1986.*
[16]*The Office of the Banking Ombudsman Terms of Reference April 1997, para 1.*
[17]*para 29(c).*
[18]*Defined as a company with an annual turnover of less than £1 million, and not part of a group of companies, ibid para 29(a).*
[19]*para 12.*
[20]*para 14.*

arose in law – in effect applying Latent Damage Act principles to claims based in contract. Note that a case before the courts may now be stayed pending a complaint being considered by the Ombudsman. He is not bound by the precedent of his own previous decisions and he may reject a complaint as frivolous or vexatious.

There are two ways in which a complaint may be removed from consideration by the Ombudsman. First, the Ombudsman may do so if he considers it more appropriate for the matter to be heard by a court or other forum.[21] Second, a bank may give the Ombudsman written notice that it wishes a complaint against it to be withdrawn under the 'test case' procedure as the bank believes the complaint involves an issue of general importance to the bank or involves an important or novel point of law.[22] If the Ombudsman finds the bank's case to be reasonable he shall cease to consider the complaint on the bank's undertaking to pay the complainant's costs in any subsequent case in the courts, including the costs arising from any appeal by the bank. It should also be noted that the Ombudsman will not hear complaints based purely upon a bank's commercial judgment such as whether to make a loan or how much to charge for a loan.

The Banking Ombudsman scheme is non-statutory and as such, banks join the scheme voluntarily. Once in the scheme, a bank is considered to be legally obliged to pay any award made against it. It is free to leave the scheme afterwards, however.[23] By contrast, the Building Societies Ombudsman is a statutory scheme under which building societies must be in the scheme but are not bound to pay an award so long as they publish their reasons for refusal to do so.

The Banking Code is limited to banks' dealings with their 'personal customers in the United Kingdom'. This term is defined in the Code as a 'private individual who maintains an account including . . . an account held as an executor or trustee but excluding the accounts of sole traders . . . or who receives other services from

[21]*para 16(e).*
[22]*para 20.*
[23]*In 1997, 111 banks and subsidiary companies were in the scheme and less than 4 complaints in 1,000 were received against banks not in the scheme, The Banking Ombudsman Scheme Annual Report 1996–1997.*

a bank or building society'.[24] The Ombudsman will thus hear a complaint from a business customer and from small companies but will not apply the Code in deciding the case. He may, however, apply any Business Customer Code which the respondent bank may have issued. The Mortgage Code applies to all loans, other than overdrafts, secured on the home which a personal customer owns and occupies, unless the loan is governed by the Consumer Credit Act.

It is an interesting question whether the courts will apply the Codes in a case concerning the banker-customer relationship. They may be taken to be part of the implied terms of the contract even though they are not themselves of direct legal effect. It is assumed, however, that the express intention of the Codes to limit themselves to non-business customers would prevent them from being taken as an implied term of category (a) and (b) relationships.

1.2 DEFINITION OF A BANK

The legal definition of a bank is relevant because certain rights and obligations attach to a bank at common law, e.g. a bank enjoys the right to exercise the banker's lien[25] and a bank is entitled to the protection of statute when paying and collecting cheques.[26] Similarly a bank is impliedly obliged to observe the duty of confidentiality.[27]

The Banking Act 1987 establishes a framework whereby the Bank of England authorises institutions to refer to themselves as banks and under this Act, the definition of a bank for the purposes of certain specific statutes (such as the Agricultural Credits Act 1928) is simply an institution authorised under the Banking Act. For the purposes of what constitutes a bank when applying the protective provisions of the Bills of Exchange Act 1882 and the Cheques Act 1957, the definition of a bank is not based upon authorisation under the Banking Act 1987 but upon common law. This common law

---

[24]*Banking Code, 'Useful Definitions'.*
[25]*See 1.15 below.*
[26]*See chapter 5.*
[27]*See 1.9 below.*

definition of a bank is provided by United Dominion Trust Ltd v Kirkwood.[28] It was held that there are three essential characteristics of a banking business:

(a) collecting cheques for customers;
(b) paying cheques drawn by their customers;
(c) keeping current accounts for their customers.

It appears that all three must be satisfied in order for an institution to be considered a bank at common law.

1.3 DEFINITION OF A CUSTOMER

A person becomes a customer of a bank when an account is opened for him, and at the same time a contract is formed.[29] In Woods v Martins Bank[30] it was held that the contract was formed well before an account was opened. The branch manager of M Bank advised W to invest in a company customer of the same branch. This advice was held to be grossly negligent but as this case predated the decision in Hedley Byrne v Heller,[31] there was no question of liability on the part of the bank unless a contract existed between W and the M Bank. It was held that W became a customer when the bank accepted his instructions to collect money from his account with another institution and to pay it to the company and to retain the balance to W's order.

Since the *Hedley Byrne* decision it is open to the courts to find a bank liable in tort for negligent advice to a non-customer. Indeed, as a matter of general law, a bank may be liable to any person against whom it commits a tort. A person may only become a customer, however, when a contract is formed with the bank.

The principal reason from a bank's point of view for determining when a person is a customer is for the purposes of section 4 of the Cheques Act 1957 where a bank may be protected in collecting a

[28]*[1966] 2 QB 431 CA.*
[29]*Commissioners of Taxation v English, Scottish and Australian Bank [1920] AC 683 PC.*
[30]*[1959] 1 QB 55.*
[31]*[1964] AC 465 HL, see 1.11 below.*

cheque when it does so for a customer. It is thus protected whenever it collects a cheque for someone who has an account with it. This is so even when the stolen cheque was the first and only cheque ever paid into the account.[32] Cashing a cheque for a person who does not have an account with the bank was not considered to be collecting a cheque for a customer in Great Western Railway Co. v London and County Banking.[33]

It was suggested by Lawrence LJ in the Court of Appeal in Lloyds Bank v E.B. Savory & Co.[34] that a bank is not collecting a cheque for a customer when a person pays in a cheque at a different bank from the one where he has his account, and that this is so even where the cheque is paid in at a different branch of the same bank. If this is correct, the customer must be considered a customer of an individual branch, not of the whole bank.

1.4 THE DEBTOR-CREDITOR RELATIONSHIP AND OTHER IMPLIED TERMS

In Foley v Hill,[35] it was held that when a customer pays money into his account, the bank becomes a debtor to the customer creditor. The money becomes the property of the bank and the bank has borrowed the money from its customer. In Balmoral Supermarket Ltd v Bank of New Zealand[36] the timing of the ownership of the money passing to the bank was considered. An employee of the plaintiff was depositing a substantial sum of cash with the defendant bank and had emptied his bag onto the counter midway between him and the cashier. The cashier had picked up one bundle of notes and counted them. At that moment robbers entered the bank and stole the uncounted cash. It was decided that this money was still the property of the customer as the bank had not indicated its

---

[32]*Commissioners of Taxation case, see above.*
[33]*[1901] AC 414 HL.*
[34]*[1932] 2 KB 122 CA; on appeal to HL [1933] AC 201 where this point was not considered.*
[35]*(1848) 2 HL Cas 28 HL.*
[36]*[1974] 2 NZLR 155.*

acceptance of it. In Chambers v Miller,[37] the payment was being made in the other direction in that the plaintiff was cashing a cheque drawn on the defendant. He was given the cash and was counting it when the defendant banker realised there was insufficient funds in the account to cover the transaction. The defendant asked for the money back, which the plaintiff refused to do. The defendant proceeded to detain him and take it from him by force. This resulted in liability for false imprisonment and assault.

Certain important matters flow from the principle that deposited money becomes the property of the bank. First, the bank is free to do what it likes with the money and is not bound to account to its customer for what it does with it. The bank is merely liable to repay the money to the customer when he demands it. Second, if the bank fails to repay on demand, the customer ranks only as an unsecured creditor in any claim against an insolvent bank. In these circumstances, however, a customer may benefit from the statutory set-off provisions of section 323 of the Insolvency Act 1986 so that, for example, if he owes a debt to the bank on another account which exceeds his credit balance, his loss may be nil.

The Deposit Protection Board operates a scheme under the Banking Act 1987 which will refund 90% of eligible deposits with an authorised bank, up to a maximum deposit of £20,000. Thus the maximum compensation is £18,000. To qualify for compensation, the deposit must be in a currency of the European Economic Area and be made with an office of the authorised bank in the EEA. Deposits with banks whose home state is elsewhere in the EEA are normally covered by the deposit scheme operated by the home country even if the deposit is made with a branch in the UK. The Credit Institutions (Protection of Depositors) Regulations 1995 direct all EEA-based institutions to implement a deposit protection scheme of a minimum standard. Banks from outside the EEA with branches in the UK must join the UK scheme unless they can show that a scheme in their home country covers the deposits made with their UK branch. Non-EEA currency deposits are not protected under the UK scheme. Deposits in the same name with a bank are aggregated (i.e. the limit is £20,000 per person not per account) and

[37]*(1862) 13 CBNS 125.*

joint accounts are divided equally between the account holders. Companies[38] enjoy protection in the same way as individuals.

The earliest reported case to deal with the generality of implied terms in the banker-customer contract was Joachimson v Swiss Bank Corporation.[39] They included:

(a) the bank will receive the customer's deposits and collect his cheques;
(b) the bank will comply with written orders (i.e. cheques) issued by its customer, assuming there is sufficient credit in the account;
(c) the bank will repay the entire balance on the customer's demand at the account holding branch during banking hours;
(d) the bank will give reasonable notice before closing a customer's account, at least if it is in credit;
(e) the customer will take reasonable care when writing his cheques.

It was also stated that the relationship between bank and customer is contained in one contract which may encompass a variety of matters, as opposed to there being separate contracts for each service offered by the bank to a customer.

In Libyan Arab Foreign Bank v Bankers Trust,[40] L had Eurodollar deposits amounting to over $300 million with the bank. There were two accounts, one was held in New York and one at a London branch. The bank refused to repay the deposit on L's demand as a US Presidential order had sought to freeze the accounts. It became important to decide whether the contract was subject to English or to New York law. It was held that there was one contract between the parties, although the New York account was subject to New York law and the London account was subject to English law. It was also decided that, in the absence of any express agreement to the contrary and applying *Joachimson* term (c) above, L was entitled to demand the balance held on the London account in cash. This was despite evidence that it would involve seven plane journeys from New York to bring over the necessary dollar bills.

In the English law of contract, any implied term can normally be

---

[38]*Not including other financial institutions.*
[39]*[1921] 3 KB 110 CA.*
[40]*[1989] QB 728.*

negated or altered by an express agreement between the parties to the contract. This and other important issues arose in Tai Hing Cotton Mill Ltd v Liu Chong Hing Bank,[41] a case which underlines the implied term that a bank must only act on its customer's valid instructions and not on any forgery of those instructions.

T Ltd had a current account with three different banks in Hong Kong. It had mandated the banks to pay cheques which were signed by its managing director. L, the accounts clerk of T Ltd, forged the managing director's signature on 300 cheques which totalled $HK 5.5 million and these were all paid by the banks. The forged cheques were payable to companies and L set up accounts into which these were paid. When L's fraud was exposed after five years, he fled to Taiwan and the money was not recovered from him. T Ltd therefore claimed recovery of the money from the banks.

Prima facie the banks were liable to T Ltd since the cheques were forged, T Ltd had given no authority to pay and no estoppel could arise since T Ltd as a company customer had no knowledge of the forgeries.[42] The banks raised a number of points in their defence, however:

(a) they claimed there should be an implied term to the effect that a customer has a duty to take reasonable precautions to prevent forged cheques being presented for payment on his account. It was clear that T Ltd's accounting system was lamentably negligent in allowing L to cover his tracks in perpetrating his fraud;

(b) they claimed there should be an implied term that a customer has a duty to check the statements of account which his bank sends him and where the unauthorised debits will appear. If the customer fails to raise queries, his claim against the bank should be prejudiced. Nobody in T Ltd, apart from L, had examined the bank statements for the five years that the fraud was going on;

(c) alternatively to the above, they claimed the customer should be under a duty in the tort of negligence to take care to prevent forgeries and check his statements.

All of the above submissions were dismissed by the Privy Council

[41] *[1986] AC 80 PC.*
[42] *See 5.9 below.*

who reiterated the principles established in London Joint Stock Bank v Macmillan and Arthur[43] and in Greenwood v Martins Bank[44] that a customer only has duties:

(a) to exercise reasonable care when drawing cheques to prevent forgery and alteration, and
(b) to notify the bank if he knows of forgeries on his account.

A customer therefore is not liable if he walks along the street tearing off unsigned cheques from his cheque book and scattering them around. However, if he sees someone pick up a cheque and start to complete it, he then has a duty to inform his bank forthwith. If he fails to do this, he may be liable for the forgery.

Equally a customer is not liable simply because he ignores all statements of account which he receives from his bank even when a cursory examination would reveal unauthorised debits. If he does look at his statement and notices unauthorised debits but does not inform the bank then he may be estopped from claiming on the basis that he then knows of the forgeries.

In the White Paper[45] it is stated that the government considers this area of the law to be unfair to banks. It proposed legislative change to make the customer bear some of the loss where he has been negligent. This proposal has not been implemented but the Banking Ombudsman will apply contributory negligence rules against a complainant in the appropriate circumstances.

The view of the Privy Council in Tai Hing that the banker-customer relationship was entirely a contractual one and its consequent rejection of the bank's argument that a customer owes a duty in tort not to act negligently has been put in some doubt by the decision in Henderson v Merrett Syndicates Ltd,[46] where it was held that concurrent duties in contract and tort could co-exist in a relationship in the insurance industry.

---

[43]*[1918] AC 777 HL.*
[44]*[1933] AC 51 HL.*
[45]*Cm 1026, see 1.1 above.*
[46]*[1995] 2 AC 145 HL.*

1.5 EXPRESS TERMS

The banks in the *Tai Hing* case, in fact, had incorporated express terms into their contracts with their customer, which in various ways had sought to place an express duty on the customer to examine his statements of account and to raise queries within a given period, failing which the statements were to be deemed to be correct.

It was held in *Tai Hing* that at common law there is nothing to prevent such terms being effective (they may be referred to as 'conclusive evidence clauses'), but as terms which seek to exclude rights which the customer would otherwise enjoy, they can only be effective if the effect of them is clearly brought home to the customer; it was held that the banks in *Tai Hing* had not done so. It is suggested that banks would be unwise to incorporate such a term in any case, since it may happen that the account is wrongly credited with a large sum which could also be treated as conclusive. A better term from the bank's point of view would be one which obliges a customer specifically to inform the bank of unauthorised debits within a certain period.

As explained above,[47] any express term which seeks to exclude liability on the part of one party to a contract may be rendered void by the Unfair Contract Terms Act 1977 if it is considered to be an unreasonable exclusion of liability.

The Banking Code declares that all written terms should be fair in substance and set out the customer's rights and responsibilities clearly and in plain language, with legal and technical language used only where necessary.[48] It further provides that banks should tell customers how any variation of the terms will be notified and that reasonable notice of variation be given. Banks should also issue customers with a consolidated set of express terms whenever there have been sufficient changes in any 12-month period to warrant this.[49]

Other terms of the banker-customer contract such as the duty of

---

[47]*In 1.1.*
[48]*Section 2.6.*
[49]*Section 2.9.*

confidentiality and charges to the account are discussed under separate headings.[50]

1.6 THE BANK'S DUTY OF CARE

When a bank pays a cheque it does so as agent for its customer. Also, when it collects a cheque it does so as agent.[51] It has already been observed[52] that a bank may be liable to its customer if it pays a forged or altered cheque. There are also circumstances where a bank may be liable for paying a cheque which is drawn in accordance with the mandate from the customer and where there has been no alteration.

In Lipkin Gorman v Karpnale Ltd[53], LG were a firm of solicitors who held a client account at a branch of Lloyds Bank. Any one partner of LG was mandated to operate the account. One of the partners (C) also had a personal account at the same branch. C withdrew and used over £200,000 of client account money in gambling at the Playboy Club (then owned by Karpnale Ltd). He had removed the client account funds largely by signing cheques payable to cash and sending a clerk to the bank to cash the cheques. LG made a series of claims against Karpnale Ltd and Lloyds Bank for recovery of the money. The Court of Appeal found against LG on almost all of its claims but recognised that there can be circumstances which make a bank liable even if it has complied with the written mandate.

In this helpful decision for banks, May LJ declared:

'In the simple case of a current account in credit, the basic obligation on the banker is to pay his customer's cheques in accordance with his mandate. Having in mind the vast numbers of cheques which are presented for payment every day in this country . . . it is my opinion only when the circumstances are such that any reasonable cashier would hesitate to pay a cheque at once . . . that a cheque should not be paid immediately upon presentation.'

---

[50]See 1.8 and 1.9 below.
[51]See 5.4 below for a bank's duties in this event.
[52]See 1.5 above.
[53][1989] 1 WLR 1340 CA; varied but not on this point [1992] 2 AC 548 HL.

The court conceded that just one telephone call by the bank manager to the senior partner in Lipkin Gorman to inform him of C's gambling would have put a stop to the fraud but held that this would have been a flagrant breach of the bank's duty of secrecy to its customer C.

The test to be applied to determine whether a bank is in breach of its duty as agent was stated by Parker LJ as follows:

'If a reasonable banker would have had reasonable grounds for believing that C was operating the client account in fraud, then, in continuing to pay the cash cheques without enquiry the bank would, in my view, be negligent and thus liable for breach of contract, albeit neither Mr Fox (the bank manager) nor anyone else appreciated that the facts did afford reasonable grounds and was thus innocent of any sort of dishonesty.'

Later he stated:

'The question must be whether, if a reasonable and honest banker knew of the relevant facts, he would have considered that there was a serious or real possibility that C was drawing on the client account and using the funds so obtained for his own . . . purposes.'

Another case which was decided in favour of the bank is Barclays Bank v Quincecare Ltd.[54] S approached the bank for a loan of £400,000 in order to purchase some chemists shops. An account was opened in the name of Q Ltd and a guarantee for the loan was obtained from Unichem Ltd. S asked the bank to transfer a large sum of money from Q Ltd's account to the firm of solicitors which (he said) was acting in the purchase of the shops. This was done, whereupon S instructed the solicitors to transfer the money to the USA from where it was never recovered. The bank sued Q Ltd for the debt and Unichem Ltd on their guarantee. It was held that there had been no suspicious circumstances which should have alerted the bank before it transferred the money to the solicitors and that it was not liable. The law relating to unauthorised debits is summarised in Figure 1.

There are other cases of interest concerning a bank's liability to its customer. In Box v Midland Bank,[55] B approached the bank for a loan facility in order to finance an export contract. The bank

[54]*[1992] 4 All ER 363.*
[55]*[1979] 2 Lloyd's Rep 391.*

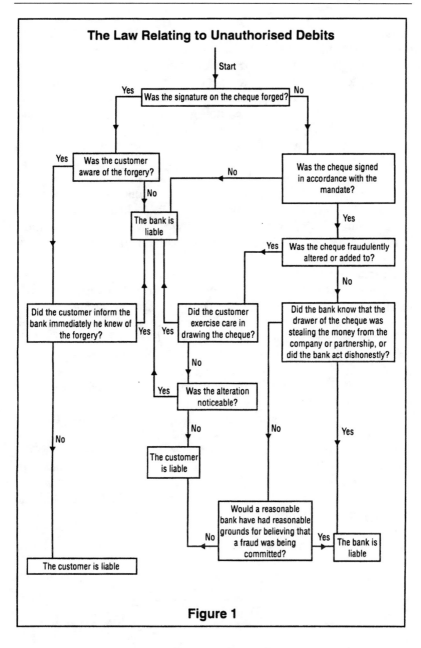

Figure 1

manager explained that the Regional Head Office would have to approve the facility but that this would be a mere formality if an ECGD policy was obtained. B acted on this assurance and incurred expenses setting up the contract. In fact Regional Head Office would not have granted the facility under any circumstances and the facility was not granted. B sued for his loss and succeeded on the basis of the bank's liability for tortious negligent misstatement under the principle established in Hedley Byrne v Heller.[56]

In Redmond v Allied Irish Banks,[57] R was a customer of the bank. G approached R, asking him to put two cheques through R's account; G said he did not want to put the cheques through his own account for tax reasons. The cheques were payable to individuals who appeared to have indorsed them in blank; they were crossed 'not negotiable'. They had been obtained by fraud. R did pay them into his account, withdrew the funds when they cleared and paid G, whereupon G disappeared. R did not acquire good title to the cheques because of the fraud and the 'not negotiable' crossing. R contended that his bank owed him a duty to warn him of the risks of paying in indorsed cheques which were crossed 'not negotiable'. The court dismissed this argument and found in favour of the bank.

In Verity and Spindler v Lloyds Bank,[58] the plaintiffs obtained a loan from the bank which was used to renovate a property which was eventually sold at a loss. The manager of the bank had advised the plaintiffs that the project was viable. It was held that the bank had assumed the role of financial adviser in this case because of the obvious financial naivety of the plaintiffs, the business nature of the project, the bank's marketing leaflet which had offered free financial advice, and the fact that the manager had inspected the property and pronounced it viable after having inspected others which he advised the plaintiffs against buying. The case appears to establish that where a bank assumes the duty of financial advisor

---

[56]See 1.11 below.
[57][1987] 2 FTLR 264. See also Schioler v National Westminster Bank [1970] 2 QB 719.
[58][1995] CLC 1557.

(which does not automatically follow from the fact that it has lent money for a particular project) then it must be sure that any advice it gives is not negligent. A mere approval of a loan could constitute negligent advice if the duty to advise has been assumed.[59]

An interesting question of a bank's duty of care to a non-customer arose in Gold Coin Joailliers SA v United Bank of Kuwait.[60] A fraudster devised a scam whereby he would impersonate a wealthy customer of the defendant bank as a means of obtaining valuable goods on credit. He telephoned the bank (impersonating their customer) and instructed it to give a telephone reference to the victim of the scam. The victim duly phoned the bank for a reference and was given a favourable reply. He therefore released watches priced at $450,000 to the fraudster, accepting payment in the form of a payment instruction signed by the fraudster but in the name of the customer of the defendant bank who had been impersonated. The bank dishonoured the payment instruction as a forgery and the victim sued it for causing his loss by their misrepresentation. It was held on appeal by the bank that the bank owed no duty of care to the victim.

1.7 THE BANK AS TRUSTEE

A bank's liability under an express trust

Banks commonly act as trustees appointed as such under an express trust set up by a customer. In this event the bank is subject to all the general law concerning powers, duties and liabilities of trustees and this includes the duty to take care of the trust property to the standard of a prudent business person. It has been held, however, that a bank trustee is under a greater duty as it holds itself out as a trustee with a special degree of care and skill.[61] This duty appears

---

[59]*Williams and Glyn's Bank v Barnes [1981] Com LR 205. See the Encyclopaedia of Banking Law at C100.*
[60]*[1997] 7 Bank LR 60 CA.*
[61]*Bartlett v Barclays Bank Trust Co. Ltd [1980] 2 WLR 430.*

only to extend to preserving the fund and not to the achievement of growth.[62]

Constructive trusts

The constructive trust is a general principle which is not confined to banking law. It arises when a person who has not been appointed to act as a trustee becomes involved in the affairs of the trust and thus becomes liable to the beneficiaries of the trust in the same way as an appointed trustee who acts in breach of trust. It can also arise when there is no formal trust but a fiduciary duty is owed, for instance by a partner to his other partners.

A bank may be liable as constructive trustee if it either:

(a) receives trust funds with actual or constructive notice that they are trust funds and that the transfer of the funds to the bank constitutes a breach of trust, or

(b) knowingly assists a trustee of the trust to dishonestly misapply trust funds.[63]

In the banking context, it has been seen that a bank is liable as a debtor to a customer for the balance on his account[64] and it is not normally liable as trustee unless it has been appointed as such. It might become a constructive trustee if it permits an authorised signatory to withdraw funds from an account in circumstances where it knows that the funds are being misapplied. This was an alternative ground of claim in the *Lipkin Gorman* case.[65]

In *Lipkin Gorman*, the Court of Appeal came to the conclusion that there is no possibility of a bank being liable as a constructive trustee of funds which have been fraudulently misapplied with the knowing assistance of the bank, without it also being liable in simple breach of contract for not conducting a customer's account with sufficient care. On the other hand, it might be liable in breach of

[62]*Nestle v National Westminster Bank [1993] 1 WLR 1260 and N. Clayton [1994] JIBFL 352.*
[63]*Belmont Finance Corpn v Williams Furniture Ltd [1980] 1 All ER 393 CA.*
[64]*See 1.4 above.*
[65]*See 1.6 above.*

contract for conducting the account negligently, in circumstances when it had insufficient knowledge to make it liable as a constructive trustee. In other words, liability to a customer in breach of contract is more extensive than liability as a constructive trustee. This renders the constructive trust remedy irrelevant to a customer claiming in respect of funds misapplied from his account by an authorised signatory, such as occurred in *Lipkin Gorman*.

However, it could arise that the bank is accused of assisting in the misapplication of funds which in equity belong to a third party (i.e. to a non-customer). In Agip (Africa) Ltd v Jackson,[66] Z, the chief accountant of A Ltd, fraudulently altered the payee's name on payment orders validly signed by a director of A Ltd. One such payment order (payable for over $500,000) was altered to be payable to B Ltd, which held an account at Lloyds Bank, to which the funds were paid by A Ltd's bank. J was a director of B Ltd and he authorised Lloyds Bank to transfer the money through a network of companies so that eventually little of the money remained under J's control. It was held that a fiduciary relationship existed between Z and A Ltd and that strangers to this trust could be liable in equity if they knowingly received trust property or knowingly assisted in its fraudulent misapplication. In this case, J was held to have so assisted and to have had the requisite degree of knowledge; he was thus fully liable for A Ltd's losses on the transaction. No action was brought against Lloyds Bank but it is clear that in principle a bank could find itself in the same position as did J in this case (i.e. if it paid away the money with a sufficient level of knowledge). It would then similarly be liable as a constructive trustee for the third party's losses even though the third party is not a customer of the bank.

The question of liability as a constructive trustee on the basis of knowing assistance is clearly of vital importance to banks and can render them liable whenever stolen money is laundered through them. The Privy Council shed further light on the matter in the recent case of Royal Brunei Airlines v Tan.[67] It held that liability depends upon dishonesty of the person who provided the assistance.

[66]*[1989] 3 WLR 1367; affirmed [1991] 3 WLR 116 CA.*
[67]*[1995] 2 AC 378 PC.*

Thus previous cases which hinged upon the necessary degree of knowledge[68] now appear to be of less significance. A bank will only be liable for assisting a theft or breach of trust if it has acted dishonestly. Dishonesty is judged objectively, based on the standards of an ordinarily honest person. Thus it is no defence to say that an action was subjectively regarded as honest if most people would have seen it as dishonest.

The circumstances which would render a bank liable as constructive trustee for assisting in a breach of trust have been listed as follows:[69]

(a) there must have been a breach of some fiduciary duty. This might be a partner's duty to his fellow partners or a company director's duty to his company as well as a breach of trust by an appointed trustee or a breach of trust by an appointed trustee, note there is no requirement that the trustee was acting dishonestly, he might have committed the breach innocently;
(b) the bank must have assisted in the breach, such as by accepting money into an account and subsequently paying it away;
(c) the bank must have acted dishonestly. This is further defined as commercially unacceptable conduct.

An unusual form of constructive trust claim against a bank was recently heard in Box v Barclays Bank.[70] The plaintiff deposited money with an unauthorised deposit-taker. The latter had deposited the funds with the defendant bank. The unauthorised deposit-taker had acted illegally in taking the deposit but the plaintiff had a statutory right to recover the funds from him under section 3(3) of the Banking Act 1987. It was argued that the defendant bank was at fault in receiving the funds and liable as a constructive trustee but the court held that liability as a constructive trustee could only exist on these facts where the illegality led to there being no remedy against the deposit-taker. The statutory right to recover

---

[68]Such as Belmont Finance Corpn v Williams Furniture [1979] Ch 250, Baden v Societe General [1983] BCLC 325 and Agip (Africa) Ltd v Jackson, see above.
[69]By M. Hapgood in Paget's Law of Banking, 11th edition, 1996 at p401.
[70](1998) The Times, 30th April.

against the deposit-taker (although in practice useless) negated any liability of the defendant bank as constructive trustee.

'*Quistclose*' trusts

Somewhat similar to the constructive trust is the '*Quistclose*' trust, which arises when money is paid to a bank which, to the bank's knowledge, is to be used for a special purpose. In Barclays Bank v Quistclose Investments Ltd,[71] RR Ltd had a large overdraft with the bank. The company borrowed a sum of money from Q Ltd in order to meet a dividend it had declared. Q Ltd lent this money to RR Ltd on condition that it was used to pay the dividend. The money it lent was placed in a special account opened in RR Ltd's name with the bank. The bank was aware of the condition attached to the loan. RR Ltd went into liquidation before the dividend was paid; the bank claimed that the money in the special account had belonged to RR Ltd and could therefore be set-off against the company's overdraft debt. It was held that, as the bank knew of the purpose of the loan, the money was held on trust primarily to pay the dividend, but if that purpose failed, then secondarily for the benefit of the lender, Q Ltd. Thus the bank was unable to set off the money against the overdrawn account and had to return it to Q Ltd.

1.8 THE BANK'S RIGHT TO INTEREST AND TO CHARGES

Interest

A bank may compound interest on a longstanding debt, i.e. it will add the interest to the capital at intervals so that interest is charged on unpaid interest. This right to compound is an implied contractual right arising from the custom and usage of banks.[72] The right to compound interest survives the making of demand by the bank and the closure of the overdrawn account.

---

[71]*[1970] AC 567 HL.*
[72]*National Bank of Greece SA v Pinios Shipping Co. [1990] 1 AC 637 HL.*

The Banking Code[73] obliges banks to tell new customers the interest rates applicable to their accounts, the basis on which interest is calculated and when it will be charged to their accounts.[74] Banks must also inform all customers of any change in interest rates either by letter or by notices in branches and advertisements in the press.[75]

Charges

It is nowadays common for banks to express the circumstances in which customers may be charged and the Banking Code requires that new customers be given a tariff covering basic account services.[76] Where this has occurred the tariff would form part of the express terms of the contract. Where no tariff has been issued or where the bank seeks to charge for a service which is not listed on the tariff, it could rely on custom and usage.[77] The Supply of Goods and Services Act 1982 provides that where, under a contract for the supply of a service, the price for the service is not expressed, there is an implied term that the party contracting with the supplier will pay a reasonable charge.[78]

Besides requiring banks to provide their personal customers with a tariff of charges for basic account services (which is not defined), the Banking Code states that customers will be told of any additional charges or interest the customer may have to pay in the event of an unauthorised overdraft, exceeding an overdraft limit, a loan falling into arrears or the early termination of a fixed term product.[79] Before taking out a mortgage and at any time the customer asks, he should be given a tariff of charges and additional interest payable if it falls

[73]*Where it applies, see 1.1 above.*
[74]*Section 2.1.*
[75]*Section 2.11. The Banking Ombudsman takes the view that customers with postal accounts should also be informed of interest rates at least annually by post.*
[76]*Section 2.1. The tariff must also be available in branches.*
[77]*See M. Hapgood – Paget's Law of Banking 11th ed at p187.*
[78]*Section 15.*
[79]*Section 2.3.*

into arrears.[80] Customers must be told the charge for any other service or product before or when it is provided or at any other time the customer asks.[81] The Code also states that if charges or interest arise on an account, the customer should be given 14 days' notice of the amount to be deducted.[82] Neither the Code nor the law limit the amount of any charge which a bank may wish to make, although an excessively high charge might be considered to offend the Code's general requirement that banks' dealings with customers be fair and reasonable. The Code follows the spirit of the Jack Report which supported the notion of banks being required to give information to customers who can then shop around for the best deal, rather than directly controlling the behaviour of banks.[83]

1.9 THE BANK'S DUTY OF CONFIDENTIALITY

A bank owes an implied duty to its customer not to divulge information about its customers to third parties. In Tournier v National Provincial and Union Bank of England,[84] T had an overdrawn account with the bank. The branch manager spoke to T's employers in order to find out T's home address. In the process the manager revealed that T had defaulted on his obligation to the bank and was suspected of being a heavy gambler. T was dismissed from his job and successfully sued for his losses.

The *Tournier* case also lays down four exceptions to the duty of secrecy:

(a) where disclosure is under compulsion of law;
(b) where there is a duty to the public to disclose;
(c) where the interests of the bank require disclosure;
(d) where disclosure occurs with the express or implied consent of the customer.

---

[80]*Section 2.4 and section 6 of the Mortgage Code.*
[81]*Section 2.5.*
[82]*Section 3.4. The 14 days runs from the day the notification is posted.*
[83]*Cm622, recommendation 13(2).*
[84]*[1924] 1 KB 461 CA.*

Disclosure under compulsion of law

It is helpful to sub-divide this exception into four parts:

(a) where the compulsion takes the form of a court order to disclose. Examples of this include (amongst others):

  (i) an order to permit the inspection of entries in a banker's book[85] under section 7 of the Bankers' Books Evidence Act 1879 on the application of a party to any legal proceeding;

  (ii) an order under section 9 of the Police and Criminal Evidence Act 1984 to assist police in the investigation of a criminal offence;

  (iii) discovery orders made in aid of a party seeking a Mareva injunction;

  (iv) an order for obtaining evidence in a foreign trial under the Evidence (Proceedings in Other Jurisdictions) Act 1975;

  (v) a writ of subpoena or a witness order compelling a bank employee to give evidence in a civil or criminal trial;

  (vi) an order by the court under section 55 of the Drug Trafficking Act 1994 to assist a police investigation into a suspected drug trafficking offence;

(b) where the compulsion takes the form of a valid request from an official and no court order is necessary. Examples include:

  (i) information required by the Inland Revenue under the Taxes Management Act 1970 and the Income and Corporation Taxes Act 1988, e.g. concerning interest credited to customers' accounts;

  (ii) information required about a company by the Department of Trade and Industry acting under powers granted in the Companies Act 1985;

  (iii) under the Criminal Justice Act 1987, the Director of the Serious Fraud Office may require a person to attend to answer questions;

(c) where there is no direct compulsion to divulge information

---

[85]*This includes microfilm, magnetic tape or any other data retrieval mechanism, section 9(2).*

about a customer but the bank is in danger of committing an offence and there is specific statutory protection if information is divulged. Examples are:

(i) section 50 of the Drug Trafficking Act 1994 makes it an offence to enter into an arrangement whereby the retention or control of the proceeds of drug trafficking is facilitated, knowing or suspecting that the person concerned has carried on drug trafficking. Clearly a bank can commit this offence by operating the account of a drug trafficker if it has the necessary knowledge or suspicion. Disclosure to the police of a suspicion or belief relating to funds derived from illegal drug trafficking will not constitute a breach of the implied duty of secrecy[86] and provides a defence for a bank so long as the disclosure is made before it does the assisting in the retention or control by the trafficker and acts with the consent of the police or it informs the police as soon as reasonable to do so after it acts. The effect of this provision is of course to encourage banks to volunteer information about a customer;

(ii) the Criminal Justice Act 1988[87] extends the above rule to the proceeds of any criminal conduct. Thus a bank can commit an offence by operating the account of an armed robber or any thief if it has the necessary knowledge or suspicion but it commits no offence if it informs the police as described above and no breach of secrecy is committed;

(iii) sections 11 and 12 of the Prevention of Terrorism (Temporary Provisions) Act 1989 provides almost identical rules applicable to the bank account of a terrorist. Interestingly this offence is committed if the bank knew or had *reasonable* cause to suspect. The addition of the word reasonable may indicate that an offence is committed even where the bank did not itself suspect but a reasonable banker would have;

---

[86]*Section 50(3)(a).*
[87]*Section 93A.*

(d) where the law compels a bank to disclose information and an offence is committed if does not do so:

  (i) section 52 of the Drug Trafficking Act 1994 makes it an offence to fail to report a knowledge or suspicion of a person's engagement in drug money laundering when the information is acquired in the course of his trade, profession or employment. No offence is committed if the information is disclosed as soon as is reasonably practicable after it came to his attention. No offence is committed if there was a reasonable excuse for not disclosing and legal advisers enjoy a defence if the matter arose in privileged circumstances. Perhaps rather unnecessarily, it is provided that any disclosure under this heading will not constitute a breach of the duty of confidentiality;

  (ii) section 54A of the Northern Ireland (Emergency Provisions) Act 1989 creates a similar offence to section 52 above but in relation to knowledge or suspicion of laundering of terrorist funds. Similar defences are provided as above.

Note that it is only an offence to fail to report the knowledge or suspicion of money laundering if the knowledge arose in the course of a trade, profession or employment and it is only drug trafficking or terrorist funds which are included. Knowledge of laundering of the proceeds of armed robbery and other offences is not included under this heading.

Other money laundering provisions:

  (i) under section 53 of the Drug Trafficking Act 1994 it is an offence to tip-off a person that a drug money laundering investigation is being conducted or to disclose that information has been passed to disclose that fact. It is a defence that the discloser did not know that disclosure would prejudice the investigation;

  (ii) section 17 of the Prevention of Terrorism (Temporary Provisions) Act 1989 provides similarly in relation to tipping-off persons under investigation for terrorist money laundering. Once again, these offences are limited to drug money and terrorist money laundering and no offence is committed for tipping-off other kinds of money launderer;

(iii) the Money Laundering Regulations 1993[88] make it an offence for banks not to set up procedures for identification, record-keeping, internal reporting, internal control and communication. They must also train staff to be familiar with the procedures and with the law on money-laundering and to enable them to detect money laundering operations.

Duty to the public to disclose

This has not been a well used exception to the duty of secrecy and its parameters are unclear. It has been suggested that it might apply to permit disclosure in wartime when a customer has dealings with the enemy.[89] In Libyan Arab Foreign Bank v Bankers Trust[90] the court neither confirmed nor denied that the exception applied where immediately prior to the making of a US Presidential Order freezing Libyan assets in the hands of US persons in 1986, the US authorities requested and obtained information about Libyan government accounts with the defendant bank.

Disclosure in the bank's interest

This exception was successfully invoked by a bank in Sunderland v Barclays Bank.[91] S telephoned her bank to complain about its dishonour of her cheques. The bank was justified in dishonouring the cheques as there were insufficient funds but it was also concerned about S's gambling. S's husband took the telephone from S to add his views whereupon the bank informed him of his wife's gambling. The court held the bank was entitled to disclose in its own interest and expressed the view that it would also be justified under this exception for disclosure in the common situation of it suing a customer for the balance of an overdrawn account. This is

---

[88]*Regulation 5. This is discussed further in 2.2 below.*
[89]*Lord Chorley, Law of Banking, 6th edition 1974 at p23.*
[90]*[1989] QB 728.*
[91]*(1938) 5 Legal Decisions Affecting Bankers 163.*

necessary as legal action in these circumstances will reveal to the public the balance on the customer's account. For similar reasons, a bank may claim from a guarantor of the customer's debt without breaching the duty of confidentiality, although if the guarantee is limited and the debt exceeds the limit the guarantor should only be informed he is fully liable up to his limit. Where the loan agreement is regulated by the Consumer Credit Act 1974, the guarantor has a statutory right to know the state of the bank's account with the customer.[92]

The Banking Code declares that information about personal debts owed to a bank may be disclosed to credit reference agencies where the loan is in arrears and the amount is not in dispute and the customer has not made proposals satisfactory to the bank for repayment following formal demand and the customer has been given 28 days' notice of the bank's intention to disclose.[93] It appears that any such disclosure could only be justified under this exception to the duty of secrecy.

The Banking Code reiterates the common law duty of confidentiality and declares that banks will not attempt to use the third exception to justify the disclosure of information for marketing purposes, including to companies in the same group.[94] It further provides that new customers will have the opportunity to give instructions that they do not wish to receive any marketing material[95] and that all customers will be reminded of this right at least every three years.[96]

Disclosure with the customer's consent

In *Tournier* it was stated that if a customer gives his bank as a reference, there is implied consent to disclosure of information. The court in *Sunderland* also considered that the disclosure in that case

---

[92]*See 3.5 above. This must come under the compulsion of law exception.*
[93]*Section 4.2.*
[94]*Section 4.1. The Mortgage Code contains an identical provision (section 7.1).*
[95]*Section 2.13.*
[96]*Section 2.14*

was justified on the basis of implied consent as well as being in the bank's interest.

The traditional system of bankers' opinions operates whereby one bank may make a status enquiry to another bank concerning the credit standing of a customer of the second bank.[97] In some cases the customer will not be aware that the status enquiry has been made nor even that a system for giving information in this way exists. It is difficult to argue that a customer impliedly consents to something of which he is not aware. This traditional practice has yielded to a modern system where a customer's consent is always sought before a banker's reference is given. The latest edition of the Banking Code confirms this.[98]

It was stated in *Tournier* that the duty of secrecy commences when the banker-customer relationship (presumably the contract) is formed. The duty extends to information which the bank has obtained from other sources whilst acting as banker to the customer, e.g. information about its customer which it obtained from a reference on him provided by another bank. It was also stated that the duty does not cease on termination of the banker-customer contract.

Liability for breach of the duty of confidentiality will be based upon general principles of liability for breach of contract and therefore the customer will usually have to prove actual loss in order to obtain more than nominal damages. In both the *Sunderland* and *Libyan Arab Foreign Bank* cases, the court considered there had been no such loss and that only nominal damages would be awarded even if the plaintiff established a breach of the duty. It would appear therefore that in the majority of situations where an unjustified disclosure occurs there will be no significant damages awarded against the bank. Figure 2 illustrates a banker's duty of confidentiality.

1.10 THE DATA PROTECTION ACT

A new Data Protection Act is being introduced in order to comply with the European Union Data Protection Directive (95/46/EC). The

[97]*See 1.11 below.*
[98]*In section 4.5.*

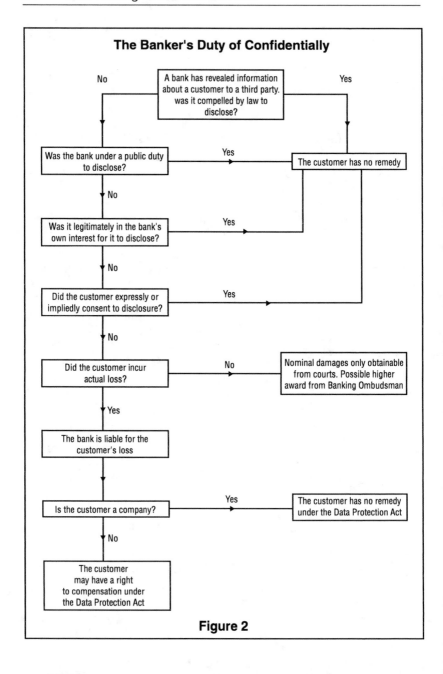

The Banker's Duty of Confidentially

A bank has revealed information about a customer to a third party. was it compelled by law to disclose?

No — Yes

Was the bank under a public duty to disclose? — Yes → The customer has no remedy

No

Was it legitimately in the bank's own interest for it to disclose? — Yes →

No

Did the customer expressly or impliedly consent to disclosure? — Yes →

No

Did the customer incur actual loss? — No → Nominal damages only obtainable from courts. Possible higher award from Banking Ombudsman

Yes

The bank is liable for the customer's loss

Is the customer a company? — Yes → The customer has no remedy under the Data Protection Act

No

The customer may have a right to compensation under the Data Protection Act

Figure 2

new Act will contain a mix of existing and new features. The system of registration will be replaced by a system of notification to the data protection authorities. Data processors will continue to be obliged to process data concerning individuals fairly and lawfully and for purposes they have notified to the authorities. Data processing will only be legitimate where one of the following criteria applies:

(a) where the individual has consented;
(b) where it is necessary for the performance of a contract with the individual;
(c) where it is required under a legal obligation;
(d) where it is necessary to protect the vital interests of the individual or to carry out public functions;
(e) where it is necessary to pursue the legitimate interests of the business (unless prejudicial to the individual).

Appropriate measures must be taken to prevent the unlawful or unauthorised processing or disclosure of data.

Individual data subjects will have the right to a description of any data concerning them, a description of the purposes for which it is being processed, a description of any potential recipients of the data and information as to its source. Where the data is processed automatically and is likely to be the sole basis for a decision significantly affecting the data subject, he can request the logic involved in that decision. In this way, a lender may be obliged to give reasons for refusing a loan application which was processed by computer. The data subject will also have the right to prevent processing which will cause damage and distress and a specific right to prevent processing for the purposes of direct marketing. The courts will be able to award compensation to data subjects by any breach of the Act.

The new Act will extend coverage to manual filing systems, where information to an individual is readily accessible. This part of the new law is not expected to come into force until 2007, however.

A bank's common law duty of confidentiality (i.e. the rule of *Tournier's* case) applies only to the disclosure by a bank to a third party of information known by the bank about both its personal and corporate customers. In contrast, the Data Protection Act regulates the obtaining by and use within a bank, as well as the disclosure to third parties, of information about non-corporate customers only.

An interesting effect is produced by a combined effect of the data protection principles and the rule in *Tournier*. A bank must process personal information fairly and lawfully. This presumably means it must not breach its duty of confidentiality to its customer.[99] If a bank uses computers to pass personal information about customers to another company in its group, this would be an unlawful processing of information and thus a criminal offence under the Data Protection Act.

1.11 BANKERS' OPINIONS

A bankers' opinion is a reference which a bank provides about its customer. The traditional practice is that the reference is requested by and given to another bank who then pass it on to the ultimate recipient (a customer of the requesting bank). This customer of course has no contractual relationship with the bank giving the reference unless he is charged by it for the service. Figure 3 illustrates the legal relationships involved when a reference is given. In the diagram, Y Bank is providing the reference on its customer (B) after a request is made by A, through his bank (X).

A banker must give a reference on the basis of facts actually known to him at the time; he is not obliged to make enquiries to ascertain new facts or other people's opinions.[100] He is required to conform to the standard of skill and competence and diligence which is generally shown by persons who carry on the business of providing references of that kind.[101] The bank giving the reference is concerned about potential liability to two different parties:

(a) the ultimate recipient of the reference; and
(b) its own customer.

---

[99]*Note the principle says 'lawfully' not 'legally' so a breach of the civil law infringes the principle.*
[100]*Parsons v Barclay & Co (1910) 103 LT 196 CA.*
[101]*Mutual Life and Citizens Assurance Co v Evatt [1971] AC 793 PC.*

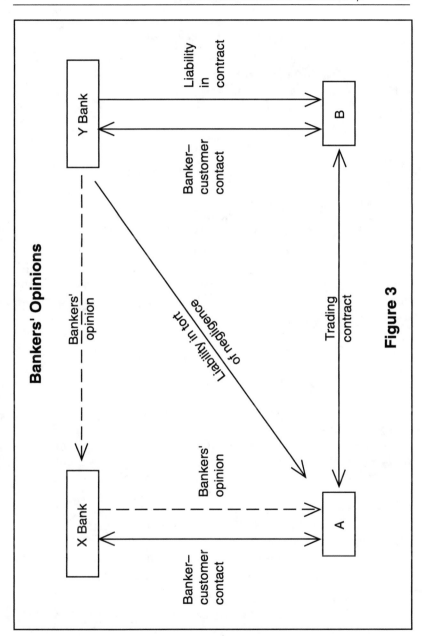

Figure 3

Liability to the ultimate recipient

This may arise because the bank has given an unduly favourable reference about its customer, and the recipient, relying on this, extends credit to the customer who defaults. Liability may occur in fraudulent misrepresentation and in negligence.

Fraudulent misrepresentation

Liability under this head requires that the misrepresentation by the bank was made knowingly or recklessly, that the bank intended to deceive and that it intended that it should be acted upon by someone and that someone did act upon it and as a result suffered loss.[102] This will always be difficult to prove in practice. In any case, section 6 of the Statute of Frauds Amendment Act 1828 provides that no liability arises from a fraudulent misrepresentation as to someone's credit standing unless the statement is in writing and signed by the maker. By the simple expedient of not signing opinions, therefore, banks are able to exclude any possibility of liability under this head. If the statement is signed by an employee of the bank acting within his authority, liability is not excluded.[103]

Negligence

Liability under this head was the issue in Hedley Byrne & Co. Ltd v Heller & Partners Ltd,[104] where a negligent bankers' opinion was given, causing loss to the recipient. The court opened up the possibility of liability for negligence in these circumstances, but it had to be established that the bank, when giving its opinion, was willing to accept responsibility for its statement. The bank had followed the usual practice of incorporating a disclaimer of liability in its opinion, which made it clear it was not prepared to assume responsibility for its statement.

The law would thus be clear were it not for the subsequent

---

[102]*Derry v Peek (1889) 14 App Cas 337 HL*
[103]*UBAF Ltd v European American Banking Corpn [1984] QB 713 CA.*
[104]*[1964] AC 465 HL.*

enactment of the Unfair Contract Terms Act 1977, which renders ineffective any attempt to exclude liability for negligence unless the exclusion can be justified as reasonable.[105] A bank's liability therefore now depends on whether its exclusion of liability is deemed to be reasonable. No reported decision has been made on the matter.

Liability to the customer

There are two areas of potential liability here. One is for breach of secrecy and the second is for damaging the customer by giving an unduly poor reference. It is now standard but not universal practice for a bank to seek and obtain the express consent of its customer before it provides an opinion.[106]

The banker's duty of secrecy to its customer has been discussed in 1.9 above. The giving of information in the form of a bankers' opinion has to come within one of the exceptions in *Tournier*, if it is not to amount to a breach of contract. The only exception which can apply is that of the customer's consent, express or implied. Where the customer is unaware that the opinion is being given or that the system of status enquiries exists, it is hard to argue that he impliedly consents. However, assuming there is a breach of contract, the customer will have to establish loss if he is to be entitled to more than nominal damages.

In order to sue his bank for libel, the customer would have to establish that his bank gave an unduly unfavourable reference which reduced his standing in the eyes of right-thinking people. It appears, however, that the bank can claim privileged statement as a defence if it gave the opinion bona fide.[107] In order to sue his bank for breach of contract, the customer could rely on the implied term brought in

---

[105]*Section 2(2). Despite the name of this Act, it does cover exclusions of liability in non-contractual relationships.*
[106]*The Banking Code requires this for references given on personal customers, section 4.5.*
[107]*London Association for Protection of Trade v Greenlands Ltd [1916] 2 AC 15 HL.*

by the Supply of Goods and Services Act 1982 that the bank should carry out its service with a reasonable degree of care and skill.[108]

1.12 REPAYMENT ON DEMAND AND LIMITATION

Where a bank permits a customer to borrow by overdrawing his current account, the bank is entitled to require repayment on demand.[109] Where, however, the bank has expressed that the facility is available for a specific time period then the bank will not be able to demand repayment before this period has expired.[110] Where there are conflicting provisions in the facility letter, so that in one place it says that the overdraft is repayable on demand and in another that the facility is available for a certain period, then it is a question of construction of the true intention of the parties. On these facts in *Titford Property*, the repayment on demand clause was held to be subordinate to the term provision.

The Limitation Act 1980 statute-bars legal actions in simple contract when the cause of action arose more than six years previously. When the debt is secured by a mortgage, the limitation period extends to twelve years. In the case of a bank overdraft on a current account, the cause of action arises in respect of each debit entry on the account and time runs from the date of each debit.[111] If the account is active, however, the limitation period runs from the date of the last movement on the account.[112] Thus there is a greater limitation risk for banks in respect of dormant overdrawn accounts.

A customer who wishes to sue for recovery of a credit balance owed to him by a bank can do so within six years of his demand

---

[108]*Section 12.*

[109]*Titford Property Co. v Cannon Street Acceptances Ltd (1975) unreported, see M. Hapgood, Paget's Law of Banking, 11th edition 1996 at p167.*

[110]*Williams and Glyn's Bank v Barnes [1981] Com LR 205.*

[111]*Parr's Banking Co Ltd v Yates [1898] 2 QB 460 CA.*

[112]*This is the effect of section 29(5) of the Limitation Act 1980. The inclusion of a debt within a Sundry Creditors figure contained in a company's balance sheet was held to constitute acknowledgement of the debt and accordingly time ran from the data of acknowledgement, Jones v Bellgrove Properties Ltd [1949] 2 KB 700 CA.*

for repayment from the bank. In National Bank of Commerce v National Westminster Bank,[113] the defendant bank made some debit entries on the plaintiff bank's account with them between 1978 and 1980. These were disputed by the plaintiff bank in 1988 and the legal action began in the same year. It was held that the claim was not statute barred since, irrespective of the debiting of the accounts at an earlier stage, the demand was not made by the customer until 1988 and the six years started running then.

1.13 APPROPRIATION OF PAYMENTS

Appropriation of payments may arise in two distinct situations:

(a) where a customer has two or more accounts with the same bank and he (for example) pays money in. The money will be appropriated to one of the accounts;

(b) where a customer has one account and he pays money into it as well as drawing cheques on it. Appropriation will settle the issue of which payment in relates to which payment out.

In the vast majority of situations it will not matter in the least what appropriation takes place. Where there are two or more accounts, the bank normally enjoys a right to combine the accounts, and the only relevant issue is the combined balance. In the case of a single account, the relevant matter will normally be the bottom line balance, and the issue of which debits relate to which credits will be quite academic.

There are a number of situations where the appropriation is crucial, however. For instance, where there are two accounts, one of which is a wages account and entitles the bank to claim as a preferential creditor, the bank will be keen that a payment in is appropriated to the general account. This will reduce the bank's unsecured claim without reducing its preferential claim.

In the case of a single account, there are a number of situations where the appropriation that takes place will have an impact.

First, a statement of the general law on appropriation. When a customer pays money in, he has the first right to appropriate the

[113]*(1990) Financial Times, 16 March.*

payment.[114] It follows from this that a customer with an overdrawn account is entitled to pay in a cheque and appropriate it to a cheque he has drawn, and his bank will not be able to use the credit to reduce the overdraft.

If the customer does not appropriate, the bank may make an appropriation. In the case of appropriating between two accounts, the bank will normally make an appropriation simply because it has to make a credit entry somewhere.

If, in the single account case, the bank also does not appropriate, the rule in *Clayton's case*[115] is used to determine the issue. This rule essentially says that the first payment in relates to the first payment out. In *Clayton's case*, Devaynes was a banking partnership. One of the partners, D, died. The surviving partners continued the business for a year, at which point it became bankrupt. D's personal estate, however, was solvent. Clayton had an account with the partnership which had always been in credit. Clayton was obviously keen to claim against the estate of D. As a matter of partnership law, the estate of a deceased partner is jointly liable for debts existing at the date of death but not for subsequent debts. The credit balance on Clayton's account at the date of D's death was £1,713. Subsequent to the death, Clayton had paid in and withdrawn sums exceeding £1,713, and the ultimate credit balance was greater than £1,713. Neither Clayton nor the banking partnership had expressed any appropriation when debits and credits occurred.

It was held that D's estate was not liable at all. This was because each debit was deemed to have been set against the earliest available credit. Thus on an active account, the credit items which pre-dated D's death were extinguished by debits, and the ultimate credit balance was represented by the most recent credits, all of which post-dated D's death, and for which D's estate was therefore not liable. It can help to understand the rule if one thinks of its effect as simply moving forward the date of the debt, which is always represented by the most recent items on the relevant side of the account. Where the date of the debt does not matter, which will be the usual case, *Clayton's case* will be quite irrelevant. Where a

[114]*Deeley v Lloyds Bank [1912] AC 756 HL.*
[115]*Devaynes v Noble, Clayton's case (1816) 1 Mer 529 and 572 CA.*

partner has died, however, and his estate is therefore not liable for debts incurred after his death, the date of the debt will be crucial.

Other examples of the operation of *Clayton's case*

In Deeley v Lloyds Bank,[116] the bank had taken a second mortgage from a customer to secure an overdrawn current account. The bank subsequently received notice from D that she had taken a third mortgage over the same property. The current account continued to be operated, and by the time the bank sought to enforce its mortgage, the total credits on the account had exceeded the debit balance as at the date it received notice of the third mortgage. The bank's mortgage covered the later debits since it contained a continuing security clause, but the sale of the property did not achieve sufficient funds to repay D. The issue therefore was, which had priority? Held D, because the payments into the running account had extinguished the debt owed at the time notice of third mortgage was given and the ultimate debt was represented by the latest debits, all of which arose after the notice was received. This was so even though the account had never moved into credit. In other words there is a notional repayment of the earlier debt.

The operation of the rule can also prejudice a bank's claim when a partner dies or retires and the bank continues the partnership account, and later it wishes to claim against the deceased or retired partner. Once again, even though the account has remained in debit, there is a notional repayment of the debt that existed at the relevant time. This situation is, of course, the reverse of the facts in *Clayton's case* itself. Instead of a bankrupt bank, there is a bankrupt customer.

The rule can improve a bank's claim in some circumstances where it is beneficial for the bank that the date of the debt is moved forward. These situations are explained in 16.6 below,[117] and 2.7 below.[118]

Where, however, the bank wishes to prevent the date of the debt moving forward in time, it may freeze the debt in time by simply

[116]*[1912] AC 756 HL.*
[117]*see Re Yeovil Glove Ltd [1965] Ch 148.*
[118]*see Re Primrose Builders Ltd [1950] Ch 561.*

ruling off the account and continuing the account by starting with a nil balance. It is therefore standard practice to rule off a partnership account when a partner retires or dies, or a secured account when notice of second mortgage is received.

It is also possible for a bank to insert a clause in a security document, to the effect that there will be deemed to be a ruling off of the account when the relevant event occurs. For example, in a mortgage form, a clause may say that if notice of second mortgage is received, there will then occur an automatic ruling off of the account. Such a clause has not been tested in the courts, however. A somewhat similar clause in a guarantee form has been upheld.[119]

Limitations to the operation of the rule

(1) The rule only applies to a running account.[120]
(2) The rule does not apply when a customer mixes his personal funds and funds he holds on trust in the same account. In this event the rule in Re Hallett's Estate[121] applies. The effect is that the personal funds are deemed to be withdrawn first.

1.14 COMBINATION OF ACCOUNTS AND SET-OFF

A banker's right to combine accounts

Where a customer has two different accounts with the same bank, the bank has a common law right to combine them without giving notice to the customer. This is so even if the accounts are with different branches of the bank.[122] To give an example, if the credit balance on a customer's account at branch A is £100 and his debit balance at branch B amounts to £90, branch A can refuse payment of more than £10. The first the customer need know is that his cheque has been dishonoured.

---

[119]see *Westminster Bank v Cond (1940) 40 Com Cas 60*, discussed in 12.7 below.
[120]*Re Sherry (1884) 25 ChD 692.*
[121]*(1880) 13 ChD 696.*
[122]*Garnett v McKewan (1872) LR 8 Exch 10.*

On the other hand, a customer has no such right to instantly combine accounts. Therefore a customer who has a credit balance at the A branch of a bank and nil balance at the B branch, has no right to demand payment at the B branch.

If there are three or more accounts, the bank is free to combine any accounts of its choice and to leave others intact. For example, where an employer customer has three accounts, one in credit, one overdrawn wages account and one overdrawn general account, the bank will choose to combine the credit account and the overdrawn general account, leaving the overdrawn wages account intact, as this enables the bank to claim as a preferential creditor.

Limitations on the bank's right to combine accounts prior to insolvency

(1) Where the debit balance account is not yet a debt due and payable by the customer. Therefore a loan account which is repayable at a future date cannot be combined. Nor may a contingent liability, such as a customer's potential liability as a guarantor.[123]

(2) Where the debit balance is on a loan account which is presently due and payable, there will still be no right to combine instantly due to an implied agreement to keep the accounts separate.[124] The rationale behind this is that a customer in these circumstances should not have his cheques dishonoured without any warning. This implied agreement does not extend to the case of an overdrawn current account which has been frozen.[125] In the usual case the bank will still be able to combine after giving a short period of notice. This may of course defeat the object of the combination if, during the notice period, the customer quickly withdraws the balance of the account in credit. It has also been suggested that the customer has the right to with-

---

[123]*Jeffryes v Agra and Masterman's Bank (1866) LR 2 Eq 674.*
[124]*Bradford Old Bank v Sutcliffe [1918] 2 KB 833 CA.*
[125]*Halesowen Presswork and Assemblies Ltd v Westminster Bank [1972] AC 785 HL.*

draw, at any time, the credit balance as at the date he received notice to combine.[126]

(3) Any express agreement not to combine the accounts will negate the bank's right to do so.

(4) Where one account represents funds held on trust by the customer. If the bank is aware that the funds are held on trust, it is unable to combine. This principle extends to the case where the funds have been lent to the customer for a special purpose – the *Quistclose* trust.[127] Where the bank is unaware of facts which expressly or impliedly indicate that the funds are held on trust, however, it enjoys the right to combine.

The equitable right of set-off

Two recent cases have dealt with this issue: Bhogal v Punjab National Bank[128] and Uttamchandani v Central Bank of India.[129] They had similar facts which essentially were as follows. The bank holds two accounts. One in the name of X which is in credit and one in the name of Y which is overdrawn. The bank believes that both accounts are nominee accounts operated on behalf of a third party, Z. The bank therefore seeks to combine X's and Y's accounts and refuses to honour X's cheques, whereupon X sues. In both cases the bank lost. The relevant general principles are:

(a) a bank has a duty to pay within a reasonable time all cheques properly drawn by its customer; and

(b) an equitable set-off is available only if there is clear and indisputable evidence of the nomineeship. An arguable case of nomineeship is insufficient as whilst the case is pending trial, the customer is denied his funds.

The banks in these cases could have protected their positions by

---

[126]*Halesowen Presswork and Assemblies Ltd v Westminster Bank [1972] AC 785 HL.*
[127]*see 1.7 above.*
[128]*[1988] 2 All ER 296 CA.*
[129]*[1989] NJLR 222 CA.*

having X sign a letter of set-off expressly permitting his account to be used as security for any debt owed to the bank by Y or Z.

Set-off following insolvency

All of the above comments are based on the assumption that neither the customer nor the bank has become subject to the insolvency regime. If one or other is insolvent then the following principles apply.

(1) At the relevant time there will be a statutory set-off under the provisions in section 323 of the Insolvency Act 1986 (individuals) or rule 4.90 of the Insolvency Rules 1986 (companies).

(2) The statutory set-off is automatic and unexcludable so any express or implied agreement not to set-off or combine will become void.[130]

(3) Any agreement to extend the right of set-off will also become void; the assets of the debtor must be distributed in accordance with insolvency law.[131]

(4) Debts which were not yet due and payable become due and payable on the onset of insolvency and are therefore subject to statutory setoff. Contingent debts are also included, the amount can be estimated if the contingency has not occurred by the time the debtor's account is taken.[132]

(5) Where debits on a customer's account take place after the bank had notice of a petition for bankruptcy of an individual customer, or a petition for winding-up or the summoning of a meeting of creditors of a company customer, then these debits will not be set-off. Equally, where a customer has notice of a petition to wind-up the bank or of the summoning of a meeting

---

[130]*Halesowen Presswork and Assemblies Ltd v Westminster Bank [1972] AC 785 HL.*
[131]*British Eagle International Airlines Ltd v Cie Nationale Air France [1975] 1 WLR 758 HL.*
[132]*Stein v Blake [1995] 2 WLR 710 HL.*

of its creditors, any subsequent credits into his account will not be set-off when he proves against the bank's liquidator.

(6) Where the customer has three or more accounts, the statutory set-off will take place to effectively combine all the accounts. If there is one credit balance account and two debit balance accounts, one of which is a wages account, the credit balance will be allocated rateably to the two debit balances in proportion to their respective sizes.[133] For example, if the No. 1 account has a credit balance of £100, the No. 2 account a debit balance of £100 and the wages account a debit balance of £100, statutory set-off will apply so that the bank will claim in the insolvency of the customer for £100. It will claim £50 as a preferential creditor and £50 as an unsecured creditor. If the wages account balance had been £300, the bank would claim a total of £300, £225 as a preferential creditor and £75 as an unsecured creditor.

(7) Part VII of the Companies Act 1989 sets up a new set of insolvency rules which apply when a member of a 'recognised investment exchange', such as the Stock Exchange, becomes insolvent. The relevant exchanges are obliged to have default rules dealing with the insolvency of any member. In a complete reversal of the *British Eagle* principle (point (3) above) these default rules then take precedence over the general insolvency law. The effect is that when a member becomes insolvent, the first stage is a set-off exercise involving that member's debts to and credits from other members of the exchange. Any credit balance resulting can be used for the insolvent member's liabilities to the outside world. Any debit balance resulting is provable by the liquidator. There are also provisions conferring special rights on an exchange holding a charge over a member's assets.

1.15 THE BANKER'S LIEN

A lien generally is a type of security which carries the right to retain property belonging to another pending satisfaction of a debt owed by the owner of the property. For example, when goods are put in for repair, the repairer has a lien over the goods until the repair is

[133]*Re Unit Two Windows Ltd [1985] 3 All ER 647.*

paid for. The goods remain the property of the original owner but the repairer has rights over them. In R v Turner,[134] it was held that the owner of a car who removed it from the repairer's workshop without paying the bill and without permission, could be guilty of theft of his own car. The repairer's lien does not carry a power of sale at common law, although a statutory power can arise under the Torts (Interference with Goods) Act 1977.

A pledge is a different type of security which is more akin to a mortgage. For example, a pawnbroker has a pledge over goods deposited with him. The pledge carries a power of sale of the goods, which in the pawnbroking example, will be deferred pending possible repayment of the debt.

The banker's lien is a special type of lien which is equivalent to an implied pledge. It therefore carries a power of sale.[135]

Property which may be the subject of the banker's lien

In Brandao v Barnett it was stated that the lien could apply to 'securities' in the possession of a bank. Other cases restrict this to 'paper securities'. Share certificates are included[136] as, it seems, is an insurance policy.[137] A dearth of modern cases and a degree of contradiction in the older cases make it somewhat uncertain what other assets are capable of being subject to the lien. It would seem that government stock, Eurobonds, commercial paper and certificates of deposit would qualify. It seems doubtful that the lien can apply to documents of title to land.

Limitations on the operation of the banker's lien

(1) Cheques and bills paid into the bank for collection. The bank may in fact have a lien over cheques paid into an overdrawn account but it is also under a contractual duty to collect the

---

[134][1970] 2 All ER 281 CA.
[135]Brandao v Barnett (1846) 12 Cl & Fin 787 HL.
[136]Re United Service Co., Johnstone's Claim (1870) 40 LJ Ch 286.
[137]Re Bowes, Earl of Strathmore v Vane (1886) 33 ChD 586.

cheque and credit the proceeds to the customer's account. In practice this hardly matters as the proceeds of the cheque will reduce the overdrawn balance. If there are multiple accounts, the bank usually has rights both to appropriate the cheque to a specific account[138] and to combine accounts.

(2) The lien does not apply to securities which are deposited with the bank for safe custody.[139]

(3) The lien does not apply to securities which, to the bank's knowledge, are held in trust by the customer.[140] If, however, the bank is not aware of the trust, the lien does arise.

(4) The lien does not arise if there is any agreement to the contrary between bank and customer.

In Halesowen Presswork and Assemblies Ltd v Westminster Bank,[141] it was held that a lien does not apply to an in-credit bank balance in the customer's name. This was because the money in question in fact belongs to the bank and it is not possible to have a lien over one's own property. This view is now doubtful since the decision in Re Bank of Credit and Commerce International SA (No. 8).[142] In any case, a bank may of course enjoy a right to combine the relevant accounts and there are alternatives to taking a charge over a customer's bank balance.[143]

1.16 SAFE CUSTODY

It is a long established part of a bank's business to accept property from customers for the purposes of safe custody. When one party has possession of property belonging to another in this way, the law describes this as a voluntary bailment. The law further categorises this into a bailment for reward and a gratuitous bailment, depending on whether the bailee (the person accepting the property) is paid by the bailor. It is established, however, that a bank is always to be

---

[138]*Unless the customer has already appropriated, see 1.13 above.*
[139]*Brandao v Barnett, see above.*
[140]*Brandao v Barnett, see above.*
[141]*See above.*
[142]*[1997] 3 WLR 909 HL.*
[143]*See chapter 17.*

regarded as a bailee for reward when taking its customer's property for safe custody, whether or not it is specifically paid for this service.[144] This is because the safe custody arrangement is seen as part of the broader contract between bank and customer.

Liability of a bank bailee

A bank accepting property for safe custody is under a duty to take proper care of it. A bank will be liable in breach of contract if it negligently allows the item to be stolen and it will be liable in conversion if it hands the item to the wrong person.

Other points in relation to safe custody

(1) Where an item has been deposited by two or more bailors jointly, delivery should be made only on the authority of all the bailors.[145] On the death of one bailor, a right of survivorship may accrue to the survivors. Otherwise the personal representative of the deceased should give a receipt.

(2) Where the bank is under some bona fide doubt as to who has title to the goods, it may refuse to hand them over on demand and may detain them for a reasonable time in order to clear up that doubt.[146]

(3) Where the items are stolen by an employee of the bank, there are cases which suggest the bank will only be liable if the employee was acting in the course of his employment in the sense that he was performing his normal duties, albeit dishonestly. This is the test of vicarious liability in tort. The effect of this doctrine is that a bank will only be liable for a theft by an employee whose duties included looking after the property and not for a theft by an employee whose duties did not include supervision of it.[147] It is suggested, however, that a bank will in

[144]*Port Swettenham Authority v TW Wu and Co. (M) Sdn Bhd [1979] AC 580 PC.*
[145]*Brandon v Scott (1857) 7 E&B 234.*
[146]*Hollins v Fowler (1875) LR 7, HL 757.*
[147]*Morris v Martin & Sons Ltd [1966] 1 QB 716 CA.*

any case be liable in breach of contract for negligently permitting an unauthorised employee access to the property or for negligently employing a dishonest employee.

(4) A bank is free to take a mandate from joint bailors to the effect that any one may give a receipt for the property. Even so, by analogy with the cases on duty of care when making payment of cheques, a bank will presumably be liable if it hands over the property with knowledge that a breach of trust is being committed.

(5) A bank is free to disclaim liability for negligence and this was found to be effective in Coldman v Hill.[148] The Unfair Contract Terms Act 1977, however, requires that such an exclusion of liability has to be justified as reasonable. Liability for fraudulent conversion may not be excluded.

(6) Items deposited for safe custody are not subject to the banker's lien.[149]

1.17 TERMINATION OF THE BANKER-CUSTOMER CONTRACT

It is considered that it is preferable to refer to termination of the banker-customer contract, rather than termination of the banker-customer relationship because the relationship may survive indefinitely, e.g. the bank's duty of secrecy.

Termination by customer

The customer may at any time demand full repayment of his credit balance.[150] It is suggested that if the customer reduces the account to a nil balance, the account should not be closed without confirmation from the customer that this is his intention. It would seem that a customer with an overdrawn account may not terminate the banker-customer contract without repaying the debt.

---

[148][1919] 1 KB 443.
[149]Brandao v Barnett, see above.
[150]Joachimson v Swiss Bank Corporation [1921] 3 KB 110 CA.

Termination by bank

It was stated in Joachimson that a bank may only close an account after giving reasonable notice and making provision for outstanding cheques. In Prosperity Ltd v Lloyds Bank,[151] it was held that one month's notice was insufficient, but here the customer's banking arrangements were unusually complex. The Banking Code declares that a customer should be given reasonable notice before his account is closed – and this appears to include overdrawn accounts.[152]

It has been observed that a bank's duty of secrecy survives the termination of the contract. The customer may make claims arising from unauthorised debits (such as forged cheques), which the customer raises for the first time after termination of the contract.[153]

Termination by operation of law

The following events will terminate the contract:

(a) death of the customer;
(b) mental incapacity of a customer;
(c) bankruptcy or insolvency of bank or customer.

---

[151](1923) 39 TLR 372.
[152]Section 2.8.
[153]Limpgrange Ltd v Bank of Credit and Commerce International SA [1986] FLR 36.

2 Types of customer

2.1 INTRODUCTION

Chapter 1 dealt with the banker-customer contract in general terms. This chapter examines six different types of account-holder, each of which is commonly encountered in practice, namely individual customers, joint accounts, minors, trustee accounts, partnerships and companies.

The law relating to the following matters is dealt with for each of the six types of customer, where relevant: the opening of the account, the general conduct of the account, operation of the account by an agent of the customer, insolvency of the customer, mental incapacity of the customer and death or dissolution of the customer.

2.2 INDIVIDUALS

A primary consideration for a bank when opening an account for an individual is to ensure that the person concerned gives his true name. If he does not, and the bank collects cheques which he has stolen, then the bank faces liability in conversion to the true owner of the cheques. It has a defence if it has acted without negligence.[1] Furthermore the bank commits a criminal offence under the Money Laundering Regulations 1993 if it does not follow the identification procedures laid down in those regulations. Also the Banking Code declares that a bank will tell new customers what proof of identifi-

---

[1] *Section 4 of the Cheques Act 1957. See 5.6 below.*

cation is needed from them and what checks may be made with credit reference agencies.[2]

A bank should also ask a new customer for the identity of his employer.[3] There is no duty to keep track of changes of employer, however.[4] In Robinson v Midland Bank,[5] an account was opened for an individual, without his permission, on the application of a third party. Not surprisingly, the practice was disapproved.

Where the new customer is an employer, the bank should consider opening a separate wages account so that it can make a claim as a preferential creditor in the event of the customer's insolvency. The law relating to wages accounts is considered in detail in 2.7 below.

The Money Laundering Regulations require that identity be verified when an account is to be opened, or a significant one-off transaction or series of linked transactions are to be undertaken.[6] It is also required that records be maintained to indicate the nature of the evidence of identity obtained and a copy of that evidence kept. These records must be kept for five years after the relationship with the customer has ended. Guidance Notes issued by the Joint Money Laundering Steering Group[7] indicate that ideally the name of the customer should be verified by a document from a reputable source which bears a photograph. Wherever possible this should be a passport but each bank can decide on the appropriateness of documents in the light of other security procedures operated at account opening. The Guidance Notes suggest that in addition to name verification, the address of the customer should also be verified. Suggested means are checking the electoral roll, making a credit reference agency search, checking the phone book or requesting sight of a recent utility or council tax bill or a bank or building society statement.

---

[2]*Section 4.6.*
[3]*Lloyds Bank v E.B. Savory & Co. [1933] AC 201 HL.*
[4]*Orbit Mining and Trading Co. Ltd v Westminster Bank [1963] 1 QB 794 CA.*
[5]*(1925) 41 TLR 402.*
[6]*Verification is not normally necessary when there is to be a single one-off payment by or to a person of less than ECU 15,000.*
[7]*Originally known as the 'Red Book' – the current edition is named the 'Money Laundering Guidance Notes', published August 1997 by the British Bankers Association.*

Operation of the account by third parties

It may happen that an individual customer authorises another to operate his account. He may do this by specifically informing the bank, in which case he will be asked to sign a mandate form, or by executing a power of attorney. In either case an agency is set up.

Where a bank mandate form is signed by the customer, the powers conferred on the agent will be clearly set out and will normally be in broad terms. The bank must, however, operate the account strictly within the powers granted. Where the agent operates the account for his own benefit and the bank knows this, the bank will not be able to rely on the mandate form and will be liable in breach of contract to its customer and as a constructive trustee.[8]

Powers of attorney

Similar considerations apply when the account is operated by the donee of a power of attorney. Under the Powers of Attorney Act 1971, a power must be executed as a deed by the donor. If he is incapable of signing, it may be signed on his behalf in his presence. In this case, two witnesses must attest the deed. A bank may rely on a photocopy of the deed if it is certified by the donor or by a solicitor or stockbroker. A power may be expressed as a general power in accordance with section 10 of the Act in which case the bank may assume that the donee has the widest possible powers.

A mandate or a power of attorney will be revoked under general principles of agency law by:

(a) death of the principal or agent;
(b) mental incapacity of principal or agent;
(c) insolvency of principal;
(d) notice by principal or agent;
(e) fulfilment of the purpose of the agency;
(f) expiration of the term of the agency; or
(g) illegality or frustration of the agency.

If any of the above occurs, therefore, the authority of the agent is

[8]*Lipkin Gorman v Karpnale Ltd [1989] 1 WLR 1340 CA.*

terminated. However, a bank which deals with the donee of a power, after the power has in fact been revoked, is protected by the Act, so long as it did not know of the revocation.[9] When a bank mandate is used, the bank will not enjoy this protection.

There are, however, two ways in which the agency will not necessarily be revoked by some of the above.

Enduring powers of attorney

A particular problem with powers of attorney is that where a donor becomes mentally incapable, the power is automatically revoked at a time when it is likely to be needed the most.

Under the Enduring Powers of Attorney Act 1985, an individual may grant a power which can survive his mental incapacity. He must, of course, be mentally competent when he grants the power. The power must be in the precise form required by regulations made under the Act (this means that the standard form, including marginal notes, must be used), executed by donor and by donee and witnessed. When the donor becomes mentally incapable, the donee must apply to the court for registration of the power. Meanwhile, pending the court hearing, the power enters a hiatus period during which time the donee has limited authority in order to maintain himself and the donor. If and when the power is registered by the court, the donee reassumes the power he had before the onset of incapacity.

Irrevocable power of attorney

An equitable mortgage under seal is discussed in 13.11 (note that section 1 of the Law of Property (Miscellaneous Provisions) Act 1989 does away with the need for sealing a document, so long as the parties to it intend it to be a deed). The system relies upon a power of attorney being granted by the mortgagor in favour of the mortgagee, along with deposit of the title deeds to the asset being mortgaged; a full memorandum of deposit signed by both parties is also required in the case of a mortgage over land, in order to comply

[9] *Section 5(2) Powers of Attorney Act 1971.*

with section 2 of the Law of Property (Miscellaneous Provisions) Act 1989. The memorandum of deposit should be executed as a deed. By these means, the mortgagee acquires a power of sale over the asset. Clearly the security would be vulnerable if the power could be revoked, and thus the Powers of Attorney Act 1971 recognises an irrevocable power when it is granted to secure the performance of an obligation owed to the donee. Until this obligation is performed, the power may not be revoked by notice from the donor, nor by his death, mental incapacity or insolvency.

Death or mental incapacity of an individual account-holder

It has been noted,[10] that either of these events will have the effect of terminating the banker-customer contract. By section 75 of the Bills of Exchange Act 1882, however, a bank's authority to pay a customer's cheques is terminated when the bank receives notice of the customer's death. Presumably this statutory provision overrides the common law, and a bank is protected paying a customer's cheques until it knows of the death.

Bankruptcy of an individual account-holder

The bankruptcy regime set up by the Insolvency Act 1986 provides for the process to begin with a bankruptcy petition presented to the court. This may be presented by the debtor himself on the ground of his inability to pay his debts or it may be presented by a creditor on the ground of the debtor's inability to pay his debts or of the debtor having no reasonable prospect of paying his debts. The creditor can establish these grounds either by delivering a statutory demand to the debtor which is not complied with within three weeks or by unsatisfied execution of a judgment debt. When the court considers the petition, it may then make a bankruptcy order against the debtor. A trustee in bankruptcy will be appointed to supervise payment to the creditors. Finally, three years after the

[10]*In 1.17 above.*

bankruptcy order (two years in the case of a 'small bankruptcy'), the debtor is normally discharged from bankruptcy.

The essential feature of the law is that on the making of the bankruptcy order, all property which at that time belongs to the debtor automatically vests in the trustee in bankruptcy who holds it on behalf of the creditors. It matters not that the trustee is in fact appointed some time after the making of the order, since his title relates back to the date of the order. The bankrupt is allowed to retain the tools of his trade, clothing, household equipment, etc. Also any assets he holds on trust do not pass to the trustee. It follows from the above that where an individual has a bank account and he becomes bankrupt, on the date of the bankruptcy order any credit balance will cease to belong to the individual and will pass to the trustee. The bank should not therefore honour any cheques after the making of the bankruptcy order but should await the instructions of the trustee. Where the account is overdrawn the bank will make its claim as a creditor in the bankruptcy.

Where there is an overdrawn balance on the wages account of a sole trader customer, the bank may make a claim as a preferential creditor. The full legal position relating to wages accounts is discussed under company customers.[11]

Where the bank holds some form of mortgage from the bankrupt customer, it will be unable to claim in the bankruptcy except in as much as the security is insufficient (it can prove in the bankruptcy in full if it releases its security). The law relating to the bank as secured creditor is discussed in chapter 13.

Conduct of the account after presentation of the bankruptcy petition but before the making of the bankruptcy order

Section 284 of the Insolvency Act states that payments and dispositions of property by the debtor that take place after the presentation of the bankruptcy petition and before the making of the bankruptcy order are void unless ratified by the court. Bankruptcy petitions are not published in the London Gazette so a bank may not be aware of

[11]*See 2.7 below.*

the petition. If it is aware, however, it should not pay any cheque from an account in credit. Where it has paid in ignorance of the petition, it must hope that the court will ratify the payment.

Where an account is overdrawn when the bank hears of a bankruptcy petition, the bank should not pay any further cheques for obvious practical reasons but in addition, the bank will find it is unable to even claim for the debt. If a bank pays in ignorance of the petition, it is considered that it will be able to claim for the debt.

In respect of payments into the debtor's account between the presentation of the petition and the making of the order, in practical terms the bank will have no reason to refuse to accept these, so long as it declined to allow the debtor to withdraw the funds. Once the bankruptcy order is made, any credit balance will vest in the trustee in bankruptcy. Payments into an overdrawn account will serve to reduce the sum owed to the bank if the bank is in ignorance of the petition and acts in good faith.[12] Payments into an overdrawn account where the bank knows of the petition will have to be returned to the trustee unless the court ratifies this disposition of the debtor's property.

Operation of the account after the bankruptcy order is made

The Act permits a bankrupt to retain property which he acquires after the making of the bankruptcy order, unless the trustee serves notice under section 307 to claim the property. On the other hand, section 284 still applies to render void dispositions and payments that take place after the order. The safe course for a bank is therefore to refuse to allow the bankrupt to operate his account until a validation order is made by the court.

Where the court has ordered that the bankruptcy order should not be advertised, e.g. pending an appeal by the debtor, and the bank in ignorance of the order operates an account, some protection may be afforded by section 284(5). This permits a bank to claim for a debit on the debtor's account which took place after the order if the bank was unaware of the bankruptcy and it is reasonably practi-

[12]*Section 284(4) of the Insolvency Act 1986.*

cable to recover the money from the recipient (i.e. the payee of the cheque).

Once the bankrupt has been discharged from bankruptcy, all debts are permanently discharged. The debtor will remain liable, however, for debts which have arisen since the date of the bankruptcy order.

2.3 JOINT ACCOUNTS

When a bank opens an account in joint names, it will need to establish true identities and to find out the names of the new customers' employers in the same way as with an individual account.

A mandate will normally be taken. This will render the customers jointly and severally liable for any debt owed to the bank.[13] It will also establish whether the account may be operated by either one on his own or only by both acting jointly. In the absence of an agreement to operate by either one, the presumption will be that both signatures are required.[14] The mandate will in any event separately declare that a right of survivorship applies, so that on the death of one of them the bank may pay the whole balance to the survivor. Even without such a clause, the law would normally, but not always, assume that the survivor of a joint account would be beneficially entitled to the whole balance. In an exceptional case, the law may conclude that the whole balance accrues to the deceased, even when there is a survivorship agreement. In McEvoy v Belfast Banking Co. Ltd,[15] a father opened a joint account in his name and that of his son. He deposited £10,000. Payment was mandated to either or to the survivor. The father died and over some years the bank paid the money away to his executors who were continuing the father's business and in which the son played a part. The son then sued for the money. In a case where the plaintiff's case had few merits in non-legal terms, the court came to the conclusion that, in equity, the money had passed to the father's estate.

Where the mandate requires both signatures to operate the account, the bank will be liable to the non-signing party if it pays

---

[13]See 2.6 below for an explanation of the effect of this.
[14]Husband v Davis (1851) 10 CB 645.
[15][1935] AC 24 HL.

on the signature of only one. This liability will amount to half the sum that was withdrawn.[16] However, if payment of the cheque in question served to discharge a debt for which both of the account-holders were liable, the bank may rely on the subrogation principle to debit the account.[17]

On the death of the first account-holder, assuming the normal survivorship agreement, it is considered that the bank will always be safe in paying the survivor, irrespective of the decision in McEvoy, unless it is restrained by court order.

If the account is overdrawn at the time of death, the bank may wish to rule off the account in order to preserve its claim against the estate of the deceased, as otherwise the rule in *Clayton's case* will operate so that subsequent credits will extinguish the pre-death debt. Cheques signed by the deceased but presented after his death should not be paid, applying section 75 of the Bills of Exchange Act 1882.

The mandate will authorise either account-holder to countermand payment of a cheque, even if cheques require both signatures.

If one account-holder becomes mentally incapable, the bank should not pay any further cheques until the Court of Protection has appointed a Receiver to manage his affairs. Payment can then be made on the joint instructions of the Receiver and the other account-holder. This is so even if the mandate permitted payment on either signature. Where the other account-holder holds an Enduring Power of Attorney, the position will differ.[18]

If one account-holder is made bankrupt, no further cheques should be paid pending the appointment of a trustee in bankruptcy, and then the bank should act on the joint instructions of the solvent account holder and the trustee. This is so even if the mandate permitted payment on either signature. The considerations discussed in 2.2 above apply so payments after notice of the bankruptcy petition should not be made. In the event of mental incapacity or bankruptcy occurring when the account is overdrawn, the account should be ruled off before fresh credits are entered on the account.

[16]*Catlin v Cyprus Finance Corpn (London) [1983] QB 759.*
[17]*B. Liggett (Liverpool) Ltd v Barclays Bank [1928] 1 KB 48.*
[18]*See 2.2 above.*

This is to preserve the bank's claim against the trustee in bankruptcy or the Receiver.

2.4 MINORS

A minor is a person under the age of 18 years.[19] Special rules apply to a minor's ability to enter into contracts. Briefly, a minor's contracts will be enforceable only if they are for 'necessaries' as opposed to luxuries.[20] As explained in chapter 1, the banker-customer relationship is not entirely concerned with contract. The position with respect to liability in other branches of the law is different. A minor can be liable for negligence and other torts and also may be prosecuted for crimes he has committed as young as the tender age of ten years.

The contract between bank and a minor customer is thus enforceable if it is considered one for 'necessaries'. In the unlikely event that it is not considered to be for 'necessaries', the contract is still enforceable by the minor but not by the bank. If the account is in credit, the bank would in practice only need to sue for its charges.

If money is lent to a minor, the lender has no right to recovery even if the borrowing was intended for the purchase of 'necessaries'. However, if the loan is in fact spent on 'necessaries', the lender can recover the amount so spent under the subrogation principle, and where a cheque is drawn by a minor to pay for 'necessaries', the bank is entitled to debit the minor's account by operation of the rule of subrogation. This is analogous to the facts in B. Liggett (Liverpool) Ltd v Barclays Bank[21]. If the cheque was not for 'necessaries', the court has power to order that the money (or what has come to represent the money) be returned if it considers this just and equitable.[22]

When money is lent to a minor and a guarantee is taken from an adult, the guarantee is enforceable notwithstanding that the minor

[19]*Family Law Reform Act 1969.*
[20]*Nash v Inman [1908] 2 KB 1.*
[21]*See above.*
[22]*Section 3 of the Minors Contracts Act 1987.*

may not be liable to repay.[23] A guarantee taken from a minor, however, remains void.

A minor has no capacity to draw or indorse a cheque and can thus never be liable as party to a cheque even if it was drawn to pay for 'necessaries'.[24] However, for reasons explained above, a minor can still be liable to his bank for the debt the cheque creates and also to the payee under the underlying contract. The minor cannot be liable to remoter parties, however, such as an indorsee of the cheque. When a cheque is drawn or indorsed by a minor, the holder is still entitled to payment from the other parties to the cheque.

The Banking Code requires banks to be selective and careful when sending marketing material to minor customers.[25]

2.5 TRUSTEE ACCOUNTS

Where two or more trustees are appointed under the terms of an express trust, the law generally requires them to act jointly. Delegation of the powers of a trustee is only permitted within the strict limits of sections 23 and 25 of the Trustee Act 1925. It is considered that these powers to delegate do not extend to the signing of cheques, and that therefore a bank should always insist that all the trustees sign every cheque. This would not be necessary, however, when the trust deed expressly permits signature by less than the full number. It is different in the case of a charitable trust. Statute permits the trustees to delegate the signing of cheques to any two or more of their number.[26]

Where trustees have power under the trust to apply capital, they are also permitted to raise capital by mortgaging trust property.[27] A mortgagee of trust property is not concerned to see that the money

[23]Section 2 of the Minors Contracts Act 1987.
[24]Section 22 of the Bills of Exchange Act 1882.
[25]Section 2.17.
[26]Section 82 of the Charities Act 1993.
[27]Section 16 of the Trustee Act 1925.

so raised is wanted by the trust or as to the application of the money.[28]

Under general principles of trust law, a bank is safe in permitting the trustees to breach the strict terms of the trust if this is done with full consent of all the possible beneficiaries, all of whom are over 18 and mentally capable.[29] Where a bank pays away money on the instructions of the trustee or trustees when he or they are acting in breach of trust, it faces liability towards the beneficiaries. The bank has a duty to make inquiry if it knows of the breach of trust. The principles of law discussed in 1.7 above in relation to constructive trusts are relevant here, in particular the concept of liability when the assistor has acted dishonestly.[30] Where the bank has not been specifically informed of the existence of the trust, it is nevertheless deemed to know that the account is a trust account if that is suggested by the name of the account or any other circumstances.[31]

On the death of a trustee, the surviving trustee or trustees have power to operate the account.[32] On the death of the last surviving trustee, the account may be operated by his personal representatives. A trustee who becomes bankrupt may continue as trustee and his trustee in bankruptcy does not take the property which he holds on trust. A new trustee may be appointed in place of a retiring trustee under section 36. The bank will wish to see the deed of appointment and to have him sign the mandate.

Where there are two or more executors then, unlike trustees, they do have power to act on their own. Like trustees, however, they have no power to delegate to third parties.

2.6 PARTNERSHIP ACCOUNTS

A partnership is defined by section 1(1) of the Partnership Act 1890 as 'the relationship which subsists between persons carrying on a business in common with a view of profit'. No formal procedure is

---

[28]*Section 17.*
[29]*Saunders v Vautier (1841) [1835-42] All ER Rep. LCCt 58.*
[30]*See Royal Brunei Airlines v Tan [1995] 2 AC 378 PC.*
[31]*Rowlandson v National Westminster Bank Ltd [1978] 1 WLR 798.*
[32]*Section 18 Trustee Act 1925.*

required to set up a partnership and one can be inferred from conduct. It can thus happen that the persons concerned are not even aware that they are considered in law to be partners.

Where the partnership is formalised it is common to find articles or a deed of partnership which sets out the rights of the partners and the extent of their authority. In the absence of express provision on any matter, however, the Partnership Act (supplemented by case law) lays down implied rights, duties and powers.

As affects a third party, such as a bank maintaining a partnership account, the relevant rules are:

(1) Any partner has implied authority to bind the firm, as agent of it, when acting in the course of the usual business of the firm.[33] Any restriction on a partner's powers will not affect a third party unless he is aware of the restriction.

(2) More specifically, any partner has implied power to draw cheques.[34]

(3) In a trading partnership (one whose main activity is buying and selling goods) any partner has implied power to borrow money and charge security on behalf of the firm. In a non-trading partnership these implied powers do not apply.[35]

(4) There is no implied power to give guarantees on behalf of the firm. Any partner purporting to do so will only render himself liable under the guarantee.[36]

(5) Partners are jointly liable for debts owed by the firm.[37]

(6) There is no concept of limited liability, except in the rare example of a Limited Partnership set up under the Limited Partnership Act 1907, where some but not all of the partners may have their liability limited to their initial contribution. General partners may therefore lose their personal assets if required to meet the debts of the business.

Some of the above law is modified by the standard bank mandate

---

[33] Section 5.
[34] *Backhouse v Charlton (1878) 8 Ch D 444.*
[35] *Alliance Bank v Kearsley (1871) LR 6 CP 433.*
[36] *Brettel v Williams (1849) 4 Ex 623.*
[37] Section 9.

which expressly deals with operation of the account, borrowing money, etc. It is common to find that at least two partners must authorise transactions and, if so, the bank is bound by this. If only one partner signs but does so using the firm's name or signs a cheque with the firm's name printed on it, section 23(2) of the Bills of Exchange Act 1882 has the effect of making all the partners liable on the cheque to the payee, irrespective of any mandate requiring two or more signatures.[38] It does not necessarily follow that the paying bank can use this principle of law to justify paying in breach of mandate requiring two signatures. However, the subrogation principle exemplified in B. Liggett (Liverpool) v Barclays Bank[39] entitles the bank to debit the partnership account if the payment discharged a legal liability of the partnership.

Invariably, the mandate will extend the joint liability of the partners into joint and several liability. Joint liability permits the creditor to claim the full debt owed by the partnership from any one partner, assuming that partner is solvent and alive. It is possible to claim from and sue several partners simultaneously, each for the full amount of the debt. Once the debt has been satisfied, the remaining claims would be abandoned. Judgment against one partner (which has not been satisfied) is no bar to fresh proceedings against another.[40] The advantage of joint and several liability, from the bank's point of view, is that the bank is able to claim against the personal estate of a deceased partner as well as against the estate of the partnership.[41] Additionally, the bank may set-off a partner's individual account against a partnership debt and prove against a bankrupt partner alongside his personal creditors. The ability to

---

[38]*Central Motors (Birmingham) v P.A. & S.N. Wadsworth [1983] C.A.T. 82/ 231; Ringham v Hackett (1980) 124 SJ 201.*
[39]*[1928] 1 KB 48.*
[40]*Section 3 of the Civil Liability (Contribution) Act 1978.*
[41]*The risk is that the estate of a deceased person who was merely jointly liable for the debt would not be liable at all on the basis that the survivor of a jointly owed debt acquires it in full, just as he would acquire a jointly owned asset in full under the right of survivorship. Section 1(1) of the Law Reform (Miscellaneous Provisions) Act 1934 may render the estate liable, however.*

do these things can on occasions significantly improve the funds repayable to the bank.

Any one partner may countermand payment of a partnership cheque.[42]

When opening a partnership account, the bank will ensure that the mandate form is completed. The bank may prefer not to see a copy of the articles of partnership as, if it does, it will have notice of the contents, which may include a restriction on the powers of the partners.

If the partnership is an employer, the bank should consider opening a separate wages account.[43]

Dissolution of the partnership

If the articles do not provide to the contrary, dissolution will occur by operation of law when, *inter alia*, a partner retires, dies, is made bankrupt, or when a new partner joins the firm. Dissolution may also occur by court order under section 35, e.g. on mental incapacity of one partner, or on just and equitable grounds.

On dissolution, the bank will wish to rule off the account if it is overdrawn, in order to prevent the operation of the rule in *Clayton's case*[44] serving to reduce the debt owed at the time of dissolution. This is because normally partners are not liable for debts incurred by the firm after they left it.[45] The surviving partners will be under a duty to wind up the business of the old partnership, and in doing so, they have a residual power to deal with partnership property, including mortgaging it.[46] This permits the bank to continue the operation of the account and to accept mortgages from the members

---

[42]*Gaunt v Taylor (1843) 2 Hare 413.*

[43]*See 2.7 below.*

[44]*See 1.13 above.*

[45]*A retired partner must notify existing creditors of the firm and also publish in the London Gazette if he is not to be liable under the 'holding out' principle, section 36. In the case of a partner who dies, or who becomes mentally incapable or bankrupt, it automatically follows that his estate is not liable for future debts. No notice is necessary.*

[46]*Section 38 and Re Bourne [1906] 2 Ch 427 CA.*

of the now dissolved partnership. There is no residual power to continue the business, however, when the entire partnership is made bankrupt. Where the dissolved partnership is reformed or where a new partner is admitted to the firm (even if this does not involve dissolution), the bank will wish to take a fresh mandate from the partners.

Insolvency of the partnership

The Insolvent Partnerships Order 1986 provides that a court may order a partnership to be made bankrupt, or wound up, or both. In any event there will be an automatic dissolution.

A winding-up of the partnership does not necessarily involve bankruptcy of the partners, but the effect of a bankruptcy order against the partnership is to make all the partners individually bankrupt. All of their personal assets are then available to pay both their personal debts and the firm's debts. The order provides that the partnership assets are used to pay the firm's debts, but that each partner's personal assets are firstly used to pay off his personal debts; only if there is a surplus remaining is the balance then used towards paying the firm's debts.

The result is that a partner's personal creditor is likely to receive a better payment than a creditor of the firm. As explained above, the bank mandate provides that partners will be severally as well as jointly liable for the firm's debts. This has the effect of entitling the bank to claim as a personal creditor of each partner, in addition to claiming as a creditor of the firm. The bank's prospects of debt recovery are thus vastly improved.

Where a wages account has been operated, the bank may make a claim as a preferential creditor.

2.7 COMPANIES

It is a fundamental principle of English company law that a company is a separate legal entity from its shareholders and may sue and be sued in its own name. It can also be prosecuted for crimes it has committed.

The vast majority of companies in England and Wales are registered companies limited by shares. Such companies may be public or private; a public company must have 'plc' at the end of its name and a private company must have 'limited' (Welsh language equivalents are acceptable). The principles examined here are identical for public and private companies.

Until recently, banks had to be concerned about a company customer's capacity to open an account, to borrow money, give security etc. and about the directors' powers to bind the company (the *ultra vires* rules). The Companies Act 1989, however, has effectively repealed these rules[47] and a bank need not be concerned about powers of the company or of its agents so long as it deals with the directors of the company, either directly or with someone authorised by them. New rules also deal with company seals and the way that company documents may be executed.[48]

Despite the new rules on corporate capacity, a bank still owes a duty of care to a company customer when paying its cheques.[49] Thus if a bank has paid a company cheque (drawn by a director acting fraudulently), when a reasonable banker would have been suspicious in the circumstances, the bank is liable to the company, by analogy to the facts of Lipkin Gorman v Karpnale Ltd.[50]

There are further possibilities with company accounts, however. The Companies Acts set out a number of criminal offences which only companies, or those associated with them, may commit. Thus it is a crime for a company to provide financial assistance for the purchase of its own shares.[51] In Selangor United Rubber Estates Ltd v Cradock (No. 3),[52] a bank was held to be unable to debit the account of a company customer in respect of a cheque to buy shares in the company in contravention of the rule in section 151. It is submitted that, following *Lipkin Gorman*, a bank would now only

---

[47]*See 16.2 below.*
[48]*See 16.3 below.*
[49]*See 1.6 above.*
[50]*See 1.6 above.*
[51]*Section 151 of the Companies Act 1985. This was the main charge in the Guinness trial in 1990.*
[52]*[1968] 1 WLR 1555.*

be liable in these circumstances if it failed the 'reasonable banker' test.

It is an offence for a company to lend money to its own directors (subject to numerous exceptions).[53] A danger area would be when a bank lends money to a company customer, knowing that the company will onlend the funds to a director.

Company cheques

As the company customer is an inanimate object, all of its cheques must be signed by a human being acting as its agent. If the company's cheque bears a printed 'signature' the instrument would not be within the legal definition of a cheque and the rules described here therefore might not apply. The printed signature can be a valid instruction to the bank to pay the funds stated on the instrument, however, and to debit the company's account, this would depend on the terms of the banker-customer contract.

A cheque is deemed to have been made by a company if made in the company's name, or on its behalf, by a person acting under the company's authority.[54] Further, every company must have its name on all cheques purporting to be signed by or on behalf of the company.[55] Section 26 of the Bills of Exchange Act 1882 provides that a person who signs a cheque on behalf of a stated principal shall not be personally liable on the cheque. He may be liable, however, if the principal is not stated. Where a director signed a company cheque in his own name, but the cheque was printed with the company's name and account number, the company and not the director was liable on the cheque.[56] The company name must be printed in full and without any abbreviation, failing which the signatory will be personally liable on it.[57] 'L R Agencies Limited' will not suffice for 'L & R Agencies Limited'[58] and 'M. Jackson (Fancy

---

[53]See the Companies Act 1985, sections 330 to 347.
[54]Section 37 of the Companies Act 1985.
[55]Section 349 of the Companies Act 1985.
[56]Bondina Ltd v Rollaway Shower Blinds Ltd [1986] 1 WLR 517 CA.
[57]Section 349(4) of the Companies Act 1985.
[58]Hendon v Adelman (1973) 117 Sol Jo 631.

Goods) Limited' will not suffice for 'Michael Jackson (Fancy Goods) Limited'.[59] The abbreviations 'Co' and 'Ltd' are acceptable, however, as is any unambiguous abbreviation.[60]

Company insolvency

The insolvency regime pertaining to companies extends to a number of possibilities. A company may set up a voluntary arrangement, it may go into liquidation, it may go into administration and administrative receivers may be appointed to manage its affairs. The voluntary arrangement is briefly discussed in 10.3 below and administration orders are dealt with in 16.10 below. Administrative receivers may only be appointed by a holder of a floating charge and are discussed at length in 16.8 below.

A company going into liquidation must be wound-up. The winding-up process may be voluntary or compulsory. A voluntary winding-up commences with the appropriate resolution at the company's general meeting of shareholders. The company must immediately cease to carry on its business, except for the purpose of a beneficial winding-up. A liquidator is usually appointed at the meeting and the powers of the directors cease on this appointment.

A compulsory winding-up consists of a court order to that effect. Seven different grounds for this are set out in section 122 of the Insolvency Act 1986. The ground relating to insolvency states simply 'the company is unable to pay its debts'. This ground is established by any one of four alternative routes:[61]

(a) a statutory demand is served on the company and no payment is received within three weeks;
(b) a judgment creditor attempts to enforce his judgment by having court officers seize the company's assets but insufficient assets are found;

[59]*Durham Fancy Goods Ltd v Michael Jackson (Fancy Goods) Ltd [1968] 2 QB 839.*
[60]*Banque de l'Indochine et de Suez SA v Euroseas Group Finance Co. Ltd [1981] 3 All ER 198.*
[61]*Section 123.*

(c) the company is unable to pay its debts as they fall due; or
(d) the company's liabilities exceed its assets.

The compulsory winding-up commences with a petition to the court. Sometime later the court hears the case. If the petition is dismissed, there is no winding-up. If the order is made, however, the winding-up is deemed to commence on the date the petition was presented.

By section 127 any disposition of the company's property after the commencement of the winding-up is void, unless the court otherwise orders. It has been held that the effect of this is that payments by a company into its overdrawn bank account constitute a void disposition of the company's property, and also that payments out of a company's bank account constitute a void disposition of property.[62]

Petitions to wind-up a company are published in the London Gazette and it is important for a bank to search each issue for names of its corporate customers. Once the petition has been presented, the bank should not pay any more of the company's cheques. If it does so, the liquidator may later obtain a court order requiring the bank to repay the funds to him. The court is empowered, however, to sanction a disposition under section 127. A bank is likely to obtain this sanction retrospectively in two situations:

(a) if it paid cheques after the petition was presented but before it was published; and
(b) if the disposition did not prejudice the position of the unsecured creditors of the company.[63]

The bank's liability as a shadow director

Section 214 of the Companies Act 1985, dealing with 'wrongful trading', empowers the court to make an order requiring a director to make a contribution to the assets of the company in the following circumstances:

[62]Re Gray's Inn Construction Ltd [1980] 1 WLR 711.
[63]Re Gray's Inn Construction Ltd [1980] 1 WLR 711 and Denney v John Hudson & Co Ltd [1992] BCLC 901 CA.

(a) the company has gone into insolvent liquidation; and
(b) at some time before the commencement of the winding-up, the director knew or ought to have concluded that there was no reasonable prospect that the company would avoid going into insolvent liquidation.

A shadow director is defined as a person in accordance with whose instructions the directors of the company are accustomed to act.[64] The risk for a bank is that it will set out a rescue package for a financially troubled company customer. The company unsuccessfully follows the rescue plan, leaving the bank potentially liable for wrongful trading as a shadow director.[65]

In assessing (b) above, a director is assumed to be a reasonably diligent person with both the knowledge, skill and experience that may reasonably be expected of a person carrying out the same functions as carried out by that director in relation to the company and the knowledge, skill and experience that that director actually has. Since it is the corporate entity of the bank which could be deemed to be the shadow director, the level of skill and experience that that director has would inevitably be considered to be very high. The level of knowledge about the company's finances would depend on the degree of access to the facts that the bank actually had, bearing in mind it was not a *de jure* director sitting at board meetings. A director will not be liable, however, if he took every step with a view to minimising the potential loss to the company's creditors which he ought to have taken.

Wages accounts

The priority of creditors' claims in the event of a company's insolvency is set out in 10.2 below. The category of preferential creditor ranks higher than the unsecured creditor and also higher than the floating charge holder. A bank creditor is therefore pleased to rank

---

[64]*Section 251 of the Companies Act 1985.*
[65]*Re a Company (No. 005009 of 1987) ex p Copp [1989] BCLC 13. Also relevant is Re Tasbian Ltd (No.3) [1993] BCLC 297 CA, cf Re Hydrodam (Corby) Ltd [1994] 2 BCLC 180.*

as a preferential creditor, if only partially, unless it is fully secured with fixed charges.

Schedule 6 of the Insolvency Act 1986 declares that preferential claims include those who have lent money which has been used to pay:

(a) employees' wages in respect of any period of employment in the four months prior to the resolution to wind-up the company (if a voluntary winding-up) or prior to the winding-up order (if compulsory). There is an upper limit of £800 per employee;

(b) accrued holiday remuneration in respect of any period of employment at any time before the winding-up and without financial limit.[66]

Where a company has a single bank account, the bank's ability to prove as a preferential creditor will depend on whether the most recently paid cheques include a cheque to pay wages. This is because the rule in *Clayton's case*[67] applies to appropriate the debits. For example, if the overdrawn balance at winding-up stands at £5,000, and the last cheque was for £5,000 to pay general trade creditors, and the one before was for £5,000 to pay wages, the bank is not a preferential creditor. If the final cheque was the one to pay wages, however, the bank is a preferential creditor.

The advantage of opening a separate wages account is that any overdrawn balance on that account at the start of the winding-up constitutes a preferential claim, subject to the limits stated above, i.e. not more than £800 per employee and employment in the previous four months. The balance on the general account will indisputably constitute a non-preferential claim.

Clayton's case operates on the wages account, so that the relevant debits are always the most recent, and these will tend to be preferential because they represent employment in the previous four months.

A number of cases have decided points relating to wages accounts. It is not essential that a wages account be opened in order for the bank to be a preferential creditor, it is just that it avoids the

---

[66]*Lending money to discharge other preferential claims such as Value Added Tax liability does not entitle the lender to preferential creditor status.*
[67]*See 1.13 above.*

risk of the adverse operation of *Clayton's case* as explained above.[68]
It is, however, essential that the debits on the wages account constitute genuine loans to the customer. If the bank insists on credits to
the general account before it permits a wages cheque to be drawn,
there is no loan entitling the bank to claim preferentially.[69] The bank
has a right of appropriation, so that if it holds fixed security, it may
realise this and appropriate the proceeds to the general account,
thus leaving it with a full preferential claim in respect of the wages
account. It may do so even after the winding-up of the company has
commenced.[70] It may also combine accounts as it wishes, and may
choose to combine a credit balance account with an overdrawn
general account, leaving a separate overdrawn wages account to
constitute a preferential claim. This right of combination ceases on
commencement of the winding-up, however, and on the above facts
there would then have to be a rateable abatement of the preferential
claim.[71] A bank can claim as a preferential creditor, after lending
money which the customer uses to pay wages, in respect of partnership and sole trader customers as well as company customers.

[68]*Re Primrose (Builders) Ltd [1950] Ch 561.*
[69]*Re E.J. Morel (1934) Ltd [1961] 3 WLR 57.*
[70]*Re William Hall (Contractors) Ltd [1967] 1 WLR 948.*
[71]*Re Unit Two Windows Ltd [1985] 3 All ER 647, explained in 1.14 above.*

3 Consumer credit act lending

3.1 INTRODUCTION

The Consumer Credit Act 1974[1] (referred to hereafter in this chapter as the 'Act') has three basic functions:

(a) to supervise those involved in granting credit by means of a licensing system;
(b) to place controls on the advertising and canvassing of credit; and
(c) to regulate individual credit agreements and to provide the debtor with certain rights, irrespective of express agreement between him and the creditor.

This chapter deals mostly with the last of these functions since it is this which has the greatest effect on the legal relationship between banks and their borrower customers. The Act is concerned with agreements for consumer hire as well as those for consumer credit but the former are outside the scope of this book. The Act also covers credit-brokers but it is assumed in this chapter that a bank is acting on its own behalf and not broking credit on behalf of another, nor using a credit-broker to introduce it to customers.

Anyone carrying on a consumer credit business requires a licence.[2] This is issued by the Director General of Fair Trading who must be satisfied that the applicant is fit to be engaged in the activities to be licensed and that the name under which he applies to be

---

[1] *The Act was preceded by the Crowther Committee on Consumer Credit (1971) Cmnd 4596.*
[2] *Licensing is covered in Part III of the Act.*

licensed is not misleading or undesirable.[3] The Director General has powers to refuse an application for a licence, and to vary, suspend or revoke existing licences. It is a criminal offence to engage in consumer credit business without holding a licence and any agreement entered into is only enforceable against the debtor if the Director General so orders.

In the Act, the borrower is referred to as the debtor and the lender referred to as the creditor. This terminology is adopted in this chapter.

3.2 THE DEFINITIONS OF REGULATED LENDING

A regulated agreement is a consumer credit agreement[4] which is not an exempt agreement. A consumer credit agreement is an agreement for the provision of credit where the debtor is an individual and the amount of credit does not exceed £25,000.[5] Interest due on the loan and arrangement fees are ignored in determining the amount of the credit. Loans to companies are not regulated but loans to unincorporated businesses are capable of being regulated, including those to partnerships.[6]

Consumer credit agreements must be categorised into:

(a) running-account credit or fixed-sum credit;
(b) restricted-use or unrestricted-use credit;
(c) debtor-creditor or debtor-creditor-supplier credit.

Running-account credit is defined as a facility where the debtor receives from time to time cash, goods or services up to any applicable credit limit[7] and in the retail banking context is exampled by the current account overdraft and the credit card account. Fixed sum is defined as any other form of credit[8] and is exampled by a

---

[3] Section 25.
[4] Or consumer hire agreement.
[5] Section 8. The amount of £25,000 is effective from 1st May 1998 (SI 1998/996).
[6] Unless all the members of the partnership are corporations, section 185.
[7] Section 10(1)(a).
[8] Section 10(1)(b).

personal loan. Running-account credit is within the £25,000 limit for regulated agreements if the credit limit does not exceed £25,000, or even if it is over £25,000 the debtor is unable to draw more than £25,000 at any one time, or the rate of interest steps up at £25,000 or below, or at the time the agreement is made it is probable that the debtor will draw more than £25,000.

Restricted-use credit is essentially that where the creditor retains actual control over the use that the debtor makes of the funds, disregarding any contractual promise the debtor makes concerning use of the funds.[9] A bank overdraft is typically unrestricted-use credit because the debtor can withdraw cash or write cheques payable to whomever he pleases. A personal loan is also usually unrestricted-use credit because the funds are advanced to the debtor without any real control over what he uses them for. If under a term of the loan he is supposed to use it to buy a car and he uses it for some other purpose, it is still unrestricted-use credit. Contrast a mortgage loan where the creditor retains control by advancing the funds to a solicitor so that he can be sure that the funds will be used to purchase the property as intended in the loan agreement. There does not have to be any pre-existing arrangements between the creditor and the recipient of the funds, it is purely a matter of whether the creditor retains this control.

Debtor-creditor-supplier (DCS) agreements[10] can take two different forms. In one, the creditor himself is supplying the goods or services to the debtor (known as two-party DCS credit). This form is not typically provided by banks. In the other, the creditor has pre-existing arrangements with the supplier of the goods and services with whom the debtor spends the borrowed funds (known as 'three-party DCS credit'). This is not usually the case with borrowing by bank overdraft or even bank personal loans[11] but it is the case with credit cards when they are used to purchase goods or services. All other agreements are debtor-creditor (DC),[12] and this

---

[9]*Section 11.*
[10]*See section 12.*
[11]*Contrast finance houses which are introduced to the debtor by the supplier of the goods or service.*
[12]*See section 13.*

includes the typical bank overdraft, the bank personal loan and the credit card when the card is used to obtain cash. Note that three-party DCS agreements can be either restricted-use or unrestricted-use depending on the degree of control that the creditor exercises over the use of the funds; the operative factor is whether there are pre-existing links between the creditor and supplier.

The following are exempt agreements and are thus excluded[13] from regulation:[14]

(a) agreements secured on land where the creditor is a bank or building society and the funds are used to purchase land, e.g. house-purchase mortgage loans;

(b) agreements supplemental to those described in (a) which provide further funds for improvement or repair of property and which are secured on that property, e.g. additional loans for home improvement;

(c) an agreement which re-finances (a) or (b) above;

(d) DCS agreements for running-account credit where repayments are related to specified periods and the credit advanced in period must be repaid in a single amount, e.g. charge cards when used to obtain goods and services;

(e) agreements where the maximum charge for credit is the higher of 13% or 1% over base rate. Thus when base rate is 12% or less, loans with an interest rate of 13% or less are exempt.

3.3 CREDIT-TOKENS

Section 14(1) defines a credit-token as

'a card, cheque, voucher, coupon, stamp, form, booklet or other document or thing given to an individual by a person carrying on a consumer
credit business, who undertakes:

(a) that on production of it (whether or not some other action is also

---

[13]*By regulations made under section 16. There are other kinds of exempt agreement of less relevance to retail banking.*
[14]*Except for the rules relating to prohibiting the sending of unrequested credit-tokens and to extortionate credit transactions.*

required) he will supply cash, goods and services (or any of them) on credit; or

(b) that where, on production of it to a third party (whether or not any other action is also required), the third party supplies cash, goods and services (or any of them), he will pay the third party for them (whether or not deducting any discount or commission), in return for payment to him by the individual.

(2) A credit-token agreement is a regulated agreement for the provision of credit in connection with the use of a credit-token.

(3) ... the person who gives to an individual an undertaking falling within subsection (1)(b) shall be taken to provide him with credit drawn on whenever a third party supplies him with cash, goods or services.

(4) For the purposes of subsection (1), use of an object to operate a machine provided by the person giving the object or a third party shall be treated as the production of the object to him.'

Banks issue a variety of plastic cards to customers. It is important to know which give rise to regulated agreements and when they do, whether the agreement is DC or DCS as this determines whether connected lender liability applies.

There is no doubt that credit cards are credit-tokens as defined by section 14, whether used to buy goods or services from retailers[15] or to obtain cash from the card issuer.[16] In the former case the credit is DCS and in the latter it is DC. Due to the similarity with credit cards, there can also be no doubt that store cards are also credit-tokens, and if a separate financial institution provides the credit to the debtor this will be a three-party DCS agreement. If the store itself extends the credit to the debtor, this is a two-party DCS agreement. The use of credit and store cards also undoubtedly gives rise to a regulated credit-token agreement since the provision of the credit is connected to the use of the card. These cards would only escape regulation if the credit limit were over £25,000 (and not even then if the qualifications listed in 3.2 above apply) or the customer is a company (notwithstanding the card is used of course by an individual).

Charge cards are effectively the same as credit cards except that

[15]*Section 14(1)(b).*
[16]*Section 14(1)(a).*

no extended credit is offered, the cardholder is supposed to pay the full amount of the statement within a given number of days. This requirement brings charge cards within an exemption which applies to DCS agreements for running-account credit which require the debtor to repay the whole amount of credit provided in a specified period by one payment.[17] Charge cards are thus exempt from regulation under the Act but not if they are used to obtain cash as this would constitute a DC agreement and thus not within the exemption.

Cheque cards are considered not to be credit-tokens for the reason that they are not in themselves used to obtain credit, so one cannot say that on production of the card cash etc is supplied. Rather they are used to guarantee that the cheque is paid and if any overdraft exists on the customer's account that may be regulated credit but it is not a credit-token agreement.

The position with ATM cards and with debit cards is complex and is discussed more fully in 8.2 and 9.2 below.

The Act contains important protection for holders of credit-tokens which are misused. The starting point is that the debtor is liable for all transactions he has authorised and he is also liable for transactions made by his agent or someone who is treated as acting as his agent.[18]

If the credit-token is used by another whilst it is in the hands of another person (e.g. following a theft) the debtor can be made liable by the terms of his contract with the card issuer for a sum not exceeding £50. The contract can also make the debtor liable to an unlimited extent if the credit-token is misused by a person who acquired possession of it with the debtor's consent,[19] but the debtor cannot be liable for loss arising from use by another (except where that other is his agent or to be treated as acting as such) if the use occurs after he has notified the issuer of the loss of the card.[20] Oral

---

[17] *Consumer Credit (Exempt Agreements) Order 1989, SI 1989/869.*
[18] *Section 83.*
[19] *Section 84(1) and (2).*
[20] *Section 84(3).*

notice is permitted but it must be confirmed in writing within seven days.[21]

Thus where a fraudster simply uses information copied from the debtor's credit-token to order goods by telephone or he manufactures a replica card, the debtor cannot be liable for any such use (unless the fraudster is his agent or is treated as acting as such) as the credit-token has not left the debtor's possession. If the debtor allows a person to have the credit-token, he can be made liable (if the agreement so provides) to any extent for use of the credit-token by that person (but not use by any other person). This raises the interesting issue of the debtor who gives the credit-token for instance to a waiter to settle a restaurant bill and the waiter misuses the card and returns it. Arguably, the debtor can be made liable for the full amount of such loss. Interestingly, as negligence is not an issue under these rules, writing the PIN on a credit-token does not of itself render the debtor liable for any misuse of the card.[22]

These rules in the Act limiting a cardholder's loss apply to credit cards and store cards, and to ATM cards in some circumstances,[23] but not to debit cards,[24] nor to cheque cards.[25] It is generally assumed they do not apply to charge cards but a case can be made to the contrary on the basis that charge cards are not exempt when they are used to obtain cash.

Interesting issues arise from the practice of issuing credit-tokens to additional cardholders. The liability remains solely that of the debtor and he is liable for all use by the additional cardholder. If he wishes to terminate that liability, he can give notice to the creditor but the card is in the possession of someone who has it with his consent. This means the debtor can be made liable for all use by the additional cardholder up to the time he notifies the creditor. This is reasonable but it can also be argued that the additional

---

[21]*Section 84(5). The creditor cannot impose these terms on the debtor unless he has provided a name, address and telephone number for reporting of lost cards.*
[22]*Unlike the position under the Banking Code, see 8.3 and 9.3 below.*
[23]*See 8.2 below.*
[24]*See 9.2 below.*
[25]*As cheque cards are not credit-tokens, see above.*

cardholder is his agent and is to be treated as his agent even after he has notified the creditor. If so, the debtor is liable for all use by the additional cardholder without any limit, temporal or financial, and this would be so even if the additional cardholder no longer had possession of the card.

Finally, it is an offence to give a credit-token to a person unless he asked for it in a signed document. This does not apply to renewal and replacement cards.[26]

3.4 CONNECTED LENDER LIABILITY

Section 75 provides as follows:

> '(1) If a debtor under a debtor-creditor-supplier agreement . . . has, in relation to a transaction financed by the agreement, any claim against the supplier in respect of a misrepresentation or breach of contract, he shall have a like claim against the creditor, who, with the supplier, shall accordingly be jointly and severally liable to the debtor.'

Under subsection (3) the above does not apply to any claim so far as the claim relates to any single item to which the supplier has attached a cash price not exceeding £100 or more than £30,000.

A debtor who purchases goods and services with his credit card will thus be able to claim against the creditor (the card issuer) on a joint and several basis[27] in respect of any claims for misrepresentation or breach of contract that he has against the supplier of the goods or services. It is clear that whatever the claim that he has against the supplier, he has exactly the same claim against the creditor. In some circumstances this may exceed the amount of credit obtained in the transaction and the cash price of the item.

Where the debtor purchases an item priced at £120, paying £100 cash and putting £20 on his credit card, the creditor is jointly and severally liable under section 75 because the cash price of the item exceeds £100. Other matters are less clear-cut. For instance, where

---

[26]*Section 51. There is an argument that renewal debit cards and charge cards must be requested in a signed document but the original agreement can include a reference to renewal and replacement cards.*
[27]*Joint and several liability is explained in 2.6 above.*

the debtor buys two items in the same transaction each priced at £60. It is submitted that the reference in subsection (3) to the 'single item' suggests that this transaction would not be within the scope of the section.

Where the transaction takes place outside the UK, it has been argued that the transaction is outside the scope of the section. It is submitted that in order to reach this conclusion one would have to put words into the section which are not there. The Banking Ombudsman operated a compromise arrangement in respect of transactions between 15 May 1995 and 31 December 1996 whereby foreign transactions were considered within the section but that the maximum liability of a bank was not to exceed the amount of credit provided and UK law was deemed to apply. He has stated that he believes foreign transactions are not within the section and that sometimes foreign transactions are inappropriate for him to investigate because of lack of evidence. He further believes that the applicability of foreign law raises further difficulty for him.[28] In Jarrett v Barclays Bank,[29] the defendant bank argued that a section 75 claim following use of a Barclaycard to purchase a timeshare in Portugal would have to be heard in Portugal under Article 16 of the Brussels Convention.[30] The bank's argument was not successful.

It has also been suggested by those wishing to limit the scope of section 75 that it does not apply in some circumstances because the necessary pre-existing arrangements between creditor and supplier to render the agreement DCS are lacking. For instance, where the supplier does not deal directly with the creditor but through an intermediary such as a transaction acquirer (which is often the case).[31] It is submitted that this argument has some force but the counter-view is that the transaction acquirer acts as agent of the creditor. Also in some cases the debtor transacts with someone who is not the actual supplier of the goods or service. For instance if he buys a holiday from a travel agent when the holiday is supplied by

[28]*Annual Report 1995–96, Appendix V.*
[29]*(1996) The Times, 18th November, CA.*
[30]*Article 16 in essence provides that legal proceedings which relate to rights in land must be heard in the courts of the country where the land is located.*
[31]*Sometimes referred to as 'four-party DCS credit'.*

a travel company. Once again the counter-view is that the travel agent acts as the agent of the holiday company.[32] Finally there is the question of an item being purchased by a deposit paid for by credit card, where the item (such as a holiday) is priced at over £100 but the deposit is less than £100. It is submitted that section 75 focuses on the price of the item, not of the deposit.

Those wishing to extend the ambit of section 75 suggest that the scope of section 75 should be extended to debit card transactions where the item purchased costs over £100. This view is explored further in 9.2 above.

If a creditor is obliged to pay damages to the debtor as a result of his joint and several liability under section 75, he has a right of indemnity for that sum against the supplier, including reasonably incurred costs expended in defending the claim from the debtor.[33]

In practice, section 75 is used against creditors mostly when there is an insolvency of a supplier who sold goods or services which were paid for in advance. Examples are furniture and carpet retailers and airlines and travel companies. Consumers are well advised to pay for such purchases by credit card in preference to cheques, debit cards or charge cards.

3.5 THE FORMS AND FORMALITIES

The Act lays down detailed requirements relating to the content of the agreement, copies of the agreement that must be given to the debtor, information that must be provided to the debtor and the procedure for termination by the creditor if the debtor defaults on the loan. In some circumstances, failure to adhere to the formalities has the effect of making the loan unenforceable by the lender. A key concept is that of the Annual Percentage Rate (APR) which must be calculated in accordance with a prescribed formula so that the debtor can assess the interest rate charged by reference to an objective criterion.

In the case of bank overdrafts, the creditor is released from these

---

[32]*This is less obvious than it sounds since a travel agent is normally thought of as being agent of the customer.*
[33]*Section 75(2).*

detailed requirements and only need tell the debtor the credit limit, the APR (and how it can be varied) and the procedure for termination (which in the normal case will simply be on demand). If the overdraft is unauthorised, the debtor only need be informed within seven days of the overdraft continuing for three months.[34]

All other regulated agreements must be in the prescribed form (regulations lay down the heading it must have, the size of the print used, the colour contrast between the print and the paper it is printed on, the size of the signature box amongst many others, and if the agreement is cancellable this must be stated). The agreement must contain all the prescribed terms (these are the specific financial terms which must be included such as the total charge for credit, the APR and the repayment schedule and these prescribed terms must be presented together, unmixed with other terms and be positioned near to the signature box) and it must embody all the express terms of the agreement, although this can be achieved by reference to another document. The agreement must be signed by the debtor and by someone acting on behalf of the creditor.[35]

Where the agreement is sent through the post for the debtor to sign, he must be given a copy of the agreement in addition to the agreement which he signs and returns. A further copy must be sent to the debtor within seven days of the creditor signing the agreement. It is not necessary to send a further copy to the debtor in respect of a credit-token agreement if he is sent a copy along with the credit-token. Where the agreement is presented personally to the debtor for signature, he must be given a copy then and there and he must be given another copy within seven days of the creditor signing.[36]

If the loan is secured, the security must be stated in the agreement. If the security is provided by a third party surety (i.e. a guarantor), the surety must sign a document containing all the terms of the security (this can be by reference to another document) and

---

[34]*By a determination of the Director General of Fair Trading made pursuant to section 74(3A).*
[35]*See sections 60 and 61.*
[36]*Section 62. Slightly different rules apply when the creditor has signed the agreement first, which is uncommon in practice.*

a copy must be sent to him. A further copy must be sent to him within seven days of the loan agreement being executed.[37]

Both the debtor and any surety have a right to make a written request for certain information from the creditor. A request for information can be ignored by the creditor if it is made within one month of a previous request. Both the debtor and any surety can request a copy of the credit agreement at any time together with a signed statement of the total sum paid so far by the debtor, the total of any arrears and the total still to be paid.[38] A payment of £1 must be made by the requestor.[39] A written request can be made for a copy of any surety agreement on payment of a £1 fee.

The debtor can make a written request for the name and address of any credit reference agency to which the creditor applied for information about the debtor. The creditor must reply within seven days. The debtor, or indeed any individual, can make a written request to a credit reference agency, on payment of a fee of £2, for a copy of the file held by the agency on the individual. These rights can be exercised whether or not credit has been refused.

In the event of default by the debtor, a default notice must be served by the creditor before he can terminate the agreement or take other action to demand repayment or enforce security.[40] The default notice must give the debtor a minimum seven days to remedy the breach and if the debtor does remedy it, the creditor can take no action. Where the loan is secured, a copy of the default notice must be served on any third-party surety. It is considered that no default notice need be served in relation to an on-demand overdraft because there is no specified term for the agreement and thus no demand for early repayment. The creditor is not permitted to charge a higher default rate of interest in any circumstances.[41] If the loan is secured on land, a court order is always required for any enforcement of the

---

[37]*Section 105.*
[38]*This assumes the credit is fixed sum. If it is running-account, the statement must show the state of the account. See sections 77 and 78.*
[39]*Increased by SI 1998/997.*
[40]*Part VII of the Act.*
[41]*Section 93.*

security. This is in addition to any possession order which may be required as discussed in 13.13 below.

Complex rules in the Act deal with the modification of regulated agreements. Creditors, however, are permitted to include a term in the original agreement which provides for variation of the interest rate payable where the interest rates are determined by reference to a daily balance. In this case, the interest rate can be varied following publication of the particulars of variation in advertisements of a minimum size in three national daily newspapers.

A debtor has the right to make early repayment of a loan.[42] He can make a written request to the creditor to be told the amount due and the creditor must grant a rebate for early settlement, to be calculated according to a prescribed formula. The creditor must give the information within twelve working days. In Lombard North Central v Stobart,[43] the creditor understated the early settlement figure by mistake. The debtor paid the stated sum, honestly believing it to be correct and changed his position as a result of it. It was held the creditor was estopped from claiming the true figure owed.[44]

Where the creditor has failed to comply with the Act's requirements, he is unable to enforce the loan. The non-compliance is incurable when it consisted of a failure to include the prescribed terms in the agreement, or of the debtor not having signed the agreement, or (if the agreement was cancellable) the creditor did not give the debtor notice of his right to cancel.[45] In all other cases, the non-compliance is potentially curable, either by serving the required documents on the debtor before litigation commences,[46] or by obtaining an enforcement order from the court. The court must have regard to any prejudice caused by the non-compliance and the degree to which the creditor was culpable in its non-compliance. The court has power to grant enforcement subject to a reduction in the amount payable by the debtor.[47]

---

[42] *Section 94.*
[43] *[1990] CCLR 53 CA.*
[44] *It is interesting to compare this with the cases listed in 5.14 below.*
[45] *Section 127.*
[46] *e.g. the copy of the agreement which should have been served earlier.*
[47] *Part IX of the Act.*

3.6 CANCELLATION

Regulated agreements are prima facie cancellable by the debtor by him serving notice within five days of his receipt of the copy agreement containing notice of his right to cancel.[48] If the right to cancel is exercised, the agreement is treated as if it had never been entered into. The debtor must return any credit he has received and if he does so before the first instalment was due, no interest is payable.[49]

If any one of the following apply, however, the debtor will have no right to cancel the agreement:

(1) No oral representations were made concerning the agreement by the creditor in the presence of the debtor.
(2) The agreement is signed on the creditor's business premises.
(3) If it is DCS credit, the agreement is signed on the supplier's trade premises.
(4) The agreement is for a bridging loan in connection with the purchase of land or is a restricted-use agreement for the purchase of land.
(5) The agreement is secured on land.[50]

It follows that non-cancellable agreements are commonplace. Exception (1) includes all agreements where there is no face-to-face meeting of the debtor and creditor, such as credit applied for by post or telephone. Exception (2) includes all agreements where the debtor signed the agreement on the bank's premises whether or not there were face-to-face discussions. Exception (4) applies whether or not the agreement is secured on land. Exception (5) was designed to prevent the inconvenience of registering a charge on land only to have to remove the charge shortly after when the loan is cancelled.

In the case of agreements secured on land, therefore, a special withdrawal procedure is imposed which is designed to give the debtor time to consider the merits of entering into the agreement

---

[48]Section 68.
[49]Section 71. If the credit was not repayable by instalments, the debtor must repay it within one month of serving his notice of cancellation if he is to escape paying interest on the credit.
[50]Section 67.

before doing so, rather than giving him the right to cancel it after doing so. The creditor must send the debtor an advance copy of the agreement containing notice of his right to withdraw at least seven days before the actual agreement for signing is sent. The creditor must not approach the debtor in any way except in response to a specific request from the debtor during a period which commences on the sending of the advance copy and ending seven days after he sent the agreement for signing (or on receipt of the signed agreement from the debtor). This is known as the 'consideration period'.[51] Note that signing the agreement on the creditor's trade premises (or having no face-to-face discussions) does not remove the right of withdrawal.

3.7 ADVERTISING AND CANVASSING

The rules contained in this part of the Act are of a criminal nature. Breach of them renders the creditor liable to prosecution but has no effect on the validity of any agreement made which was obtained subsequent to a breach of the rules.

Detailed regulations govern the advertising of consumer credit[52] which are considered to be outside the scope of this book. The regulations do not apply in certain circumstances. These include (amongst others) where the advertisement does not indicate that the creditor is willing to extend credit;[53] where the advertisement indicates that the credit must exceed £25,000 and that either no security is required or no security on land is required; where the advertisement indicates it is only available to companies or other corporate bodies; and where some kinds of exempt agreements are advertised.[54]

---

[51]*Sections 58 and 61. The right of withdrawal does not exist when there is a restricted-use agreement for the purchase of the mortgaged land or to an agreement for a bridging loan in connection with the purchase of the mortgaged land or other land.*
[52]*See for example SI 1989/1125.*
[53]*Jenkins v Lombard North Central [1984] 1 WLR 307 suggests that displaying only the company name and logo does not indicate a willingness to provide credit.*
[54]*See SI 1985/621.*

The Act provides that canvassing debtor-creditor credit is prohibited.[55] However, no canvassing offence is committed if any one of the following exceptions apply:

(a) where the canvassing takes place on the creditor's trade premises;

(b) where the canvassing takes place on the consumer's trade premises;[56]

(c) where there are no oral representations made during a visit by the canvasser to a place where the consumer is (e.g. telephone canvassing is permitted);

(d) where the canvasser received a prior written and signed request from the consumer;

(e) where the canvasser canvasses overdraft facilities to an existing customer;

(f) where the canvasser did not make the visit to the place where the consumer is for the purpose of canvassing.[57]

Finally, the regulations which once required providers of consumer credit to issue quotations to applicants have been revoked.[58]

3.8 EXTORTIONATE CREDIT BARGAINS

The Act defines a credit bargain as extortionate when it requires the debtor to make payments which are grossly exorbitant or it otherwise contravenes ordinary principles of fair dealing.[59] A number of factors must be taken into account in deciding if it is extortionate including (among others) the interest rates prevailing at the time, the degree of risk accepted by the creditor and the degree to which the debtor was under financial pressure. Every case thus depends on its facts

---

[55]*The canvassing rules do not apply at all to the canvassing of DCS credit.*
[56]*The Act refers to the debtor as the consumer as no agreement would have been entered into at the canvassing stage.*
[57]*Sections 48 and 49. Other exceptions less relevant to retail banking also apply.*
[58]*SI 1997/211 effective 10th March 1997.*
[59]*Section 138.*

but in A. Ketley Ltd v Scott,[60] an interest rate of 48% p.a. was held not to be extortionate whilst in Castle Phillips Co Ltd v Wilkinson,[61] an interest rate set at 3.5 times the building society re-mortgage rate was held to be extortionate.

An application to the court may be made by the debtor or by a guarantor. The court has power to re-open any agreement made by an individual including one which is not regulated because it exceeds £25,000 or one which is exempt from regulation. The debtor can be relieved of paying sums due and he can have sums already paid returned to him. Security can be released wholly or partly, as can guarantors.[62]

If the debtor has become bankrupt, his trustee in bankruptcy may make a similar application to the court in respect of an extortionate credit transaction which the debtor had entered into in the three years before the bankruptcy commenced.[63]

---

[60]*[1981] ICR 241.*
[61]*[1993] CLY 472.*
[62]*Section 139.*
[63]*See 10.6 below.*

4 Cheques – the basic law

4.1 INTRODUCTION

The legal principles concerning a bank's dealing with instruments which are commonly regarded as cheques are examined here. In particular, the rights and obligations of the parties will be discussed, both in the normal transaction and in the event of some irregularity such as forgery, fraudulent alteration, loss or theft.

The law relating to these matters consists of a blend of contract law and a variety of statutory provisions. It will be apparent that much of the law has developed in a piecemeal fashion and little attempt has been made, since 1882 at least, to render it coherent. Some of the more difficult areas, such as the holder for value, appear to have been almost deliberately fudged in the relevant statutes and cases. In spite of these drawbacks, there is a remarkable degree of common understanding throughout most of this area of the law, and in practice it appears to function well.

Anyone approaching this area of the law for the first time, however, may be forgiven if he finds it somewhat confusing. An attempt has been made here to place the various principles in a logical order but in many instances there is an interdependence, and a proper understanding of any part is likely only to emerge at the conclusion.

It should be noted that in March 1990 a White Paper entitled 'Banking Services: Law and Practice' was published.[1] It proposed changes to the law relating to crossings on cheques, negotiability of cheques, statutory protection of the bank paying a cheque, and

[1]Cm 1026.

truncation of cheques. Some of these have been enacted, for example, the Cheques Act 1992 created the concept of the non-transferable cheque. Further details of the proposals are contained in the relevant places in this chapter. A Review Committee[2] reported prior to the White Paper. This Report recommended more widespread changes in banking law and specifically the law relating to cheques. Most of the Report's recommendations were, however, not adopted in the White Paper.

4.2 CHEQUES AND NEGOTIABLE INSTRUMENTS

A negotiable instrument enjoys a special status in English law whereby it is not only transferable but also is negotiable, which means that a good faith taker for value of the instrument can acquire a good title to it irrespective of the quality of the title of the giver. This is in contrast to the position with goods generally, where a good faith purchaser will not ordinarily acquire a good title from a thief, and will have to return the property to the owner from whom it was stolen.

Negotiable instruments include:

(a) bank notes (currency of the realm);
(b) other promissory notes;
(c) bills of exchange;
(d) cheques (other than those crossed 'not negotiable' or 'account payee');
(e) banker's drafts;
(f) bearer bonds;
(g) certificates of deposit;
(h) commercial paper; and
(i) eurobonds.

This book is only concerned in detail with (d) and (e) above, and with instruments analogous to cheques. Cheques are negotiable instruments because the Bills of Exchange Act 1882 declares them

---

[2]*The 'Jack Report', (1989) Cm 622.*

so to be,[3] but the great majority of cheques now bear a crossing which prevents them being so. Heads (e) to (i) are either covered by this Act or are considered to be negotiable instruments by virtue of the common law doctrine of the 'law merchant'.[4]

In this context it is important to note that negotiation is not synonymous with transfer. The point can be illustrated by the following example. Suppose A sells a stolen car to B, who purchases it in good faith and pays a full market price. The true owner of the car may at any time reclaim it from B, as A did not have good title to it and B cannot acquire good title through A, however honest B is. Suppose now that A sells a genuine car to B and that B pays A with stolen bank notes. The original owner of the bank notes cannot reclaim them from A (assuming A acts in good faith) because they have been negotiated to him and he thereby acquires a good title even if B's title to them was bad. Obviously the original owner could have recovered the notes from B before they were negotiated to A.

Thus it can be seen that negotiation must involve transfer but that transfer will not necessarily involve negotiation. Put another way, negotiation is a special form of transfer.

The law relating to the use of cheques and other instruments dealt with by banks through the clearing system, includes a study of the principles of negotiability and of the Bills of Exchange Act 1882, as these can have an impact on the rights and duties of the parties. It should be clearly noted, however, that the law relating to the bank which pays cheques, and its customer who draws them, is also very much a matter of the terms of the contract between bank and customer. It is also a matter of general principles of law, such as constructive trusteeship. These matters have been dealt with in chapter 1.

---

[3] *Section 73 declares a cheque to be a bill of exchange payable on demand and it is clear from the general terms of the Bills of Exchange Act that bills of exchange are negotiable instruments.*
[4] *See Goodwin v Robarts (1876) 1 App Cas 476 HL, where Russian and Hungarian government scrip (exchangeable for bonds) were held to be negotiable under this principle.*

4.3 THE BILLS OF EXCHANGE ACT 1882

By section 73 of this Act a cheque is defined as:

'A bill of exchange drawn on a banker payable on demand.'

And applying section 3(1), which defines a bill of exchange, it must be an unconditional order in writing, signed and addressed by the drawer to the bank, requiring the bank to pay on demand a sum certain in money to or to the order of a specified person, or to bearer.

It follows that, in legal terms, a cheque is a special form of bill of exchange. Also, there must be at least three parties to a cheque:

(a) the drawer (or customer of the bank);
(b) the drawee (the bank); and
(c) the payee or bearer.

This is because a cheque must be addressed by one person to a bank and must be payable to a specified person or to bearer.

Most of the Bills of Exchange Act consists of provisions which concern bills of exchange generally and many, but not all, of these apply to cheques. Examples are the rules on indorsement, holders for value and holders in due course. Some sections are devoted specifically to cheques, such as those dealing with crossings. The Cheques Acts 1957 and 1992 contain further provisions specific to cheques. A selection of these sections is contained in Appendix 1.

It should be noted that whilst the drawer of a cheque will be liable to the payee (or subsequent holder) assuming valid consideration has been given, a drawee bank is never liable to the payee or holder, as it does not in practice accept a cheque (although it can in law do so). Special arrangements are made for cheques backed by a cheque card. Bills of exchange other than cheques are frequently accepted by banks which thereby do become liable on them.

A banker's draft does not come within the definition of a cheque, nor of a bill of exchange, because it is not addressed by one person to another (the bank is addressing itself). Nor does a cheque drawn 'pay cash' or 'pay wages' since this is not payable to a specified person or to bearer.[5] Some provisions of the Cheques Act and even some of the Bills of Exchange Act do apply to these instruments, however. References hereafter to 'cheques' are intended to include these analogous instruments unless otherwise stated and references to 'the Act' are to the Bills of Exchange Act 1882.

All cheques must have a drawee or paying bank,[6] and in the majority of instances there will also be a collecting bank involved. This is because the payee of the cheque pays it into his account with his own bank and this bank then obtains payment from the paying bank.

4.4 CROSSINGS ON CHEQUES

The provisions in the Act which deal with crossings on cheques[7] apply not only to cheques but also to banker's drafts, government payment orders and to 'cheques' drawn 'pay cash'.[8]

In practice, most of these cheques and analogous instruments are crossed and the effect of the crossing is well understood, i.e. from the point of view of the payee, the cheque must be paid into a bank account and cash cannot be obtained over the counter at the paying bank. The Act, however, expresses this as a duty of the paying bank who is obliged to pay another bank only.[9] In fact two types of crossing are recognised:

(a) general – this consists of two parallel lines, with or without the words '& Co.' or 'not negotiable';
(b) special – which consists of the name of one bank written on the face of the cheque, with or without the parallel lines and any accompanying words.

[5] *Orbit Mining and Trading Co. Ltd v Westminster Bank [1963] 1 QB 794 CA.*

[6] *Payment orders issued by government departments (which bear sort codes and in some ways are handled like cheques) are not drawn on a bank and yet are within some of the statutory rules, such as section 4 of the Cheques Act 1957.*

[7] *Sections 76 to 81.*

[8] *By virtue of section 5 of the Cheques Act.*

[9] *Section 79.*

Specially crossed cheques are rarely issued in this form but it is common practice for a collecting bank to stamp its name on a cheque paid in by its customer. The Act recognises this as a crossing and also the right of a holder to put on and to add certain crossings.[10]

By section 81, a generally or specially crossed cheque may have the words 'not negotiable' added, in which case the cheque is not a negotiable instrument. It is, however, still within the legal definition of a cheque and it also remains transferable. Uncrossed cheques which have 'not negotiable' written across their face are considered to be not transferable by analogy to the crossing having this effect on a bill of exchange.[11]

The 'account payee' crossing is now recognised by the Cheques Act 1992, section 1 of which inserts a new section into the Bills of Exchange Act. This (section 81A) declares such a cheque to be not transferable and only valid between the parties to it. This only affects the collecting bank, however, as a paying bank need not concern itself with a purported indorsement on a cheque crossed 'account payee'.[12] The paying bank enjoys the general protection of section 80 whenever it pays a crossed cheque in the appropriate manner.[13]

As section 80 (as amended by the Cheques Act 1992) refers to a cheque being not transferable under section 81A nor otherwisej, statute implicitly recognises that a cheque may be rendered non-transferable by other means than the 'account payee' crossing. This presumably includes a 'not transferable' crossing or the inclusion of 'only' after the name of the payee and/or the deletion of the words 'or order' after the name of the payee.

The Act does not permit the removal of any crossing on a cheque, even by the drawer.[14] In practice, as cheque forms are commonly issued by banks ready crossed, customers often wish to delete the crossing. This practice was recognised by the Committee of London

---

[10]*Section 77.*
[11]*Hibernian Bank v Gysin and Hanson [1939] 1 KB 483 CA.*
[12]*Section 81A(2).*
[13]*See 5.1 below.*
[14]*Section 78.*

Clearing Banks in 1912,[15] although it was stated that the full signature of the customer should accompany the 'opening' of the cheque and he, or his known agent, should be presenting the cheque for cash. In any event, if the customer himself is presenting the cheque, there is unlikely to be any objection to him receiving his own money, whatever the position under the strict terms of the Act. Cheques opened in this way, however, should not be paid to a third party payee who is not a known agent, as the bank would then be in clear breach of section 79 (this states that the paying bank will be liable to the true owner of the cheque for any loss if it does not pay another bank).

The White Paper[16] proposed that a crossing on a cheque will make it not negotiable, whether or not those words are written; that the special crossing will be discontinued; and that an open cheque will, as at present, be a negotiable instrument and one which can be presented for cash. None of these have been implemented. The introduction of the 'account payee' crossing has rendered the first proposal virtually redundant.

4.5 INDORSEMENTS ON CHEQUES

The following discussion is limited in practice to cheques which are transferrable (i.e. are not crossed 'account payee').

Section 31 of the Act provides that cheques payable to bearer may be negotiated by delivery but that those payable to order require indorsement of the holder. Negotiation is complete when the transferee becomes the holder.

Cheques which are drawn payable to a fictitious or non-existent person are by section 7(3) treated as payable to bearer. For example, in Clutton v Attenborough,[17] a cheque was drawn by a fraudulent employee in favour of 'Mr Brett' and the employer signed, believing he owed money to this person. In fact the employee had made the name up. He indorsed the cheque and obtained payment. Held,

[15]Resolution of the Committee of London Clearing Bankers, 7th November 1912.
[16](1990) Cm 1026.
[17][1897] AC 90 HL.

the cheque was payable to bearer and therefore required no indorsement in order to be transferred.

Sections 32 to 35 of the Act set out the rules relating to different types of indorsement. In practice the most common is the indorsement in blank, which consists of just the signature of the holder. An order cheque indorsed in this way becomes payable to bearer and therefore may then be negotiated by delivery any number of times without any further indorsement.

A special indorsement consists of the signature of the holder in addition to the name of the indorsee, e.g. 'Pay X, signed Y'. An order cheque so indorsed remains an order cheque and therefore may be negotiated again but only by further indorsement.

The Act also provides for restrictive indorsements, e.g. 'pay X only, signed Y'. Further negotiation of such a cheque is not then possible. A conditional indorsement places some condition on the negotiation. A drawee bank is entitled to ignore the condition, however.

Indorsements must be valid and regular in order for the indorsee to obtain the benefit of the negotiability of the cheque. A forged indorsement will have no effect (section 24 of the Act) whilst an irregular one, e.g. a signature which does not correspond fully with the name of the transferor, may transfer his title but is not negotiated, so the transferee will not obtain a good title if the transferor's was defective.[18]

Prior to the passing of the Cheques Act 1957, all cheques paid into a bank account had to be indorsed by the person paying in, and the collecting bank had the responsibility of ensuring that the indorsements of their customers were valid and regular. This Act set up a framework whereby indorsements on cheques would no longer be required, so far as the paying and collecting banks are concerned, although an order cheque which is transferred to a non-bank will still need to be indorsed if the transferee is to acquire the transferor's title, let alone obtain the benefit of negotiation.

The effect of the Cheques Act has been qualified, however, by a practice agreement made by the clearing banks in 1957. This is

---

[18]*Arab Bank Ltd v Ross [1952] 2 QB 216 CA.*

discussed below[19] in the context of the statutory protection that exists for paying and collecting banks.

It should be noted that a cheque which is not a negotiable instrument because it is crossed 'not negotiable' is subject to the same rules on indorsements in the Act when it is transferred. It cannot of course be negotiated.

4.6 HOLDERS OF A CHEQUE

A holder is defined in section 2 of the Act as the payee or indorsee (of a cheque) who is in possession of it, or the bearer thereof. Thus a thief is the holder of a bearer cheque he possesses, and the recipient of a gift (who has thus given no value for the cheque) is the holder of an order cheque payable to him. Mere holders have few rights, but the term is significant because a bank which pays a holder can be protected by section 59 of the Act.

A holder in due course is the personification of the principle of negotiability. It follows that there can never be a holder in due course of a cheque which is crossed 'account payee' or 'not negotiable'. This type of holder enjoys the following privileges:

(a) he acquires good title to a cheque even if he acquires it from a thief or fraudster; and

(b) he can claim against all other parties to the cheque, i.e. the drawer and indorsers.

To be a holder in due course, the conditions contained in section 29 of the Act must be satisfied. These are:

(1) He must be a holder of a cheque which is complete and regular. Thus the drawer's and indorser's signatures must be valid, regular and authorised. All necessary indorsements must be present. We have seen that an irregular indorsement will lead to the transferee not being a holder in due course.[20] An unauthorised alteration on the cheque will lead to it not being regular.

(2) He became the holder of it before it was overdue. By section

---

[19]See 5.1 and 5.5 below.
[20]Arab Bank Ltd v Ross, see above.

36(3) the cheque becomes overdue when a more than reasonable time has passed since it was issued. There are no modern reported cases to enlighten this point. It is suggested that a cheque would become overdue well before banks (for other reasons) ordinarily treat them as stale, i.e. after six months;

(3) He took it without notice that it was previously dishonoured (if such was the case). Previous dishonour would be evident to a transferee, by words written on the cheque.

(4) He took the cheque in good faith. This is defined in section 90 as something done honestly, whether or not it is done negligently.

(5) He took it for value. This is defined in section 2 as 'valuable consideration'. By section 27(3) of the Act, the holder of a cheque who has a lien on it, is deemed to be a holder for value, and this has been interpreted to mean that value has been given for the purposes of section 29, thus making the holder a holder in due course.[21] Where a customer pays a cheque into his overdrawn account, the bank has a lien on the cheque; it therefore gives value and can qualify as a holder in due course.[22]

(6) The cheque was negotiated to him. Since other sections of the Act imply that negotiation involves transfer to a remoter party than the payee, it has been held that the original payee may not be a holder in due course.[23] The original bearer may, however, be a holder in due course, as well as any indorsee. Clearly a cheque crossed 'not negotiable' cannot be negotiated. A cheque crossed 'account payee' cannot be transferred and therefore cannot normally be negotiated. However, such a cheque drawn payable to bearer can be negotiated to the original bearer.

(7) He had no notice of defect in the title of the transferor. The notice may be of a general or of a particular nature. A bank receiving cheques drawn by a customer in favour of himself, using his power of attorney to operate another's account, was held to have had notice.[24]

[21]*Barclays Bank v Astley Industrial Trust [1970] 2 QB 527.*
[22]*See 5.12 below.*
[23]*Jones v Waring and Gillow [1926] AC 670 HL.*
[24]*Midland Bank v Reckitt [1933] AC 1 HL.*

A holder, whether or not he gives value, who takes a cheque from a holder in due course, acquires all the rights of that holder in due course.[25] Even notice of fraud will not defeat that holder's title, unless he was a party to the fraud. Such a holder will constitute a holder for value under section 27(2), as will a holder who has a lien over the cheque he takes but who cannot be a holder in due course, as he fails to satisfy one of the conditions.[26] The Act does not state what are the precise rights of a holder for value and the reported cases do not assist greatly.

The concept of the holder in due course can be illustrated as follows. Suppose A draws a cheque[27] payable to B. B cannot be a holder in due course as he is the original payee. B indorses the cheque and transfers it for value to C. C is a holder in due course. C can enforce the cheque against A and against B. This is so even if A gave the cheque to B purely as a gift or if B obtained the cheque from A by some fraud. If A orders his bank to stop the cheque, C may enforce payment from A. This would not be possible in these circumstances if the cheque was crossed 'not negotiable'. In this event, the cheque would be validly transferred to C but C would have no better rights against A than B had.

Sometimes the bank which collects the cheque qualifies as a holder in due course.[28]

4.7 PAYMENT OF CHEQUES

The legal position of a bank paying a cheque may be considered in two separate parts:

(a) the contract it has with its customer (the drawer); and
(b) the impact of the Bills of Exchange Act and the Cheques Act.

The legal relationships involving the paying bank may include:

(a) that with its customer;

---

[25] Section 29(3).
[26] e.g. Midland Bank v Reckitt, see above.
[27] The cheque would have to be transferrable.
[28] See 5.12 below.

(b) that with some remote true owner of a cheque;
(c) that with the collecting bank.

The impact of the banker-customer contract is limited to (a) above. Heads (a) and (b) are much affected by statutory provision, whilst (c) is concerned mainly with the rules of the clearing system and with the doctrine of recovery of money paid by mistake.

The paying bank and its customer

The banker-customer contract has been fully explored in chapter 1. It will be recalled that a bank must pay within its authority (also called mandate) from its customer, otherwise it will not be entitled to debit the account. It is also liable as a constructive trustee where it dishonestly assists in a breach of fiduciary duty by another. It must exercise a reasonable degree of care and skill when conducting its customer's account.

4.8 THE FORM OF A CHEQUE

Signature

The cheque must be validly signed in order for the bank to have evidence of its customer's authority to pay, and in order for it to be covered by the Bills of Exchange Act and the Cheques Act. A forged signature is no authority (see below) and the cheque does not qualify as such legally. Where it is agreed that two or more signatures are required, there is no authority to pay on one only.[29] Likewise if one of the joint signatures is forged. It is still legally a cheque if it bears at least one genuine signature.

Date

By section 3(4)(a) of the Act, a cheque need not be dated at all. It is arguable that the paying bank has authority to insert a date under

---

[29]*Catlin v Cyprus Finance Corporation (London) [1983] QB 759. But subrogation may be available to permit the account to be debited.*

section 20(1) but it is safer for the paying bank to return it unpaid, stating 'not dated'.

A post-dated cheque should not be paid before the date stated as the bank has no authority to do so and may be liable:

(a) for wrongful dishonour of other cheques issued later but before the relevant date, and returned for lack of funds; and
(b) because the customer may countermand payment (or die, or become insolvent etc) before the relevant date. It seems from section 13(2) that a postdated cheque is within the legal definition of a cheque as there is no contradiction with it being payable on demand.[30]

A drawer remains liable on a cheque to the holder for six years under the Limitation Act 1980. The Banking Code declares that banks will keep original cheques for at least six years except where they have been returned to the customer.[31] It is normal bank practice to dishonour cheques as 'stale' which are dated more than six months in the past. There appear to be some risks in this practice, as a customer may claim that his instruction was dishonoured. The bank's only defence would appear to be that it is an implied term of the banker-customer contract not to pay six months after date. The Banking Code requires a bank to give its new customers[32] information about its practice on out-of-date cheques, which it defines as a cheque which has not been paid because it is too old, normally more than six months.[33]

Another interesting practice is that of paying those cheques, in the early days of each year, which are dated the previous year, and thus appear to be 12 months old and would otherwise be returned as stale. Where the customer's mistake is genuine, however, it can easily be established from the cheque number that it was recently issued.

---

[30]*Royal Bank of Scotland v Tottenham [1894] 2 QB 715 CA.*
[31]*Section 3.5.*
[32]*And existing customers on request.*
[33]*Section 2.1 and 'useful definitions'.*

Amount of money

In order to come within the legal definition, a cheque must be payable for a sum certain in money. It is purely a matter of practice not to pay when the amount is stated in figures only. This may amount to a breach of contract. A discrepancy between the amount stated in words and figures can be dealt with in two ways:

(a) return the cheque as an ambiguous order, 'words and figures differ'; or
(b) pay according to the words, relying on section 9(2) of the Act.

The practice of paying the smaller of the differing amounts is thus unsound.

4.9 FORGERY OF THE DRAWER'S SIGNATURE

If the customer's signature on a cheque is forged, the bank has no authority to pay and, if it does so, cannot debit the customer's account. It makes no difference that the forgery could not be detected; as a matter of the banker-customer contract the bank is in breach if it pays such a cheque. By section 24 of the Act, a forged drawer's signature is inoperative; therefore the cheque is invalid and no one can become a holder of it. For instance in Tai Hing Cotton Mill Ltd v Liu Chong Hing Bank,[34] a fraudulent employee forged the signature of his employer's managing director and thereby obtained payment of $HK 5.5 million, representing 300 forged cheques over six years. It was clear that the company had an inadequate accounting system which had facilitated the fraud. No one in the company, other than the fraudulent employee himself, had reconciled the bank statements. It was argued that the customer owed a duty to the bank to take care of its cheque-books and to inspect its bank statements, but these points were rejected. The cheques were forged and the bank had no authority to pay.

There are circumstances, however, when the law considers it inequitable for a customer to rely on the above rule. In these cases, an estoppel is said to arise to deny the customer the right to assert

[34] *[1986] AC 80 PC.*

what would normally be his right. Thus in Greenwood v Martins Bank,[35] Mr G had an account with the bank. Mrs G, without his authority or his knowledge, forged his signature on a number of cheques. Eventually Mr G became aware of this but agreed not to inform the bank if Mrs G agreed to desist. She did desist but some eight months later, Mr G informed the bank anyway and reclaimed the relevant debits. Thereupon, Mrs G committed suicide. It was held that a customer has a duty to inform his bank at once, if he is aware of forgeries on his account. As the law then stood, the bank had no right of action against Mrs G's estate and the bank suffered loss as a result of Mr G failing in this duty, and accordingly an estoppel prevented Mr G from succeeding. Since the Law Reform (Miscellaneous Provisions) Act 1934, a plaintiff has been able to take an action in tort (except for libel) against a deceased's estate. Therefore, on the same facts today, the case would presumably be decided differently.

The court defined an estoppel in this context as requiring:

(a) a representation, or conduct amounting to a representation, which was intended to induce a particular course of conduct by the other person to whom it was made;
(b) the other person, as a result of (a), acts (or omits to act) in a particular way; and
(c) detriment to the other person is caused.

Applying the test to the facts in *Greenwood*:

(a) Mr G knew about the forgeries but, by his silence for eight months, he intended to induce the bank not to claim against Mrs G;
(b) as a result the bank did not realise the truth and did not claim against Mrs G; and
(c) the bank consequently suffered loss, because by the time Mr G informed it, Mrs G was dead and there was no right of action against her estate.

It seems Mr G's best argument (not reported as raised) would have been that Mrs G would have killed herself as soon as he went to the

[35][1933] AC 51 HL.

bank, even if he had done so eight months earlier and the bank would therefore have had no claim against her estate in any case. If this was accepted, the bank would not have established the third part of the estoppel.

In Brown v Westminster Bank,[36] B's employee had forged many of her cheques. The bank was suspicious of the cheques and queried them with B, who answered that they were genuine. B later claimed recrediting of her account but it was held she was estopped from doing so, even for those paid before the bank first queried the cheques. The bank's detriment was the delay it suffered in pursuing a claim against the forger as (unlike in *Greenwood*) it had not lost its rights against him.

4.10 FRAUDULENT ALTERATION

We are concerned here with a cheque which is genuinely signed by the customer but which is altered or added to. A payee, for instance, may seek to increase the amount for which the cheque is payable. As he lacks the authority to do so, this also is a forgery, not of the signature but of the details on the cheque. Once again, the starting point is to examine the banker-customer contract and, as the customer's authority to his bank is to pay the amount he stated, the bank is not able to debit the account for the increased amount.

Again, however, an estoppel may arise to prevent the customer from asserting his right. This estoppel is based on the customer's duty to take usual and reasonable precautions to prevent forgery when he draws cheques. For example in London Joint Stock Bank v Macmillan and Arthur,[37] an employee had the task of filling in cheque forms for signature by M or A. The employee drew a cheque payable to the firm or bearer in the sum of £2, written in figures, no words being written at this stage. It was signed, and the employee later wrote 'one hundred and twenty pounds' in words and added the necessary figures. The bank was held to be entitled to debit the account for £120, as an estoppel operated when the customer failed in his duty, by signing a cheque with the amount in words left

[36] *[1964] 2 Lloyd's Rep 187.*
[37] *[1918] AC 777 HL.*

blank, and space in the figures section for the addition of more numerals.

In Young v Grote,[38] Mr Y signed some blank cheques and left them with Mrs Y to be used in his absence for paying business debts. Mrs Y asked an employee to complete a cheque for £50. The employee wrote the word 'fifty' in the middle of the line used for figures and without using a capital 'F'. The amount in figures was inserted with a gap remaining after the £ sign. The cheque was shown to Mrs Y and she asked the employee to get it cashed. Before doing so, he inserted 'three hundred' in words and the figure '3' and obtained payment for £350. It was paid by the bank and Y sued. Held in favour of the bank due to gross negligence on the part of Y and his agent, Mrs Y.

Whether or not the customer has drawn the cheque with reasonable care, the bank should not pay if there is an obvious alteration. It is normal practice not to pay unless the drawer signs next to the alteration, sometimes initials are accepted. Presumably if this signature or initialling is forged, the bank is liable. For this reason, it must be better practice to require a full signature by the alteration.

To summarise the position, on fraudulently altered cheques as between the bank and the customer:

(a) did the customer exercise reasonable care in drawing the cheque?
(b) was the alteration detectable by the bank?

If the answer to both questions is 'no', the customer must bear the loss. If the answer to either is 'yes', the loss falls on the bank.

The Act contains provisions dealing with inchoate cheques (section 20) and with material alterations (section 64). The effect of section 20 is that a signed but incomplete cheque may be completed by anyone in possession of it. It should be completed within a reasonable time and in accordance with the drawer's wishes. However, a holder in due course acquires a good title to the cheque even if it was completed for a larger sum than the drawer authorised.

A prudent drawer who wishes to leave the payee to complete the precise amount will, of course, write an amount across the top of

[38](1827) 4 Bing 253.

the cheque which is not to be exceeded. It would then be clear to a holder in due course that the cheque has not been completed within the drawer's authority.

Section 64(1) renders a cheque which has been altered in some material way (such as the amount being increased) unenforceable against the drawer. There is a proviso to this, to the effect that if the cheque has come into the hands of a holder in due course and the alteration is not apparent, it is enforceable against the drawer for the original amount. The cheque is enforceable against the person who altered it (and subsequent parties) for the new, altered, amount.

These provisions in the Act do not have any direct effect on the paying bank but merely on the position of some holder in due course of the cheque, which may include a collecting bank.[39] To illustrate the above points:

(1) Suppose A writes an open cheque drawn on the X Bank for £2 which is fraudulently altered by B to read £2,000. If B presents this for cash to the X Bank and obtains payment, the issue is simply whether A exercised reasonable care in drawing the cheque. If he did not, then he must bear the loss. If he did, the X Bank must bear the loss. Whoever loses may sue B if he can be found.

(2) Suppose that B negotiated the cheque to C, who is a holder in due course, and that he obtains payment from X Bank. The issue between X Bank and A is the same (did A exercise reasonable care) but, by section 64, C is not entitled to more than £2 from A and presumably the excess may be recovered from C as a payment made under a mistake.[40] Therefore it may not matter whether A or the X Bank must bear the loss.

(3) Suppose A writes an open cheque payable to B and leaves the amount (in both figures and words) blank. B, fraudulently, completes it for £2,000 and negotiates it to C who obtains payment from the X Bank. Once again, the issue between A and the X Bank is whether A exercised reasonable care but this time (by section 20), C as a holder in due course is entitled to the full

[39]*Assuming the cheque is transferrable.*
[40]*See 5.14 below.*

£2,000 and the money cannot be recovered from him as a mistaken payment. The position of a collecting bank which qualifies as a holder in due course will be identical to that of C.

In Slingsby v District Bank,[41] a fraudulent solicitor drew cheques for the signature of the plaintiffs. After a cheque drawn payable to JP & Co. was signed, the solicitor added 'per C and P', which was the name of his firm. The bank had no means of knowing that an alteration had been made to the cheque after it was signed, as the whole cheque (apart from the signature) was in the solicitor's handwriting. In an action against the paying bank, it was held that the drawer of a cheque was under no obligation to draw a line after the payee's name. Furthermore, the alteration had the effect of 'avoiding' the cheque under section 64(1) of the Act.[42] Consequently, the cheque was a worthless piece of paper when presented to the bank, and it should therefore not have been paid.

Some banks have for some time printed a direction in chequebooks that customers should draw a line after the name of the payee. Clearly on such facts it is open to a court to hold that it has become an express term of the banker-customer contract that customers should follow this practice.

4.11 COUNTERMAND

Section 75(1) of the Act states that a bank's duty and authority to pay a cheque are determined by countermand of payment. In other words a customer may 'stop' a cheque by giving notice to his bank.

Obviously the customer must give notice before the cheque has been paid. In Baines v National Provincial Bank,[43] B issued a cheque to X shortly before the bank's closing time. X obtained payment from B's bank five minutes after its closing time. B attempted to stop the cheque the next morning and then claimed that the bank re-

---

[41][1932] 1 KB 544 CA.
[42]The proviso to this did not apply in this case, since no one was a holder in due course of this cheque.
[43](1927) 96 LJKB 801.

credit his account. It was held that the bank was entitled to a reasonable margin of its closing time for paying a cheque.

The stop order must be clear and unambiguous; special importance is attached to the number of the cheque, as this is the one detail which is unique to it.[44] The stop order is only effective when it comes to the actual notice of the bank. In Curtice v London City and Midland Bank,[45] the notice was sent by telegram which was placed in the bank's letterbox. When the box was emptied, the telegram was left behind. Rather incredibly, it was held that the bank was justified in paying the cheque, as it had not actually received notice of countermand at the time it paid the cheque, because it had not read the telegram. It is considered, however, that the bank is liable in negligence in these circumstances, for failing to empty its letter-box.

There is no requirement in the Act that the stop notice be in writing. Naturally, for reasons of haste, the initial order is often telephoned; banks ordinarily act on this and later seek written confirmation in order to have evidence of the stop. It is considered that a bank which ignored a telephoned stop would be in breach of section 75. Under the Banking Code, banks must tell new customers about how to stop cheques.[46]

In practice stop orders seem to give rise to a number of problems including:

(a) mishearing the details of the cheque over the telephone and therefore stopping the wrong cheque;

(b) agreeing to stop a cheque which is backed by a cheque card. The customer agrees not to do this by the terms of the issue of the card, and a bank may be within its rights not to stop the cheque even where it had 'accepted' the stop order;

(c) the bank pays a stopped cheque and as a result wrongfully dishonours another cheque;

(d) the bank receives notice from the payee of the cheque that it has been lost. The bank is unable to treat this as grounds for not

[44]*Westminster Bank v Hilton (1926) 136 LT 315 HL.*
[45]*[1908] 1 KB 293 CA.*
[46]*And existing customers on request, section 2.1.*

paying, and can only advise the payee to contact the customer who may or may not choose to countermand. If the bank pays the cheque meanwhile, it may not do so in the ordinary course of business and thus may lose its statutory protection.[47] If it fails to pay it risks a breach of contract action from its customer;

(e) the bank receives notice of stop, which is later cancelled. The bank fails to pay the cheque and is liable for breach of contract.

The customer must give notice of stop to the account holding branch.[48] The exemption in Burnett v Westminster Bank[49] is based on special facts which were a product of its time, now long past. The customer appears to be able to stop a cheque up to close of business on Day Three of the clearing cycle, see 6.2 below.

Where a bank ignores a valid stop notice, it is unable to debit the customer's account. This will often be advantageous for the payee of the cheque, and the law provides three possible remedies for the bank:

(a) to recover the money as a payment made by mistake;[50]
(b) to claim from the payee any goods which have been paid for by the stopped cheque. This is an example of the principle of subrogation;
(c) (arguably) to use the principle of subrogation to debit the customer's account on the basis that a debt which he owed has been discharged;[51]

In any joint account or account which requires the signature of more than one person, a stop may be accepted from any one party.

---

[47]See 5.1 below.
[48]London Provincial and South Western Bank v Buszard (1918) 35 TLR 142.
[49][1966] 1 QB 742.
[50]Barclays Bank v W J Simms, Son and Cooke (Southern) Ltd [1980] QB 677. This is discussed in 5.14 below.
[51]By extension of the principle established in B. Liggett (Liverpool) Ltd v Barclays Bank [1928] 1 KB 48 and approved in Re Cleadon Trust Ltd [1939] 1 Ch 286 CA. Liggett concerned cheques with only one signature which required two signatures and was approved on the basis of the signatory having authority from the company to discharge its debts. It must be doubtful whether the same principle extends to a stopped cheque.

It is practice, however, only to lift a stop on the orders of all parties concerned.

From the point of view of the customer (drawer of the cheque), he is entitled to order his bank to stop payment but this does not negate any liability he has on the cheque itself. Where the cheque was given as a gift or for consideration which has totally failed, his liability to the payee will be nil. However, if the payee has negotiated it to a holder in due course, the customer will be liable to that person.

Summary of matters obliging a bank not to pay a cheque:

(1) Notice of countermand by its customer.
(2) Notice of the customer's death.[52] Actual notice is required and payment after death but before notice seems to be valid assuming the Act overrides the common law position that agency is determined on death.
(3) Notice of mental incapacity of customer, on the basis that the bank's agency to pay cheques is terminated.[53]
(4) Notice of a bankruptcy petition having been presented against a customer or against one of joint account holders.[54]
(5) Notice of winding-up petition against a company customer (this notice may be constructive as the petition is 'gazetted'), or notice that a resolution to that effect has been made.[55]
(6) Service of a garnishee order on the bank. This has the effect of freezing the account up to the amount stated in the order.
(7) Service of a 'Mareva' injunction on the bank.
(8) Service of a sequestration order on the bank.
(9) Closure of the customer's account.
(10) Adequate notice of facts which give rise either to a constructive trust or to a suspicion in the mind of a reasonable banker that the account is being conducted fraudulently.[56]

The above are in addition to matters appearing on the face of the

---

[52] Section 75(2).
[53] Drew v Nunn (1879) 4 QB 661.
[54] See 2.2 above.
[55] See 2.7 above.
[56] Lipkin Gorman v Karpnale Ltd [1989] 1 WLR 1340 CA.

cheque discussed under 4.8 above, e.g. cheque not signed, forged signature, undated etc.

4.12 WRONGFUL DISHONOUR

It may happen that a bank declines payment of a cheque when it does not have valid grounds for doing so. The reason might be:

(a) failing to realise the customer had removed a stop order;
(b) wrongly believing there were insufficient funds, or where there would be sufficient funds if the bank had not already paid a post-dated or stopped cheque;
(c) forgetting that an overdraft facility had been agreed, the bank must pay if there is an agreed overdraft facility;[57]
(d) believing the customer had closed the account when he had not.

In all of these cases the bank will be in breach of contract to its customer and may also have libelled him. First, however, Marzetti v Williams[58] is authority to the effect that a bank is entitled to a reasonable time after the receipt of funds to the credit of an account, in order to carry out the appropriate book-keeping. In this case, however, sufficient cash was paid in at 1 p.m. and payment of a cheque was refused at 3 p.m. the same day. This was held to be beyond a reasonable time and the bank was liable for breach of contract. Presumably a longer time is reasonable if cash is paid in at another branch or if a cheque is paid in which requires clearing. Established clearing custom and statements made about how many days a cheque takes to clear will have a strong influence on what is reasonable time. The Banking Code requires banks to tell new customers when funds can be withdrawn after a cheque or other payment has been credited to an account.[59]

It has been seen[60] that a bank is usually entitled to combine two accounts and thereby validly dishonour a cheque drawn on one

---

[57]*Rouse v Bradford Banking Co. Ltd [1894] AC 586 HL.*
[58]*(1830) 1 B & Ad 415.*
[59]*And existing customers on request, section 2.1.*
[60]*In 1.14 above.*

account which was in credit. It has also been seen[61] that a customer is entitled to appropriate a particular payment into his account to a particular payment out, and in this case the bank must honour the chosen cheque, whatever the general balance of the account.

If the bank pays cash for an open cheque it cannot change its mind once it discovers there are insufficient funds. In Chambers v Miller,[62] the payee had obtained payment and was counting the money when the cashier asked for it back. The payee declined to return it and the cashier took it from him by force. The bank was liable for assault and false imprisonment.

Wrongful dishonour of a cheque will always amount to a breach of contract by the bank. The long-established rule that only nominal damages are payable to non-traders unless the customer can prove special damage[63] has recently been rejected by the Court of Appeal in Kpohraror v Woolwich Building Society.[64] A trader has long been entitled to general damages amounting to reasonable compensation for the injury done to his credit, without having to prove special damage.[65]

Wrongful dishonour of a cheque may also be a libel on the customer. A libel consists of the publication to a third party of an untrue imputation against the reputation of another, ordinarily in writing. The test to be applied is – would the words tend to lower the plaintiff in the estimation of right-thinking members of society generally?[66]

It has been held that by writing 'not sufficient' on a cheque and by returning this cheque to the collecting bank or the payee, the drawee bank commits a libel on its customer's reputation (assuming of course the dishonour is wrongful). Nor is the bank able to raise

[61]In 1.13 above.
[62](1862) 13 CBNS 125.
[63]See Gibbons v Westminster Bank [1939] 2 KB 882 and National Westminster Bank v Oceancrest (No. 2) (1985) The Times, 3rd May, CA.
[64][1996] 4 All ER 119 CA. The plaintiff (a non-trader) was awarded £5,500 general damages.
[65]Wilson v United Counties Bank Ltd [1920] AC 102 HL.
[66]Sim v Stretch [1936] 2 All ER 1237 HL.

qualified privilege as a defence.[67] In Jayson v Midland Bank,[68] the words 'refer to drawer' were held to be capable of being defamatory.

In Russell v Bank America National Trust and Savings Association,[69] the words 'account closed' had been written on four business cheques. The jury awarded £50,000 damages for libel.

The award of damages for libel is not limited to the proof of real loss resulting from the bank's actions. It is open to a customer to bring an action both in contract and in libel. Damages for libel may be reduced if the defendant made an apology to the plaintiff.[70] In Baker v Australia and New Zealand Bank[71] it was said that the lack of any apology and of any explanation to the payees of the cheques, were factors in fixing the level of damages.

The Banking Code states that banks should use a letter or other private and confidential means when informing a customer that a cheque has been returned unpaid.[72]

[67]Davidson v Barclays Bank Ltd [1940] 1 All ER 316.
[68][1968] 1 Lloyd's Rep 409 CA.
[69]Unreported (1978), see Chorley & Smart, Leading Cases in the Law of Banking, 6th edition, p135.
[70]Libel Act 1843.
[71][1958] NZLR 907. The bank had written 'present again' on the cheque.
[72]Section 3.8.

5 Cheques – the paying and collecting banks

5.1 STATUTORY PROTECTION FOR THE PAYING BANK

The matters discussed in the previous chapter were largely limited to the legal relationship between a paying bank and its customer. The provisions of the Bills of Exchange Act 1882 (also referred to in this chapter simply as the Act) which are now to be examined are relevant to a paying bank because they may give it protection against two possibilities:

(a) an action for breach of contract from its customer; and
(b) an action in conversion from some third party true owner of a cheque.

Conversion is a tort which is actionable when the defendant deals with the plaintiff's goods without authority and thereby deprives the plaintiff of his property. The goods in this context consist of the piece of paper which is the cheque. A paying bank might convert a cheque as in the following example. Suppose A draws a cheque on the X Bank payable to B. C steals the cheque and opens a bank account in a false name so as to obtain payment from the X Bank. C had no title to the cheque and B remained the true owner of it. By paying C (even through another bank), the X Bank has converted B's property and is liable to him at common law.

Conversion is an absolute tort, i.e. no intention to convert or negligence need be established; if the property was in fact converted the tort is complete. In the above example, it is clear that in practice the X Bank would have no means of knowing whether the cheque was paid into the genuine B's account or some impersonator, because B is not its customer. There has long been a need, therefore, for some protection for a bank in these circumstances, and this is now contained in section 80 of the Act. The section deals only with crossed cheques (extended to crossed analogous instruments[1] and drafts by section 5 of the Cheques Act 1957). The bank must pay another bank or, if the instrument is crossed specially, it must pay the other bank named. The conditions for protection are that the bank pays in good faith and without negligence. The bank is not to be treated as having been negligent purely because it disregarded a purported indorsement on a non-transferable cheque.[2]

When a cheque[3] bears a forged or unauthorised indorsement, a paying bank is protected if it pays in good faith and in the ordinary course of business, under section 60 of the Act. The section protects when an agent places an indorsement on the cheque without authority[4] but not when there is no indorsement or the indorsement is irregular, i.e. does not correspond properly with the payee's details.[5]

A similar provision, section 19 of the Stamp Act 1853, protects a bank paying a banker's draft which purports to be indorsed by the payee but which is not made by him or by his authority. Expressed in a different way, this deals with the same situations as section 60, i.e. forged and unauthorised indorsements. In section 19, however, there is no requirement that the bank act in good faith and in the ordinary course of business.

It will be recalled that prior to 1957, all cheques had to be indorsed and that the Cheques Act 1957 was passed to enable indorsements to be dispensed with. Thus section 1 of that Act provides protection when a bank pays a cheque which is not indorsed or has an irregular indorsement. The section applies to all cheques and to analogous instruments and drafts. The conditions for this protection are identical to section 60: the bank should pay in good faith and in the ordinary course of business.

[1] e.g. 'cheques' drawn 'pay cash'.
[2] Section 81A.
[3] But not an analogous instrument or even a bearer cheque.
[4] Charles v Blackwell (1877) 2 CPD 151.
[5] Slingsby v District Bank Ltd [1932] 1 KB 544 CA.

The Committee of London Clearing Banks Circular to Branches of September 1957 contains a practice direction to the effect that paying banks should still require indorsements before paying the following:

(a) combined cheque and receipt forms marked with the letter 'R';
(b) travellers' cheques;
(c) bills of exchange other than cheques;
(d) promissory notes;
(e) cheques and other instruments cashed at the counter.

This statement of practice is relevant to the law, if it amounts to a definition of what is payment in the ordinary course of business. Suppose A draws an open cheque payable to B. C steals it and cashes it at the paying bank but is not asked to indorse it. Section 1 protects when there is no indorsement but only when the bank pays in the ordinary course of business, and the bank in this case has not followed the practice statement. Suppose C forges B's indorsement and the bank pays. It will now be protected by section 60.

Finally, it should be added that by section 59 of the Act, a bank is protected if it pays a cheque to the holder thereof in good faith and without notice that his title is defective. It has already been seen that a thief is the holder of a bearer cheque simply by having it in his possession. A bank paying a bearer cheque is protected if it satisfies the conditions of doing so in good faith and without notice of defect of title.

It will be recalled[6] that a cheque drawn payable to fictitious or non-existent persons is a bearer cheque by virtue of section 7(3) of the Act, and therefore a bank paying in the circumstances which occurred in Clutton v Attenborough[7] can be protected by section 59:

(a) if the indorsement is forged but it does not pay in the ordinary course of business, so long as it is in good faith and has no notice of defect of title; and
(b) if there is no indorsement when normally the ordinary course of business would require one.

[6] See 4.5 above.
[7] Described in 4.5 above.

In Carpenters Company v British Mutual Banking Co. Ltd,[8] the majority of the court considered that, 'in the ordinary course of business' had a different quality to that of being without negligence and, in effect, that it was an easier condition to satisfy. This case also establishes that when a cheque is paid into the same branch as that upon which it is drawn (known in practice as a 'house' cheque) and the bank involved is therefore both paying and collecting, the bank in order to be protected must satisfy the conditions, both as a paying bank and as a collecting bank.

It will be clear that there is a considerable degree of overlap between the sections protecting the paying bank. Suppose A draws a crossed cheque on X Bank payable to B. C forges B's indorsement and obtains payment. The X Bank may be protected by sections 60, 80 and arguably also by section 1. It only requires the protection of one section, however.

It should be noted that nothing in these sections protects a bank which pays a cheque where the drawer's signature is forged or some addition or alteration has been made to it. The proviso to section 79(2) of the Act does, however, protect where a crossing is altered or obliterated (if it does not appear to have been so altered or obliterated).

The White Paper[9] proposes that sections 60 and 80 of the Bills of Exchange Act, section 1 of the Cheques Act and section 19 of the Stamp Act all be repealed and be replaced by a single protective section. The condition for protection in the proposed section would be that the paying bank acted 'in good faith and without negligence'.

5.2 OTHER DEFENCES FOR THE PAYING BANK

It has already been seen[10] that a bank which pays, without authority, a stopped cheque is entitled by subrogation to any goods which were thus paid for and that it may be that this right extends to being able to debit the customer's account if the goods have passed into the customer's possession, or if payment of the cheque has discharged a

[8][1938] 1 KB 511 CA.
[9](1990) Cm 1026.
[10]In 4.11 above.

debt of the drawer. In B. Liggett (Liverpool) Ltd v Barclays Bank,[11] it was agreed that B Ltd's account would be operated by the signatures of at least two directors. The bank operated it with only one, and thereby paid creditors of B Ltd who had a genuine claim against the company. It was held the bank was entitled to debit the account, provided it appeared that the one director who signed did have authority as between himself and B Ltd to pay its debts.

5.3 THE COLLECTING BANK

There will not necessarily be a collecting bank involved in the life of a cheque but this will only occur when an open cheque is presented for cash at the drawee bank. In the great majority of cases, therefore, a collecting bank is involved. This includes house credits (where a cheque is paid into the same bank where it is payable). This bank is considered to be both a paying and collecting bank.[12]

5.4 THE COLLECTING BANK AND ITS OWN CUSTOMER

As regards its own customer, the collecting bank has a duty to exercise reasonable care and skill in collecting his cheque. Thus the collecting bank appears to have the following specific duties to its customer:

(1) To present a cheque for payment within a reasonable time. In Forman v Bank of England,[13] the bank was liable to its customer when it dishonoured a cheque for insufficient funds, two days after another cheque to cover this had been paid in. Under the practice operating at that time, the second cheque (drawn on a London bank) could have been drawn against the next day, but it was treated as a country cheque and consequently there were insufficient funds at the time the first cheque was presented for payment. It is considered that a collecting bank has a duty to

[11]*[1928] 1 KB 48.*
[12]*Carpenters Company v British Mutual Banking Co. Ltd, see above.*
[13]*(1902) 18 TLR 339.*

adhere to the current practice relating to clearing of cheques, and that the *Foreman* case does not lay down firm rules for the time which should be taken to collect a cheque. Except for house credits, all banks are reliant on the clearing system to collect cheques, and it would be most harsh if one was liable when it had simply used this system. Section 45(2) of the Act declares that a cheque must be presented for payment within a reasonable time of it being issued, if the drawer is to be liable on it. A reasonable time is to be interpreted according (*inter alia*) to the 'usage of trade'.

(2) If a cheque is dishonoured, the collecting bank (as agent of its customer) should send notice of dishonour to him by post on the same day it becomes aware of the dishonour.[14]

(3) Following the introduction of new rules permitting truncation of cheques,[15] the collecting bank's responsibility for a cheque which it is presenting for payment can now be discharged by notifying the paying bank of the cheque's essential features by electronic means. Physical presentation is no longer necessary unless this is requested by the paying bank by the day following electronic notification. When physical presentation does occur, it need not be at the account-holding branch if the paying bank has specified a central address for this purpose. The responsibilities and liabilities of the collecting bank are otherwise unaffected by these rules permitting truncation of cheques.

5.5 STATUTORY PROTECTION FOR THE COLLECTING BANK

Apart from the contractual relationship it has with its own customer, the collecting bank may have a liability to, and occasionally rights against, third parties, namely, other parties to the cheque it collects. Suppose that A draws a cheque payable to B, from whom C steals

---

[14]*Section 49(13) of the Act. Posting on the following day is permitted in some circumstances.*
[15]*SI 1996/2993, made under section 1 of the Deregulation and Contracting Out Act 1994 and discussed more fully in 6.4 below.*

it and pays it into his bank account, possibly one he has opened in a false name. When the cheque clears, he withdraws the funds and disappears. The true owner of the cheque is B but C obtained payment. B may sue C in conversion but this is rarely practicable. The paying bank is protected by section 60 of the Act if it paid in good faith and in the ordinary course of business. B has a claim against the collecting bank which has assisted C in his fraud. This claim is in conversion since the collecting bank has wrongfully dealt with B's property. In some older cases, the true owner sued the collecting bank for 'money had and received' and it appears this remains valid as an alternative remedy to conversion, although it adds nothing to the level of damages.

The collecting bank has long needed statutory protection from an action in conversion by the true owner of a cheque. With the current predomination of non-transferrable cheques, forged indorsements are not a concern since no indorsed non-transferrable cheques will be accepted – genuine or otherwise. Collecting banks still convert cheques, however, for instance by accepting them into opening false name accounts or into genuine accounts but with sufficient notice that they have been misappropriated by their customer and thus they are still grateful for statutory protection. This protection is now contained in section 4 of the Cheques Act 1957. Unlike the variety of statutes which protect the paying bank, there is only one that does so for the collecting bank, and it also deals with the abolition of the need for indorsements which occurred with the passing of that Act.

Section 4 protects a bank when it:

(a) receives payment for a customer; or
(b) having credited a customer's account, receives payment for itself.

The section applies to:

(a) all cheques;
(b) 'cheques' drawn 'pay cash';
(c) most warrants issued by government departments; and
(d) bankers' drafts.

The conditions of the protection being available are that the collecting bank:

(a) collects the cheque for a customer;
(b) does so in good faith; and
(c) does so without negligence.

The spirit of the change in indorsement practice that occurred in 1957 is reflected in sub-section (3), which declares that a banker will not be considered to be negligent by reason only of his failure to concern himself with the absence of, or irregularity in, an indorsement.

The matter of who constitutes a customer of a bank was addressed in 1.3 above. So long as the bank is collecting the cheque for someone who holds an account with it, it will satisfy this condition. This is so even if the account is opened with the very cheque which is in dispute.[16]

Sometimes, however, a cheque is paid into a different bank than the account holding branch. In the judgment of Lawrence LJ in the Court of Appeal in Lloyds Bank v Savory,[17] a bank cannot claim the protection when the cheque is paid into and collected by a different branch of the same bank, since the collecting bank is not receiving payment for a customer. The case went to the House of Lords[18] but this point was not considered there. The same circumstances did not prevent the Court of Appeal from granting the bank protection in Orbit Mining and Trading Co. Ltd v Westminster Bank,[19] although the issue was not addressed.

It may be that the customer is considered to be a customer of the whole bank for these purposes and not just of the account holding branch. It seems most unlikely, however, that a bank which collects a cheque for a customer of a different bank would come within section 4, at least if the normal procedure is followed, whereby the

---

[16]*Commissioners of Taxation v English, Scottish and Australian Bank [1920] AC 683 PC.*
[17]*[1932] 2 KB 122 CA.*
[18]*[1933] AC 201 HL.*
[19]*[1963] 1 QB 794 CA.*

bank puts the cheque into clearing directly and only a credit slip is sent to the account holding bank.

In the majority of instances the collecting bank will have no difficulty in satisfying the conditions that it must collect for a customer and do so in good faith. Proving lack of negligence is a stiffer test. There is no shortage of case law to illustrate what is negligence in this context and what is not, yet the cases are not always a model of consistency. At least part of the reason for this is that the matter of negligence turns to a large extent on the contemporary context of banking practice, and it has been said that some of the older cases may not be an accurate guide in more modern conditions.[20]

First, it should be noted that when the collecting bank is negligent, it is not liable in the tort of negligence. It is liable in conversion, but will be protected from such liability if it has not been negligent. This may seem pedantic but it does have an impact on the burden of proof. The true owner does not have to prove that the collecting bank was negligent; it is for the latter to prove it was not negligent, on a balance of probabilities.

The collecting bank is not expected to be infallible. A constant thread running through the cases is that the collecting bank is expected to make appropriate enquiries and, having done so, is not to be fobbed off with a weak reply. There will be occasions when there has been a fraud but the collecting bank has acted sufficiently carefully to absolve itself from liability. By and large, therefore, the cleverer the fraud perpetrated, or the more plausible the false explanations given in response to inquiries, the less likely the collecting bank is to be liable.

The test to be applied may be summarised thus – did the bank take reasonable care, taking into account antecedent and present circumstances?

Further relevant guidelines which emerge from *Marfani* are:

(a) when a cheque is presented by a customer who appears to be a holder of the cheque, the bank is entitled to assume the customer is the true owner, unless there are facts which are known, or

---

[20]*Marfani & Co. Ltd v Midland Bank [1968] 1 WLR 956 CA.*

ought to be known, which would cause a reasonable banker to be suspicious;

(b) the facts which ought to be known, the inquiries which ought to be made and what will cause a reasonable banker to be suspicious will depend upon current banking practice. This point was recently cited with approval in Lipkin Gorman v Karpnale Ltd;[21]

(c) such current practice will not conclusively define what the law expects of a reasonable banker but the courts will hesitate before condemning a generally adopted practice;

(d) inquiries which would probably not have prevented the fraud and would therefore only have risked offending the customer had he been honest, need not be made.[22]

Cases decided on facts which occurred before 1957 are based on the now repealed section 82 of the Bills of Exchange Act. This applied a similar test, also based on the bank being without negligence. Therefore these cases are relevant.

It is probably helpful to divide the cases into two categories:

(a) where it is alleged the bank was negligent when it opened the account, usually because this later turned out to be in a false name;

(b) where it is alleged the bank was negligent when it accepted a specific cheque or cheques for collection.

5.6 NEGLIGENCE IN OPENING THE ACCOUNT

It has long been established that a bank has a duty to obtain references before opening a new account. In Hampstead Guardians v Barclays Bank,[23] an account was opened in a false name. A reference was asked for and obtained but it was forged. The court held that some further check on identity was necessary. In Nu-Stilo Footwear

---

[21][1989] 1 WLR 1340 CA.
[22]This point was doubted in Thackwell v Barclays Bank [1986] 1 All ER 676.
[23](1923) 39 TLR 229.

Ltd v Lloyds Bank,[24] an account was opened in a false name, the customer giving his real name as a reference. The bank obtained a satisfactory reference from the bankers of the 'reference'. Held, the bank had acted without negligence in opening the account.

In Marfani & Co. Ltd v Midland Bank,[25] a false name account was opened by an employee of M Ltd. He used the name E, which was the name of a supplier to M Ltd and to whom, therefore, cheques were made payable. The new customer explained that he had no job but intended to open a restaurant. Two names were given as references. A sum of cash and a stolen cheque for £3,000 were paid into the account. The bank specially cleared the cheque (without being asked to do so). The account was credited but the bank awaited a reply from the references before allowing withdrawal of the funds. One of the references, who had an account with the branch for some years, recommended the new customer to the bank, saying that the customer had been known to him for some time. In fact this was not so. The customer had, in preparation of the fraud, introduced himself as E to this reference one month earlier. Nothing was heard from the second reference. The bank then allowed the funds to be withdrawn. Held, the bank was not negligent. Further evidence of identity was unnecessary in view of the bank having obtained a good reference from an apparently reliable source.

In Lumsden & Co. v London Trustee Savings Bank,[26] a false name account was opened by an employee of L. The name chosen was the same as one of the persons to whom the employer often made cheques payable. The new customer explained that he was a self-employed chemist and gave his real name as a reference, falsely giving himself the title of Doctor and also saying he was newly arrived from Australia. This 'reference' did not respond to the bank's request for the name of his bank. The bank had not adhered to its internal rules and whilst the court did not consider that conclusive, it held the bank should have done more to establish identity.

It may be concluded from the above cases that identity is of paramount importance and that perhaps a bank, when opening a

[24]*(1956) 7 LDB 121.*
[25]*[1968] 1 WLR 956 CA.*
[26]*[1971] 1 Lloyd's Rep 114.*

new account, would be better advised to obtain solid evidence of identity such as a passport, rather than seeking references from persons who may be spurious. Such a procedure is also likely to be less time-consuming for the bank and is now required by the Money Laundering Regulations 1993.[27] These Regulations impose criminal liability on a bank which fails to observe them so banks will clearly now require identification evidence. If a bank opened an account in a false name in circumstances where it was in breach of the Regulations, it would find it difficult to argue that it was not negligent for the purposes of section 4 if it were sued by the owner of the cheque, regardless of whether it had obtained references. The interesting question is whether obtaining evidence of identity replaces or is in addition to the civil law requirement to obtain references. The former alternative appears eminently sensible.

Whether or not a reference is taken, case law suggests that certain inquiries must be made of the new customer, such as whether he is employed and, if so, the nature of his job and the name of his employer, so that the bank may notice if he starts paying in stolen cheques drawn by or payable to that employer. In Lloyds Bank v Savory,[28] it was also held that the bank should have requested the same details concerning the customer's spouse. In Orbit Mining and Trading Co. Ltd v Westminster Bank,[29] it was stated that a bank has no obligation to keep itself up to date with the identity of a customer's employer. It is suggested that where a customer receives his pay through the BACS system, or even by cheque, his bank may be deemed to have such up-to-date knowledge.

5.7 NEGLIGENCE IN COLLECTION OF THE CHEQUE

This category may be sub-divided into:

(a) suspicious matters which are obvious, or ought to be obvious,

---

[27] See 2.2 above.
[28] See above.
[29] See above.

from the face of the cheque, possibly coupled with the information the bank has about its customer; and

(b) purely contextual matters which should arouse suspicion, in the absence of which the cheque could have been safely accepted without inquiry.

Suspicious matters on the face of the cheque

A clear example of this sub-category is the cheque crossed 'account payee' which is not originally payable to the customer. Section 81A of the Bills of Exchange Act now declares such a cheque to be not transferable and to be valid only between the parties to it. It is suggested that a bank which collects a cheque crossed 'account payee' in circumstances which would indicate to a reasonable banker that there has been a transfer of the cheque would not be protected by section 4 and that a reasonable explanation from the customer would not assist. A defence will still be available to the collecting bank if it acted in good faith and without negligence, where, for example, the account name was indistinguishable from that of the payee on the cheque and it had taken steps to establish the identity of the customer whose account had been credited.

A second example of a suspicious matter is where, on the basis that the bank does know or may be deemed to know the name of the customer's employer, it collects cheques without inquiry which are drawn by or payable to that employer. In Lloyds Bank v Savory,[30] P and S were employees of stockbrokers, which drew many cheques payable to bearer. They stole a number of these cheques; P paid some into his bank account while S paid some into Mrs S's account. All the payments in were made at other branches of the bank, i.e. not at the account holding branch. The cheques were sent to the Clearing House and the accounts credited with the appropriate amounts. The cheques never went to the account holding branches and thus, even if the latter had the relevant information about the employers, they would have been unable to connect this to the drawer's name on the cheques. Held, it was a negligent practice to not send cheques, or details of them, to the account holding branch.

[30]See above.

In Lloyds Bank v Chartered Bank of India, Australia and China,[31] L had power to draw cheques on his employer's (Lloyds Bank) account, but those for large amounts had to be co-signed by another official. L persuaded, by fraud, another to co-sign some cheques which were made payable to the C Bank, where L had a personal account. L asked the C bank to collect payment of the cheques and to credit his account with them with the proceeds. The C Bank knew that L worked for Lloyds Bank. Over two years L embezzled £17,000. Lloyds Bank sued the C Bank in conversion and succeeded, as the latter had been negligent in failing to make inquiries about the cheques.

In Orbit Mining and Trading Co. Ltd v Westminster Bank,[32] E and W were directors of O Ltd and were authorised to operate its bank account by joint signatures. W went abroad and signed some blank cheques so that E could carry on the business alone. E co-signed some cheques which he drew 'pay cash' and paid them into his personal account with the W Bank. The W Bank had asked for the name of E's employer when he opened the account and this was truthfully given, but he had changed his employment meanwhile. Held, the bank was not obliged to keep up to date with E's employment details and, as the signatures on the cheques were illegible (E's normal signature), it was not immediately obvious that E was one of the signers of the cheque, and the bank was not negligent.

In A.L. Underwood Ltd v Bank of Liverpool and Martins,[33] U had a business account at the L Bank for some years when he incorporated his business into U Ltd. He maintained a personal account with the bank but opened a company account at another bank. He paid into his personal account a number of cheques which were payable to U Ltd, which he had indorsed. Held, notwithstanding that U Ltd was a 'one person company', it had to be regarded as a separate entity even if both U and the L Bank had not done so. Some inquiry should therefore have been made as to why a director was indorsing his company's cheques and paying them into his personal account.

[31]*[1929] 1 KB 40 CA.*
[32]*See above.*
[33]*[1924] 1 KB 775 CA.*

In Morison v London County and Westminster Bank,[34] A was an employee of M and he had authority to draw M's cheques. Over 42 years, A drew a large number of cheques payable to himself, which he paid into his account with the L Bank. Held, the L Bank was negligent in collecting the cheques but that it had been 'lulled to sleep' after about two years, by the absence of any complaint from M. Thus L Bank was not liable for the later cheques. This doctrine of lulling to sleep was, however, disapproved by the House of Lords in the Savory case.

Thirdly, and similar in principle to the cases in the second category, there are those where it should be obvious to the collecting bank that its customer is paying in cheques which he has signed in his capacity as agent of the drawer. In Midland Bank v Reckitt,[35] a solicitor (T) had power of attorney from R, which authorised him to operate R's account. T's account with the M Bank was overdrawn and he drew cheques on R's account, paying them into his own account. M Bank accepted these without any inquiry. Held, it was negligent.

It can also happen that the customer has received the cheque only as agent for his employer. In Bute (Marquess of) v Barclays Bank,[36] M was an employee of B. After he left this employment he received some government warrants, payable to 'M for B'. Held, it was clear from the face of the warrant that M was entitled to payment only as agent for B, and the collecting bank was negligent in not making any inquiries.

Purely contextual matters

These are cases where negligence arose, not because of something that was clear from the cheque itself, but because the collecting bank did not take into account other information which should have aroused its suspicions. These are probably the harshest decisions from the bank's point of view. In Nu-Stilo Footwear Ltd v Lloyds

---

[34] *[1914] 3 KB 356 CA.*
[35] *[1933] AC 1 HL.*
[36] *[1955] 1 QB 202.*

Bank,[37] a false name account had been opened but the L Bank had acted without negligence in this respect, see 5.6 above. The customer then paid in a series of cheques stolen from his employer, of whom the bank knew nothing. Held, the collection of the first cheque (for £172) was not negligent but that collection of the second (for £550) without inquiry did amount to negligence, as it was inconsistent with the details the customer had given of his business.

In Motor Traders Guarantee Corporation Ltd v Midland Bank,[38] T forged an indorsement on a cheque payable to W & Co. and paid it into his account. This was collected after some superficial inquiries. Held, the duty to make further inquiry arose in this case because T's account had a history of cheques dishonoured for lack of funds.

In Thackwell v Barclays Bank,[39] S simultaneously paid two cheques into different accounts with B Bank. One was payable to himself, which he had indorsed, and the other (for £44,000) was payable to T and appeared to be indorsed by T. It was obvious from a comparison of the indorsements on the two cheques that they were written by the same person (although of course the names were different) and S had indeed forged T's indorsement on the second cheque. Held, that the circumstances of the situation were out of the ordinary and inquiries should have been made. It made no difference that S need not have put his indorsement on one of the cheques and that it would not then have been obvious that the other indorsement was forged. Also it made no difference that if the bank had asked S some questions, he would have replied convincingly. The court was unhappy with the *Marfani* principle on this latter issue.

Finally, there are cases where the collecting bank succeeded because although it had been put on inquiry, it had asked questions and received a reasonably plausible explanation. In Smith & Baldwin v Barclays Bank,[40] B paid cheques payable to a business name into his personal account. The bank asked why he was doing so and B produced a certificate under the Registration of Business

[37](1956) 7 LDB 121.
[38][1937] 4 All ER 90.
[39][1986] 1 All ER 676.
[40](1944) 5 LDB 370.

Names Act 1916 (since repealed), which showed him as the sole proprietor of the business. B had obtained this certificate by fraud but it was held the bank had acted without negligence.

In Penmount Estates Ltd v National Provincial Bank,[41] a solicitor paid a stolen cheque (drawn payable to P Ltd and indorsed) into an account he maintained at the N Bank. Inquiries were made and the solicitor explained that the cheque represented payment to a client on a matter where he had been acting, and he was paying the cheque into his own account, whereupon he would draw a cheque in favour of the client for the balance after deduction of his fees. The court held this was a plausible explanation from a solicitor and the N Bank had therefore acted without negligence.

It is clearly very hard indeed for a banker to know exactly when the law demands that he should make inquiry before accepting a cheque, and when an explanation given in reply to an inquiry is sufficiently plausible. Each situation will vary on its facts. The Committee of London Clearing Banks Circular of September 1957 is considered to be relevant in defining when a collecting bank is negligent in collecting a cheque and when it is not. This provides that the following instruments presented for collection will require indorsement:

(a) instruments tendered for the credit of an account other than that of the payee. Where the payee's name is misspelt or he is incorrectly designated, no indorsement is required unless there are circumstances to suggest that the customer is not the person to whom payment is intended to be made;
(b) combined cheque and receipt forms, marked 'R';
(c) bills of exchange, other than cheques;
(d) promissory notes;
(e) drafts drawn on the Crown Agents and other paying agents;
(f) travellers' cheques;
(g) instruments payable by banks abroad;
(h) instruments payable to joint payees which are tendered for the credit of an account to which all are not parties, e.g. a cheque payable to A and B which is paid into A's account.

[41](1945) 173 LT 344.

Having set out these rules, banks will presumably be negligent in law if they fail to adhere to them. Therefore, if a cheque is accepted which, according to the Circular, requires indorsement, and no indorsement is present or it is irregular, the collecting bank will be liable to a true owner. However, section 4(3) declares that the collecting bank will not be negligent by reason only of the absence of, or irregularity in, indorsement.

Finally, it is worth noting that in order for there to be a valid claim against a collecting bank, there must be a valid instrument which has been converted. Thus a cheque with a forged drawer's signature, or even with a material alteration which avoids it, is not valid and no claim lies against the collecting bank.[42]

5.8 CONTRIBUTORY NEGLIGENCE

Contributory negligence is a statutory defence, which for the purposes of a collecting bank is contained in section 47 of the Banking Act 1979. In any action against a bank where section 4 of the Cheques Act 1957 is used as a defence, the bank may also set up the defence that the plaintiff was contributorily negligent. The defence is only partial, and serves only to reduce the amount of damages which the bank is liable to pay. This is quantified on a percentage basis so if the plaintiff is considered to be 10% contributorily negligent, his award will be reduced accordingly.

There is only one reported case of contributory negligence being successfully raised by a collecting bank; this is Lumsden v London Trustee Savings Bank.[43] The contributory negligence in this case consisted of the employer plaintiff's practice of drawing the cheques payable to 'Brown', leaving a gap before the word 'Brown'. The intended payee was 'Brown, Mills & Co'. The fraudster inserted initials before the name Brown and opened an account in this name. The court held the employer had been contributorily negligent in the manner in which he drew the cheques. The damages were reduced by 10%.

---

[42]*Slingsby v Westminster Bank (No. 2) [1931] 2 KB 583.*
[43]*Discussed in 5.6 above.*

5.9 THE DEFENCE OF *EX TURPI CAUSA NON ORITUR ACTIO*

This translates as 'out of an immoral situation, an action does not arise'. The only reported banking case in which it arose is Thackwell v Barclays Bank,[44] discussed in 5.7 above for the relevance it has to negligence for the purposes of section 4. T and some others set up a fraud on a finance company and one result of this was that a cheque for £44,000 was made payable to T. A forged indorsement was placed on this cheque and it was paid into another account. The collecting bank was held to have been negligent due to the unusual circumstances of the cheque being paid in, but it succeeded in its defence of '*ex turpi*'.

The defence is based on it being contrary to public policy to enforce a claim which indirectly arises from a criminal act. The test is:

(a) has there been a crime which the court should take notice of (i.e. how serious is the crime?); and

(b) how proximate is the crime to the claim; if the claim is upheld would the court be seen to be indirectly assisting or encouraging the plaintiff in his criminal actions?

It was held in *Thackwell* that the underlying crime was serious and that the cheque represented the very proceeds of it. It is interesting to observe, however, that the victim of the crime was not assisted by the application of the doctrine. It was suggested, *obiter*, that even if T had been a totally innocent party to the crime, an action in conversion would not lie to recover the very proceeds of a crime.

5.10 THE COLLECTING BANK'S RIGHT TO AN INDEMNITY

Where the bank is liable in conversion to the true owner of a cheque, it is entitled to a full indemnity from its customer, on the basis that it collected the cheque as the customer's agent and an agent is

[44]*See above.*

entitled to be indemnified against losses incurred in the reasonable performance of his duties. The indemnity may not be available if the bank knew that its actions amounted to a conversion of the cheque.[45]

The Civil Liability (Contribution) Act 1978 has a similar effect as it permits recovery from a person liable in respect of the same damage, whether jointly with him or otherwise.[46]

5.11 THE DEFENCE OF ESTOPPEL

Such a defence would be based on some representation made by the plaintiff (and true owner) of a cheque to the collecting bank, which leads the latter to assume that the customer is the true owner of the cheque. The plaintiff would then be estopped from claiming. This is close to the decision in Morison[47], where a failure on the part of the drawer of the cheques to notify the collecting bank that a fraud was occurring was considered to be sufficient.

5.12 THE COLLECTING BANK AS A HOLDER IN DUE COURSE

The collecting bank will not need the protection provided by section 4 from an action in conversion by the true owner of a cheque, if it is itself the true owner. This will arise if it qualifies as a holder in due course.[48] This can only occur if the cheque is both transferrable and negotiable.

It will be recalled that two of the conditions which must be satisfied before a holder can be a holder in due course are:

(a) the holder gives value; and
(b) the cheque was negotiated to him.

The condition in (b) above requires the indorsement of the payee unless the cheque is payable to bearer. In 1957 the practice of all

---

[45]*Sheffield Corporation v Barclay [1905] AC 392 HL.*
[46]*Section 1 (1).*
[47]*Discussed in 5.7 above.*
[48]*See 4.6 above.*

order cheques being indorsed by customers before being paid into their accounts was discontinued. In order to preserve the collecting bank's rights in this situation, section 2 of the Cheques Act provides that where a bank gives value for, or has a lien on, a cheque payable to order which the holder delivers to him for collection without indorsing it, he has such rights as he would have had if the holder had indorsed it in blank. Section 2 only applies to a cheque, other instruments not being covered. Cheques payable to bearer do not require indorsement. Thus the condition in (b) above will automatically be satisfied if the condition in (a) is satisfied.

Situations where the collecting bank gives value

It is submitted that this area of the law is in a state of lamentable confusion, due to many of the cases failing to distinguish between a holder for value and a holder in due course, compounded by the fact that there is no common understanding generally of what constitutes a holder for value.

It was decided in Midland Bank v Reckitt[49] that the collecting bank did qualify as a holder for value, as it had given value for the cheque, but not as a holder in due course because it did not satisfy the condition of taking the cheque without notice of any defect of title of the transferor (see 4.6 below). If this is correct then there can be no doubt that the collecting bank must be a holder in due course in order to be protected against a claim from some other party to the cheque. Being a holder for value is insufficient.

It has been decided that a collecting bank can be a holder in due course when it allows funds to be withdrawn against an uncleared cheque[50] and when a cheque is accepted in permanent reduction of the customer's overdraft.[51] These matters may be academic, however, in view of the following. A bank automatically has a lien on cheques which a customer pays into his overdrawn account, so long as there is no agreement to the contrary.[52] Under section 27(3) of the Act,

[49][1933] AC 1 HL.
[50]Westminster Bank v Zang [1966] AC 182 HL.
[51]M'Lean v Clydesdale Banking Co. (1883) 9 App Cas 95 HL.
[52]Re Keever [1966] 3 WLR 779.

the bank thus becomes a holder for value of any cheque paid into an overdrawn account, but in Reckitt this was considered to be insufficient to defeat a claim from a true owner. However, some of the cases declare that the bank is also a holder in due course in these circumstances, as it has given value by virtue of having the lien on the cheque.[53]

The confusion arises from the fact that in A.L. Underwood Ltd v Bank of Liverpool,[54] cheques were paid into an overdrawn account, but the Court of Appeal held that the bank was not a holder in due course, in the absence of any agreement between bank and customer that the latter could draw against the cheques before clearance. This principle was cited with approval in Zang, where it was also held that the bank had not given value as it had charged interest on the amount of the cheque pending clearance. In Zang also, the account was overdrawn but the bank was held not to be a holder in due course. In Midland Bank v Harris,[55] the bank did qualify as a holder in due course of a cheque issued to its customer by H and paid into an overdrawn account, but there was an agreement that the customer could draw against uncleared effects. The lien will be irretrievably lost if the cheque is returned to the customer.[56]

The collecting bank cannot be a holder in due course when:

(a) the cheque is crossed 'not negotiable', as the collecting bank cannot then acquire a better title than its customer. If the White Paper's proposals are put into effect, all crossed cheques will automatically be not negotiable;

(b) the cheque is crossed 'account payee' as the Cheques Act 1992 renders the cheque not transferable;

(c) drafts, 'cheques' drawn 'pay cash' and government warrants are collected, as these are not covered by section 2 of the Cheques Act; thus there will be no deemed indorsement on them and the bank cannot therefore be a holder in due course unless the

[53]*Barclays Bank v Astley Industrial Trust Ltd [1970] 2 QB 527, citing dicta from Midland Bank v Reckitt.*
[54]*[1924] 1 KB 775 CA.*
[55]*[1963] 1 WLR 1021.*
[56]*Westminster Bank v Zang, see above.*

instrument has been actually negotiated to it. If the instrument happens to be indorsed by the customer, or if the customer is paying in an instrument which has been indorsed in blank by some other who is the payee, the bank may become a holder in due course if the instrument is considered to be negotiable by custom. The same applies to such an instrument drawn payable to bearer. The White Paper proposes that these instruments will be treated fully as cheques.

5.13 CHEQUE CARDS

The first cheque card was issued in 1965 in order to satisfy customers' needs to draw cash elsewhere than at the account holding branch, and to use cheques for the payment of goods where the trader would not otherwise accept a cheque, due to the risk that it might be dishonoured.

The card has proved to be an effective vehicle for fraud, however, when it is stolen with the customer's cheque book. Banks therefore now limit withdrawals of cash to one per day. Standard conditions applicable to the use of cards have been agreed by card issuers.[57] The current rules state that the issuer guarantees payment when in any single transaction only one cheque is drawn (not drawn on a company's account) if:

(1) The cheque bears the same name and code number as the card.
(2) The cheque is dated with the actual date of issue.
(3) It is signed before expiry of the card in the UK in the presence of the payee by the person whose signature appears on the card.
(4) The card number is written on the cheque by the payee.
(5) The card has not been altered or defaced.

It is clear that the guarantee is not operative if the card is used to back two cheques drawn to pay for one item. This is so even if the cheques bear different dates.

The effect of the use of the card is to set up a legal relationship between drawee bank and payee, which would not otherwise exist,

[57]*Known as the Rules of the UK Domestic Cheque Guarantee Card Community.*

since normally, a bank is not liable to the payee of a cheque. This relationship is created by the customer, acting as the bank's agent.[58] The payee has a direct right in contract to claim payment from the bank if the conditions of the use of the card are met. Unlike a normal guarantee, this obligation of the bank to pay the payee is not dependent on any default by the cardholder.

When a bank is presented with a cheque which bears the customer's card number on the reverse, there can be two reasons why it may prefer not to pay that cheque. First, it may consider the cheque to be a forgery, and second, there may be no forgery but there is insufficient credit to the customer's account. It is clear that when there is no forgery the bank must pay the cheque unless there has been some clear breach of condition of use of the card. If the cheque is forged, condition (3) appears to have been breached unless the fraudster has somehow removed the original signature on the card and replaced it with his own (the current practice of banks is to pay the cheque if the forgery is a good imitation of the customer's signature). This assumes that the payee is aware of (or deemed to be bound by) the conditions imposed by a card issuer. The current conditions are not stated on the card itself which merely states 'refer to issuer for conditions of use'.

In First Sport Ltd v Barclays Bank,[59] the conditions were printed on the card but differed in that they required the signature on the cheque to agree with the signature on the card. The defendant bank argued that a fraudster using another's card could have no authority to bind the bank to the payee and also that since the cheque was forged it was not in law a cheque and thus the bank had not guaranteed payments of it. A majority of the court rejected both arguments.

The current conditions appear to make it clear that the bank does not agree to pay if the cheque is signed by someone other than the true customer (except where the signature on the card has been changed) but as was pointed out in First Sport, it is quite unnecessary to impose a condition that the cheque be signed in the presence of the payee except to minimise the risk of fraud by a forgery of the signature as it appears on the card. If the issuer is

---

[58]First Sport Ltd v Barclays Bank [1993] 1 WLR 1229 CA.
[59]See above.

never bound to pay in these circumstances, why include it in the conditions?

A bank will set out certain conditions of use of the card when it is issued to the customer, and these will form part of the banker-customer contract. Included will be a promise by the customer not to use the card to create an unauthorised overdraft, and that the customer is unable to countermand payment of a cheque backed by the card.

Because the bank is obliged to the payee to honour the cheque, it is therefore also obliged to grant its customer an unauthorised overdraft, if the card is used when there are insufficient funds and no agreed facility. The customer will of course be liable to his bank to repay such an overdraft.

However, if the customer does use the card in this manner, he may commit an offence of obtaining a pecuniary advantage by deception under section 16(1) of the Theft Act 1968; the pecuniary advantage being the overdraft facility which his bank might not otherwise have granted him. In Metropolitan Police Commissioner v Charles,[60] the defendant visited a casino where, in order to fund his gambling, he issued an entire book of 25 cheques in one evening, backed by a cheque card, each drawn for the then maximum of £30. It was held that an implied representation to the payee is made each time a customer issues a cheque backed by the card. This is that he will have sufficient funds in his account when the cheque is presented for payment. It was also held that payees in general would refuse to accept the cheque if they know there will be insufficient funds to meet payment when the cheque is presented. Thus the deception is not of the bank which grants the overdraft, but of the payee.

In the light of this decision, a bank customer who is not certain that there will be sufficient funds to meet a cheque which he is drawing with the backing of a cheque card, should express this doubt to the retailer. This practice would negate any possibility of a criminal deception based on an implied representation.

Finally it should be noted that a cheque card, unlike a credit card, is not governed by the Consumer Credit Act 1974. This is because it is not a 'credit token' within the meaning of section 14

[60][1977] AC 177 HL.

of that Act. When the bank pays the payee, it is not paying for the goods or services on behalf of its customer, it is merely honouring his cheque, and this pertains whether or not an overdraft results from payment of the cheque.[61]

The Banking Code states that customers should take care of their cheque books and cards and should not keep them together. Customers are also told it is essential that they inform their bank if their cheque book and/or card has been lost or stolen. The bank then should take immediate steps to prevent use of the cheque book and card.[62] The legal position, however, remains that a bank is not entitled to debit its customer's account when it has paid a forged cheque,[63] and this rule is unaffected by the fact that a cheque card was presented along with the forged cheque.

5.14 RECOVERY OF MONEY PAID BY MISTAKE

The doctrine of the recovery of money paid by mistake may be relevant in the following circumstances:[64]

(a) a bank pays a forged cheque;
(b) a bank pays a stopped cheque;
(c) a bank pays a cheque with insufficient signatures;
(d) a bank pays an altered cheque; or
(e) a bank makes the same payment twice.

Recovery at common law

This area of the law is not a model of clarity and consistency but, in the light of the decisions in National Westminster Bank v Barclays Bank International[65] and Barclays Bank v W.J. Simms, Son & Cooke (Southern) Ltd,[66] it is suggested that the conditions which must be

[61]See 3.3 above.
[62]Sections 4.8, 4.9 and 4.10.
[63]Unless the customer knew of the forgery, see 4.9 above.
[64]Mistaken crediting of a customer's account, which does not involve the recovery of a payment, is treated separately in 5.15 below.
[65][1975] QB 654.
[66][1980] QB 677.

satisfied for the operation of the doctrine and to enable a mistaken payment to be recovered are:

(a) the bank pays the money to another person, doing so under a mistake of fact, e.g. it believed the signature was genuine when in fact it was forged or it believed payment had not been countermanded when in fact it had been. It does not matter whether or not the bank was negligent in paying, it must simply have been mistaken in doing so. The bank must not have made the payment under a mistake as to the law, e.g. if it knew the customer's signature was forged but considered that the law permitted payment despite this;

(b) the bank has no authority from its customer to pay. It has no authority in the five circumstances described above, but it does have authority if it pays when there are insufficient funds, and thus would not be able to recover if this is the reason for the mistaken payment.

The bank will not be able to recover if any of the following apply:

(a) it would have paid the cheque even if it had realised the truth (most unlikely in the above examples);

(b) the bank made a representation to the payee that it was making the payment (for instance, following a special presentation) and the payee has changed his position to his detriment as a result of receiving the payment and he was not at fault (e.g. by concealing facts from the bank). This would set up an estoppel preventing the bank from recovering;

(c) the bank has paid another bank as collecting agent for the payee and the latter has withdrawn the funds. The paying bank cannot then recover from the collecting bank, only from the payee. The collecting bank must have no notice of the mistake before the funds are withdrawn and have acted in good faith. In the *Simms* case, the bank paid a stopped cheque and succeeded in recovering the funds. In National Westminster Bank v Barclays Bank International, a thief removed an unsigned cheque from an unused book of cheques, taking care to remove the stub as well. Consequently the owner had no knowledge of the theft. The cheque next appeared in Nigeria where, drawn for £8,000, it was sold to

I, who bought it on the basis that if it was dishonoured, the deal was off. The cheque was specially presented and was paid. Naturally the truth began to emerge when the customer was next told his balance. It was clear that NatWest had no authority to debit its customer's account and the bank sought to recover the funds which remained in I's account with Barclays. It succeeded as I had been at fault in concealing facts from the bank;

(d) the funds have passed through a mixed fund.[67] This does not appear to prevent recovery of a payment which is made through the domestic cheque clearing system as claims for recovery were successful in these circumstances in Banque Belge pour l'Etranger v Hambrouck[68] and more recently in Trustee of the Property of FC Jones & Son v Jones.[69] In the latter case it was stated that the payer did not need to follow the funds through the clearing system, it could follow the cheques as they pass from hand to hand. In Agip (Africa) Ltd v Jackson,[70] it was stated that the funds could not be reclaimed after passing through the New York dollar clearing or where money is transferred by using electronic means. This latter objection was, however, not accepted by one member of the Court of Appeal in *Agip*;[71]

(e) a fifth principle which may prevent a bank from recovering its funds when a cheque has been indorsed emerges from Cocks v Masterman.[72] Where a bank pays a cheque and later attempts to recover the funds, it may be prevented from doing so unless it acts with great speed. This will only be so, however, if thereby the holder has lost his right to claim against other parties to the cheque as a result of his not having been given notice of dishonour. Cocks v Masterman concerned a bill of exchange with a forged acceptance, so a parallel situation could not arise with a cheque. In relation to cheques, the principle would apply in the example of an indorsed cheque, payment of which had been

[67]*Lipkin Gorman v Karpnale Ltd [1991] 2 AC 948 HL.*
[68]*[1921] 1 KB 321.*
[69]*[1996] 4 All ER 721.*
[70]*[1990] Ch 265.*
[71]*[1991] Ch 547 CA.*
[72]*(1829) 9 B&C 902.*

countermanded by the drawer, but which the bank mistakenly paid. Notice of dishonour need not be given to the drawer[73] but would need to be given to the indorser on the day of, or the day following, dishonour. The principle does not apply if the cheque either bears a forged drawer's signature, as it would not then be a valid bill of exchange, or if it bears a forged indorsement as notice of dishonour to the indorser is not then relevant.

Recovery in equity

If the paying bank is unable to recover the payment under common law as one made by mistake, it may be able to exercise a proprietary right in equity to recover the funds. This remedy, which is available in different circumstances, was traditionally referred to as the 'tracing' remedy but it has recently been suggested that tracing is not a remedy in itself but a means of identifying the person who is liable to return the funds.[74] Another traditional view was that the equitable remedy was based on the premise that the funds in equity still belonged to the payer but this also was recently rejected.[75]

The equitable remedy to reclaim funds paid by mistake is in practice most valuable to a bank when it cannot reclaim the funds at common law. This will arise in at least three situations. First, if the payee is insolvent, the remedy is considered to give the bank a claim over the money itself, as opposed to a personal claim against the payee. Thus the bank would be paid if any funds were in the hands of the insolvent payee as opposed to it claiming merely as a judgment or unsecured creditor. This conclusion may have been put in doubt, however, by the recent rejection of the view that the payer retains a beneficial ownership in the money it paid. Second, the common law is subject to a six year time limitation whereas the equitable remedy has no time limit. Third, the equitable remedy is not defeated by the money having passed through a mixed fund.

---

[73] Section 50(2)(c) Bills of Exchange Act 1882.
[74] Millet J in Agip (Africa) Ltd v Jackson [1990] Ch 265 and Millet LJ in Boscawen v Bajwa [1996] 1 WLR 328.
[75] In Westdeutsche Landesbank Girozentrale v Islington LBC [1996] 2 WLR 802 HL.

The equitable remedy suffers from several drawbacks which do not apply to the common law remedy, however. First, it has often been held that there must have been a fiduciary relationship which was breached. This is resonant of the same requirement in a claim for constructive trust.[76] In Chase Manhattan Bank v Israel-British Bank,[77] it was decided that in the case of a mistaken payment by a bank, this requirement was satisfied by the fiduciary duty of the payee to return money which in equity still belonged to the paying bank. Since the House of Lords in *Westdeutsche* rejected this equitable ownership of the payer approach, it must be doubted whether a paying bank on the facts of a simple mistaken payment could satisfy the requirement. On the other hand it is arguable that the House of Lords in *Westdeutsche* may be considered to have rejected the fiduciary duty requirement altogether.

Second, it is said that a claim in equity cannot be made against a *bona fide* purchaser for value without notice of the facts. This is assumed to mean that if the payee pays the funds into an overdrawn bank account, the bank is considered to be a *bona fide* purchaser and the claim evaporates completely so that not only can it not be made against the bank but also it cannot be made against the payee. It is also not possible to reclaim the funds in equity if the account has become overdrawn after the funds were paid into it.[78]

Finally, it is now established that a customer is also entitled to reclaim money paid under a mistake of fact. It could happen that a bank was able to debit an account in respect of a given transaction, e.g. because a cheque had been fraudulently altered for an increased sum and the customer had not exercised due care in drawing the cheque. In these circumstances the customer can set up a claim against the payee. No objection may be made on the basis that, technically, the bank when paying a cheque makes the payment with its own funds, merely debiting the customer's account.[79] In Lipkin Gorman v Karpnale Ltd,[80] the House of Lords held that a

---

[76]*See 1.7 above.*

[77]*[1981] Ch 105.*

[78]*Bishopsgate Investment Management v Homan [1995] Ch 211 CA.*

[79]*Agip (Africa) Ltd v Jackson [1991] Ch 547 CA.*

[80]*[1991] 2 AC 548 HL.*

customer with a credit balance at a bank is the owner of a form of property, i.e. a chose in action, the debt owed to him. The customer is thus able to trace that property (or any part of it) into its product, e.g. cash fraudulently drawn or funds transferred by fraudulent design into another account.

5.15 MISTAKEN CREDITING OF A CUSTOMER'S ACCOUNT

This interesting area of the law deals with a situation which is not uncommon in practice. The applicable legal principles are similar to those discussed in 5.14 above on recovery of payments made by mistake but in this case no payment has been made to a third party, it is simply a matter of whether the bank is entitled to redebit the customer's account. The bank may *prima facie* do so and therefore reclaim any funds which the customer has withdrawn from the account. An estoppel will arise, however, preventing the bank from recovering if the customer changes his position as a result of the credit and he was not at fault.

In Lloyds Bank v Brooks,[81] the bank was administering a trust and paying income from it to various beneficiaries, one of whom was B. The trust department of the bank, in error, decided that B was entitled to income from two holdings of shares, whereas in fact she was only entitled to income from one holding. The relevant income was transferred to B's account regularly for some years. The bank was unable to recover because B had altered her position as a result of her good faith belief that she was entitled to the money.

In United Overseas Bank v Jiwani,[82] the bank mistakenly credited J's account twice with the same credit of $11,000. On being told of the additional credit, J immediately issued a cheque for $11,000. The bank succeeded in recovering the funds. It was held that in order to keep the money J had to establish:

(a) the bank misrepresented the state of the account;

---

[81] *(1950) 6 Legal Decisions Affecting Bankers 161.*
[82] *[1976] 1 WLR 964.*

(b) J was misled and, in the belief that he had more money, he spent the surplus; and

(c) as a result, the customer changed his position in a way which would make it inequitable to require him to return the money.

It was held that J satisfied the first part but not the others.

In Avon County Council v Howlett,[83] an employer mistakenly credited H's account. The estoppel was here defined slightly differently:

(a) a representation of fact which led H to believe the money was his;

(b) H, *bona fide* and without notice of the employer's claim, changed his position; and

(c) the payment was not primarily caused by the fault of H.

This case was considered by the House of Lords in Lipkin Gorman v Karpnale Ltd.[84] The House was not concerned with the claim against Lloyds Bank[85] but with a claim against the operators of a casino who had received the stolen money without notice but for no consideration. It was suggested[86] that it is more helpful to consider these cases on mistaken payment not on the basis of estoppel but as claims by the payer for restitution of property. The payee has a defence to this, if he can show that he changed his position in good faith as a result of receiving the payment. If this view is adopted (it ranks as *obiter dicta*), the existence or otherwise of a representation to the payee will cease to be a factor and a partial defence would be available, in contrast to the all or nothing nature of the estoppel rule.

---

[83]*[1983] 1 WLR 605 CA.*
[84]*[1991] 2 AC 548 HL.*
[85]*See 1.6 above, this point was not pursued beyond the Court of Appeal.*
[86]*By Lord Goff.*

5.16 PRACTICAL EXAMPLES OF THE LAW RELATING TO THE USE OF CHEQUES

(1) Suppose A draws a cheque (not crossed 'not negotiable' or 'account payee') payable to B. B indorses it in blank and loses it. C finds it and asks D to cash it. Assuming D satisfies all the other conditions of being a holder in due course, he has given value and has perfect title. B cannot recover from him. If a bank cashes a cheque in a similar way, whether or not for a customer, it also is protected.[87]

(2) Suppose the same facts as in (1) but that either B's indorsement is forged or that the cheque is crossed 'not negotiable', D then is not a holder in due course. B can recover from D. Section 80 of the Act provides that where a crossed cheque is issued by a customer which comes into the hands of the payee then, assuming the customer's bank fulfils its duty to pay a bank rather than cash to the payee, the drawer is protected. The section says that the drawer can assume that the true owner of the cheque received payment, whoever in fact did.

(3) Suppose A gives B a cheque crossed 'account payee'. A is conclusively considered to have paid B and B bears the loss if the cheque is stolen. However, if the cheque is stolen before it reaches B, then A must normally bear the loss. B will bear the loss if the cheque is stolen in the post and he had authorised A to send it by post.[88] Whoever bears the loss can claim from the collecting bank, since it has collected a cheque crossed 'account payee' for another's account (or opened an account in a false name). In respect of the latter, the collecting bank may be protected by section 4 if it took appropriate measures before opening the account.

(4) Suppose B perpetrates a fraud on A, obtains a cheque from him (not crossed 'account payee' or 'not negotiable') and pays it into an overdrawn bank account. A quickly realises the truth and manages to stop the cheque. B's bank has a lien on the cheque, and therefore may qualify as a holder in due course and sue other

---

[87]*Midland Bank v Charles Simpson Motors [1960] CLY 217.*
[88]*See the Encyclopaedia of Banking Law at D1(9) and the cases listed therein.*

parties to it, including A. If A had crossed the cheque 'not negotiable' or 'account payee', this would not be possible.

(5) In all the above examples, the bank paying the cheque will be protected by one or more of sections 60 and 80 of the Bills of Exchange Act and section 1 of the Cheques Act. This is assuming it acted in good faith and in the ordinary course of business or without negligence (for section 80).

It can be seen that from the drawer's point of view it is wise to:

(a) cross the cheque;
(b) cross it 'not negotiable', to maintain his right to effectively stop the cheque if the consideration on it fails (as in (4) above) and to maintain his right to claim from some ultimate holder (as in (2) above);
(c) cross it 'account payee' in case it is stolen before it reaches the hands of the payee.

From the payee's point of view it is prudent to have cheques:

(a) crossed 'not negotiable', in case it is stolen from him and a collecting bank or some other holder qualifies as a holder in due course. This can only happen, however, if the payee has indorsed the cheque;
(b) crossed 'account payee' in case it is stolen from him, so that he should then have a claim in conversion against the collecting bank.

Note that since the passing of the Cheques Act 1992, it is unnecessary to add 'not negotiable' to a cheque crossed 'account payee' since the 'account payee' crossing prevents transfer and thus also prevents negotiation of the cheque.

As a holder of the cheque (or analogous instrument), the payee is entitled to put a crossing on it and to add 'not negotiable'.[89] There is no statutory provision authorising the addition of 'account payee' by the payee, and indeed this would be unlawful under section 78. In purely practical terms, however, it will benefit the payee to write 'account payee' on a cheque which he might lose. The reason is that, whilst if it came to litigation against the collecting

[89]*Section 77(2) and (4) of the Act.*

bank he would presumably fail because of section 78, any collecting bank would in practice be reluctant to accept the cheque.

6 Paper payment systems

6.1 INTRODUCTION

It is estimated that 70% of all transactions in the UK are settled in cash. In 1997, an average 8.4 million daily cheque transactions were recorded (41.7% of total APACS clearings).[1] Although declining,[2] cheques still represent the largest non-cash payment method. A further 1.1 million average daily transactions used paper-based credit clearing (3.6% of total clearings). By value, however, cheques represented only 3.4% of the total APACS clearings in 1997 and credit clearing only 0.2%, whilst CHAPS payments accounted for 92.7% by value.

6.2 CHEQUE CLEARING

A cheque no longer has to be presented to the branch of the bank on which it is drawn.[3] A cheque can now be presented by electronic means, i.e. the collecting bank may pass the essential features of the cheque to the paying bank and the cheque itself need never leave the collecting bank.[4] The paying bank can give notice that it requires physical presentation of the cheque in which case it may be presented to a central office of the paying bank rather than to the branch on which the cheque was drawn.[5]

---

[1] *APACS (Association for Payment Clearing Services) Annual Review 1997.*
[2] *Down 3.6% from 1996 to 1997. All the decline is presently taking place in the personal sector with business use of cheques actually increasing slightly.*
[3] *Section 74B of the Bills of Exchange Act 1882, which became law in 1996.*
[4] *See further 6.4 below.*
[5] *Section 74A.*

For the time being presentation for payment remains the essence of the cheque system of payment, albeit this is now to a central office of the paying bank. Eleven banks and one building society[6] are currently clearing bank members which operate the Clearing Exchange Centre.[7] When a cheque is paid in to a non-member of clearing, or drawn on a non-member of clearing, the non-member bank must use a clearing member as agent. A cheque which is paid into the same bank as it is drawn on does not pass through the Clearing Exchange Centre.

The sequence of presentation and payment ('the clearing cycle') is set out briefly below (assuming both paying and collecting bank are members of clearing).[8]

DAY ONE

The collecting bank credits its customer's account (as an uncleared effect) and the cheque may be encoded with magnetic characters in the codeline at the bottom of the cheque. By early evening the cheque is ready to be sent to the bank's clearing centre.

DAY TWO

The cheque is delivered to the bank's clearing centre in the early hours. The cheque is processed by high speed reader sorters which read the magnetic ink at the bottom of the cheque. The machine also sorts the cheques by paying bank. An electronic message is sent to the paying bank. The sorted cheques are delivered to the Clearing Exchange Centre where they are passed to the paying banks. The paying bank will usually retain the cheque in a central location rather than deliver it to the branch on which it is drawn, since this is now a permitted truncation.

---

[6]*Abbey National, Bank of Scotland, Barclays Bank, Clydesdale Bank, Co-operative Bank, Girobank, Lloyds/TSB Bank, Midland Bank, National Westminster Bank, Nationwide Building Society, Royal Bank of Scotland, and the Bank of England (at March 1998).*
[7]*Through a company named Cheque and Credit Clearing Co Ltd.*
[8]*The mechanics of the cheque clearing system (prior to truncation) were ably described by Bingham J in Barclays Bank v Bank of England [1985] 1 All ER 385.*

DAY THREE

The paying bank makes a decision on 'fate' of the cheque, i.e. whether it will pay it. If it decides to dishonour the cheque, it sends the cheque by first class post back to the collecting bank. The clearing members agree values between each other taking into account all the cheques presented that day, a net figure is agreed and settlement is made by a transfer between the banks' accounts at the Bank of England using the Bank Real Time System.

DAY FOUR

The collecting bank receives the cheque back in the post if the paying bank has decided to dishonour it on the previous day. Allowance is made for a cheque to be returned on day four if the paying bank has, through inadvertence, failed to return it the previous day. If the cheque's value exceeds £500, the decision to dishonour on day four must be telephoned to the collecting bank by noon. It will be posted back in any case.

Since the account of the payee of a cheque will be credited on Day 1 of the clearing cycle, it follows that this will constitute uncleared funds until Day 4. Indeed for cheques not exceeding £500, the collecting bank may not hear of dishonour until day five. It seems the drawer can 'stop' his cheque at least until close of business on Day 3. Each collecting bank is free to make its own decision when to start paying interest on a cheque paid into an account (known as the 'value' date).

The legal rights and obligations of the various parties to a cheque are discussed in detail in chapters 4 and 5.

6.3 TOWN CLEARING

This special system of clearing large value cheques was abolished in 1995. The CHAPS system of electronic funds transfer[9] had made it redundant.

[9]See 7.3 below.

6.4 TRUNCATION OF CHEQUES

Truncation of cheques has been enabled by amendments to the Bills of Exchange Act 1882 made in 1996.[10] These provide:

(a) that where a paying bank has published an address in the London, Edinburgh and Belfast Gazettes at which cheques drawn on it can be presented, a cheque is properly presented if it is presented at that address;[11]

(b) a bank may present a cheque for payment by notifying the paying bank of the essential features of the cheque by electronic means or otherwise. The essential features are stated to be the serial number, the sort code, the drawer's account number and the amount the cheque is drawn for.[12] The paying bank has until close of business on the next business day following electronic presentment to request the collecting bank to present the cheque itself. This does not constitute dishonour of the cheque but the electronic presentation of the cheque is then disregarded and physical presentation would follow.

Essentially the new rules make three changes:

(a) cheques can be presented to a central office of the paying bank;
(b) cheques can be presented by electronic communication of their essential features;
(c) the paying bank can demand physical presentation of any cheque if they make that demand within one day of electronic presentation.

To date the cheque clearing system has not moved to take full advantage of the new rules as cheques are still being presented to the paying bank, albeit at its central office. Thus only the first of the three changes listed above is being put into practice. The rules make it clear that presentation no longer need be at a reasonable hour.[13]

---

[10]*The Deregulation (Bills of Exchange) Order 1996, SI 1996/2993.*
[11]*Section 74A of the Bills of Exchange Act.*
[12]*Section 74B.*
[13]*Section 74B(2).*

6.5 CREDIT CLEARING

Credit transfers

Credit transfers, or Bank Giro Payments, enable a customer to transfer funds to a person who is a customer of the same or another bank, simply by giving his bank a written instruction on a printed standard form supplied by the banks. The paper-based clearing of credit transfers is similar to the Cheque Clearing.

Assignments and Cheques and Credit transfers

The drawing of a cheque does not constitute an assignment to the payee, either of funds in the paying bank's hands, or of the credit balance (debt) owed by the paying bank to its customer, the drawer (section 53 Bills of Exchange Act 1882). This section was necessary because an assignment of a debt can be effected by agreement between the creditor and the assignee. The agreement will be a legal assignment if it is in writing, signed by the assignor (the creditor), and notified to the debtor (the bank).[14] This definition would be satisfied every time a cheque was presented to the paying bank for payment.

A credit transfer does not normally constitute a legal or equitable assignment, since there is no agreement between the payer and the payee that payment be made from a credit balance on the payer's bank account. Where the payer requests his bank to transfer money to the payee's bank account, it is not intended that the payee or his bank should have any claim for the money against the payer's bank.[15] Even when there is agreement between payer and payee for payment directly between their accounts, this usually relates to the method of payment, it does not constitute payment by discharging the payer's liability to the payee and giving the payee an assignment of the bank's debt to the payer.[16]

---

[14]*Section 136 of the Law of Property Act 1925.*
[15]*Williams v Everett (1811) 14 East 582.*
[16]*Curran v Newpark Cinemas [1951] 1 All ER 295.*

7 Electronic payment systems

7.1 INTRODUCTION

The domestic electronic payment systems BACS and CHAPS are discussed in this chapter. SWIFT (the Society for Worldwide Interbank Financial Telecommunication) is outside the scope of this book. Electronic payment systems which are consumer-activated are covered in chapter 8 (automated teller machines) and chapter 9 (debit cards).

The phrase Electronic Funds Transfer (EFT) is often used to describe the systems of electronic payment but it is a misnomer as no funds are transferred. The various systems comprise the transfer by electronic means of payment messages and consequent adjustment, also by electronic means, of various debtor-creditor relationships. A brief description of BACS and CHAPS will show how this happens; the legal basis of the relationships and the legal rights and obligations of the parties to those relationships will then be discussed.

7.2 BACS

BACS Ltd is a clearing house through which credit or debit payments may be made electronically. Its 16 member banks and building societies have agreed rules for the system. 811 million direct credits were processed in 1997 (up 6.6% from 1996) and 1,566 million direct debits (up 9.55%).[1]

---

[1] *APACS Annual Review 1997.*

BACS transfers

Details of debit and credit transfers are transmitted to BACS in electronic form, by tape, disc or directly to BACS.[2] Banks transfer funds through BACS for themselves and their customers. Over 35,000 customers are sponsored by their banks to send transfer details directly to BACS. Transfer details received by BACS up to 9 .p.m. on any clearing day (Day 1) are processed by BACS overnight. The processing operation sorts the transfers into data files for each payee bank, which receives its files from BACS by 6 a.m. on Day 2. The payee banks debit or credit their customers' accounts at the opening of business the next day, Day 3. Net positions between member institutions are agreed each day and settlement is made over their accounts with the Bank of England.

Direct debits are subject to an agreement between all the participating institutions which offers certain protection to payers. This is known as the Direct Debit Guarantee and it provides that payers will be told in advance of any change in the amounts of payments or dates of payments. It also states that in the event of an error by the payee or the payer's bank, a full and immediate refund will be made to the payer's account on request. Payers are reminded that they can cancel a direct debit at any time by writing to their bank or building society. Companies wishing to receive payments under the direct debit system must indemnify banks against loss and authorise them to reverse credits. A payee of a mandated direct debit, however, has been held to be in an equivalent position to a payee of a cheque in that he is entitled to enforce payment directly from the payer in respect of a cancelled direct debit, without any set-off.[3]

7.3 CHAPS

Whilst CHAPS transactions only accounted for 0.3% of APACS clearing transactions by volume in 1997, this represented 92.7% of the total value of transactions.[4]

---

[2] *Using a link known as 'BACSTEL'.*
[3] *Esso Petroleum Co Ltd v Milton [1997] 1 WLR 938 CA.*
[4] *APACS Annual Review 1997.*

The Clearing House Automated Payment System ('CHAPS') is operated by the CHAPS Clearing Company Limited which has 17 member banks, all of whom agree rules for the operating of the system. There is no minimum amount of payment which can be made by CHAPS but the pricing of the service discourages small value payments. Member banks may permit their corporate customers to have access to the CHAPS system. Since 1996, CHAPS has moved to being a Real Time Gross Settlement (RTGS) System. This removes settlement risk between the member banks as the payee bank knows it has received payment as soon as it receives notice of the payment. There is no net settlement at the end of each day as with cheque clearing, credit clearing and BACS.[5] Member banks will send and receive payments on behalf of institutions which are not members of the system.

When a bank wishes to make a payment through CHAPS, it does so through its software interface to the electronic network (called a 'gateway'). Individual branches of the bank, agency banks and selected corporate customers will have indirect access to the bank's gateway. The first stage is for a part of the payment message to be sent to the Bank of England which debits the paying bank's account with the value of the payment and credits the receiving bank's account. This process ensures that the paying bank has the necessary credit in its account at the Bank of England for the payment. If the Bank of England does adjust the accounts, it sends a confirmation to the paying bank. The paying bank then sends a payment message to the receiving bank. This will go through the paying bank's gateway to the receiving bank's gateway. The receiving bank sends a Logical Acknowledgement Message (known as a 'LAK') to the paying bank. The CHAPS rules state that once the receiving bank has verified the payment order and sent the LAK, it must give same day value to its customer (or the bank for whom it is receiving the payment).

---

[5] *Although the CHAPS rules provide for a switch to daily net settlement if the real time system fails for any reason.*

7.4 THE PAYING BANK

The paying bank is considered to owe a general duty to its customers to comply with their (legitimate) instructions and in carrying out those instructions it must exercise reasonable care and skill.[6] In making a payment for its customer, the paying bank acts as its agent and is liable for the negligence of any correspondent bank it employs.[7] It should only act on genuine instructions from its customer. If it excludes liability for acting on forged instructions or for the negligence of itself or its correspondent bank, this exclusion is subject to the limits imposed by unfair contract legislation.[8] It is not necessarily liable for losses caused by failures in the payment system itself unless it should have been aware of defects in the system.

The paying bank's relationship with the receiving bank will be determined by the rules of the payment system being used. A payment made by mistake may be recoverable, this area of law is discussed in 5.14.

The paying bank's relationship with the payee is not based on any contract and therefore any liability of the paying bank to the payee would have to be in the tort of negligence. If the paying bank fails to make a payment which its customer instructed it to make, the payee would look to that customer for payment. It is arguable that if the payee cannot enforce the payment because the customer has become insolvent or has died or decided not to make a payment which was to have been a gift, the payee may have a claim against the paying bank on the basis that a duty was owed to him as beneficiary of the payment.[9]

There is no case law relating to countermand of electronic payments between banks[10] but it is generally accepted that a paying bank must act on its customer's notice of countermand of payment in a similar fashion as applies in the payment of cheques.[11] In an

---

[6]*Section 13 of the Supply of Goods and Services Act 1982.*
[7]*Royal Products Ltd v Midland Bank [1981] Com LR 93.*
[8]*Described in 1.1 above.*
[9]*By analogy to White v Jones [1995] 2 AC 145 HL.*
[10]*See the discussions in R. Goode, Commercial Law, 2nd edition at p 510 and the Encyclopaedia of Banking Law at D1 951.*
[11]*See 4.11 above.*

electronic payment, countermand can be made at any time up to the point when the paying bank becomes committed to make the payment to the receiving bank. Under the BACS payment system this will be at the beginning of Day Two when the receiving bank is told about the credit. Under the CHAPS system it will be when the Bank of England makes its adjustment of the accounts of the paying and receiving banks.

In Momm v Barclays Bank International,[12] a customer of the defendant bank ordered it to transfer funds to the plaintiff who was also a customer of the defendant. The bank made the transfer but shortly after completing it, and before the plaintiff was informed of it, the bank reversed it, the bank by now having heard of the paying customer's insolvency. The plaintiff denied the bank had the right to reverse the transfer and the court agreed with him, holding that payment was irreversible once the bank had decided to credit the plaintiff's account and had initiated the payment process. It was irrelevant that the plaintiff had not yet been told of the credit.[13] Although this case concerns reversal of payment which the bank wanted to perform, it is reasonable to assume that the same rules would apply to determine up to what point a customer could countermand an intrabank transfer.

Once it has become too late for the customer to countermand payment or for the paying bank to reverse payment, the payment is considered complete and irreversible. This does not of course prevent the paying bank (or the payer[14]) from claiming recovery of the payment as one made by mistake. The conditions for this remedy are discussed in 5.14, the objection to recovery of payments made by electronic means stated in Agip (Africa) Ltd v Jackson[15] are of particular relevance. Equitable tracing is not limited in this way but it is limited in other significant ways, primarily the requirement of a breach of some fiduciary relationship. The recovery of a simple mistaken electronic payment as was permitted in Chase Manhattan

---

[12][1977] QB 790.
[13]The plaintiff's bank statements did not show the payment or the reversal of it. The fact of the payment only emerged after litigation began.
[14]See 5.14 above.
[15][1990] Ch 265.

Bank v Israel-British Bank[16] has been placed in doubt by the decision in Westdeutsche Landesbank Girozentrale v Islington LBC.[17]

Interestingly, the court in *Momm* stated that the absolutely final time when payment had become irreversible (if it was difficult to determine an earlier decision to credit the payee's account) was close of business on the value day, at any rate if the payee's account was credited intentionally and in good faith and not by error or fraud. This suggests that payment could be reversed after this time if it had been made in error.[18]

When a payment is made in error, besides recovering a payment as one made under a mistake of fact, the paying bank could also be subrogated to the rights of the payee (if any) against the payer. Thus if the paying bank had some but insufficient authority from the payer and the payment discharged a debt owed by the payer to the payee, the paying bank could debit its customer's account in the same way as explained in 5.2 above and could arguably do so if payment had been countermanded or forged.

7.5 THE RECEIVING BANK

The receiving bank has a banker-customer relationship with the payee and accordingly owes him a duty to act with reasonable care and skill. Thus it will be liable for any negligence in its processing of the transaction and for the negligence of its agents. Any attempt to exclude such liability will be subject to the unfair contract terms legislation.[19]

It has been decided that the receiving bank receives the payment as agent for its customer, the payee.[20] In the normal case, the receiving bank has its customer's authority to receive payments to

---

[16]*[1981] Ch 105.*

[17]*[1996] 2 WLR 802 HL. See the discussion in 5.14 above.*

[18]*Note that recovery of a payment made under a mistake of fact necessitates a court action to seek repayment and would not justify a unilateral decision to reverse the payment.*

[19]*See 1.1 above.*

[20]*Mardorf Peach & Co Ltd v Attica Sea Carriers Corpn of Liberia [1977] AC 850 HL.*

his account but in some circumstances it may only have limited authority to receive payments, such as that from a ship charterer who would otherwise have established that payment had been accepted on the shipowner's behalf by its bank and thus the shipowner's right of forfeiture of the charter would have been waived.[21] However, where the payee was aware of the payment and retained the funds for three weeks before returning them without paying interest, payment is considered to have been accepted.[22]

[21]*The facts of the* Mardorf Peach *case.*
[22]*TSB Bank of Scotland v Welwyn Hatfield District Council [1993] 2 Bank LR 267.*

8 Automated teller machines

8.1 INTRODUCTION

Originally limited to dispensing cash, many Automated Teller Machines (ATMs) now fulfil some of the functions of human bank tellers, i.e. they can accept deposits, perform balance transfers, issue balances, pay bills etc. All the main banks and building societies issue ATM cards to their personal customers, on request. The same card may double up as a debit card and also as a cheque guarantee card. When this occurs, the legal consequences of the use of the card will depend upon which function it is performing on a given occasion.

ATM cards are issued together with a Personal Identification Number (PIN) which effectively replaces the signature as the means of verifying that the true customer is presenting the card to the ATM. One building society began trials in 1998 with an iris recognition ATM which uses retina scanning of the card user instead of the keying in of a PIN.

ATMs are increasingly being placed in non-bank locations such as shopping malls and railway stations. Cards can often be used in the ATMs of other banks and building societies.[1] The amounts withdrawn from ATMs are debited to the account of the customer whose card was used for the withdrawals. This is usually but by no means always a current account. Some ATM cards, especially those issued by building societies, operate savings accounts. ATM cards are particularly appropriate when issued to enable operation of a

---

[1] *An example is the LINK network which enables the cards issued by a plethora of banks and building societies to be used in each other's ATMs.*

postal or telephone account. In 1997, 57% of cash withdrawn from bank and building society accounts was by means of ATM card, from 23,193 ATMs around the UK.[2]

ATM cards are a vehicle for crime and unlike cheques, where forgery of the customer's signature however accurate renders the bank unable to debit the customer's account unless the customer knows of the forgery,[3] banks when issuing ATM cards have traditionally imposed an express term that the customer can be debited in respect of all withdrawals where the customer's card and PIN were used. The more recent practice is for the terms relating to the use of the card to mirror the provisions of the Banking Code, i.e. to render the customer liable only for a maximum of £50 unless he was fraudulent or grossly negligent.[4]

8.2 ATM CARDS AND THE CONSUMER CREDIT ACT

The definition of credit-token and the regulation of a credit-token agreement have been considered in 3.4 above. The main consequences of regulation under the Consumer Credit Act in the case of ATM cards are that the rules limiting cardholder liability for loss would apply.[5] The extent to which ATM cards are regulated by the Act depends on a technical interpretation of section 14 and there is room for different valid interpretations. There are no reported cases on section 14.[6]

Section 14(1) of the Consumer Credit Act 1974 defines a credit-token as

'a card, cheque, voucher, coupon, stamp, form, booklet or other docu-

---

[2] *APACS Annual Review 1997.*
[3] *See 4.9 above.*
[4] *Discussed further in 8.3 below.*
[5] *ATM cards which access credit in the form of a bank overdraft are exempt from the Act's documentary requirements by a determination of the Director of Fair Trading issued under section 74(3) and (3A).*
[6] *The reader is referred to chapter 6 of M. Brindle and R. Cox, Law of Bank Payments, 1st edition, 1996; the Banking Ombudsman Scheme Annual Report 1990–91 at p21; the Encyclopaedia of Banking Law at D1 1431.*

ment or thing given to an individual by a person carrying on a consumer credit business, who undertakes:

(a) that on production of it (whether or not some other action is also required) he will supply cash, goods and services (or any of them) on credit; or

(b) that where, on production of it to a third party (whether or not any other action is also required), the third party supplies cash, goods and services (or any of them), he will pay the third party for them (whether or not deducting any discount or commission), in return for payment to him by the individual.

(1) A credit-token agreement is a regulated agreement for the provision of credit in connection with the use of a credit-token.

(2) ... the person who gives to an individual an undertaking falling within subsection (1)(b) shall be taken to provide him with credit drawn on whenever a third party supplies him with cash, goods or services.

(3) For the purposes of subsection (1), use of an object to operate a machine provided by the person giving the object or a third party shall be treated as the production of the object to him.'

It is clear that an ATM card which is only used in the issuing bank's own machines and which only operates an account in credit is not a credit-token as defined in section 14. Where an ATM card is used to access credit provided by the issuing bank, however, it does appear to come within section 14(1). Where the issuing bank has not 'undertaken' to provide such credit to the cardholder but the ATM through malfunction or system design does in fact provide unauthorised credit, it is arguable that the use of the card is not within the definition.

Section 14(2) defines a credit-token agreement as a regulated agreement for the provision of credit in connection with the use of a credit-token. Thus it follows that if credit is provided which is not in connection with the use of a credit-token, this will not be a regulated credit-token agreement.[7] For instance, an overdraft which is provided to a customer who does not have an ATM card could not be a regulated credit-token agreement. If the same customer had an ATM card but never used it, it is doubtful that there is the

_____

[7]*Although it may still be a regulated credit agreement – but this will have no consequences relating to the card issuer's liability when the card is lost.*

required connection between the provision of the credit and the use of the card. It might also be argued that the required connection is lacking if the card was used to overdraw the account but there was no agreed overdraft.

Section 14(1)(b) includes as a credit-token a card which is produced to a third party who then provides cash to the cardholder and subsection (3) declares that the card issuer in these circumstances is deemed to have provided the cardholder with credit. In other words a credit-token can exist even when no actual credit has been provided. This is because of the deemed providing of credit and since this deemed providing of credit arises from the use of the card with a third party, the deemed credit must be provided in connection with the use of a credit-token. Thus there can be no room to argue that there is no credit-token agreement as defined in section 14(2).

It can, however, be argued that the use of an ATM card to obtain cash from another bank is not producing the card to a third party, but rather to a bank acting as agent of the issuer. If this is correct then the use of an ATM card with a different bank would not constitute a regulated credit-token agreement unless its use with the issuer bank in the same circumstances would make it so.

The Banking Ombudsman has issued an opinion that use of an ATM card to access an overdraft, whether agreed or not, constitutes a regulated credit-token agreement but that use of the card with a different bank does not constitute a regulated agreement if no actual credit is involved, i.e. he favours the agency interpretation of use of the card with other banks so that section 14(1)(b) is not relevant.[8]

The effect of the Consumer Credit Act on cardholders' liability is discussed more fully in 3.4 above. In summary, where the use of an ATM card is regulated by the Consumer Credit Act the cardholder *prima facie* is not liable for any transaction which he did not authorise but he can face unlimited losses if the user obtained the card with his consent and he can be liable for up to £50 in respect of transactions occurring before he notified the bank of the loss of the card. Any contractual term between the bank and the cardholder

[8]*This is the effect of the examples listed in the Annual Report 1990–91 at p21.*

which conflicts with this statutory protection for the cardholder is ineffective. Negligence on the part of the cardholder is not relevant beyond the terms of the protection. For instance, writing the PIN on the card is of no importance.

Finally, section 51 of the Consumer Credit Act prohibits the giving of a credit-token to a person unless a signed request has been made for it or it is a replacement card.

8.3 ATM CARDS AND THE BANKING CODE

The Banking Code contains a number of statements relevant to ATM cardholders. It will be recalled that the Code is only aimed at personal customers and is not directly law, although it may be considered in whole or in part to form part of the implied terms of the banker-customer contract and in any case it is enforceable by the Banking Ombudsman, assuming the issuing bank is a member of that scheme.

The Code says that customers will be told of any charges for using ATM cards when they are issued with the card.[9] It is not specifically stated that increases to charges will be notified but reasonable notice must be given of increases in charges for 'basic account services'.[10] Cardholders must be given account statements at least quarterly if there have been card transactions on the account.[11]

Cards will only be sent to customers who request one or as a replacement.[12] PINs will be advised only to the cardholder and will be issued separately from the card.[13] Customers will be told if they can select their own PIN and banks will provide this facility by 1st

[9]*Section 2.2.*
[10]*Section 2.10.*
[11]*As of 1st July 1999. This requirement compares to a minimum of annual statements for non-card accounts. The requirement to send statements does not apply to pass book accounts. Section 3.1 and 3.2.*
[12]*Section 3.9. This mirrors the rule in section 51 of the Consumer Credit Act which is backed by criminal sanctions.*
[13]*Section 3.10.*

July 2000 at the latest.[14] Cardholders can ask not to be issued with a PIN.[15]

On responsibility for losses, the bank will refund the customer the amount of any transaction together with interest and charges where the card was not received by the customer and was misused by another, for all unauthorised transactions after the customer has reported that someone else knows his PIN, and for faults which occurred in an ATM which were not obvious or subject to a warning notice.[16] If the card is misused before notification, the customer's liability is limited to £50 unless he acted fraudulently or with gross negligence.[17] Gross negligence may follow from a failure to observe the recommended safeguards in section 4.8. These are not to allow another to use the card and/or PIN, to take reasonable steps to keep the card safe and the PIN secret, never to write the PIN on the card or on anything kept with it or near it, not to write the PIN anywhere without disguising it, and to destroy the PIN immediately on receipt. The bank has the burden of proving fraud or gross negligence by the customer.[18] It is stated to be essential that the customer notify the bank as soon as he can of any loss of a card or that someone else knows his PIN[19] but failure to do so does not appear to make the customer liable for transactions on his account[20] at all in the case of someone else knowing his PIN or over £50 in the case of a lost card.

The Banking Ombudsman has given an opinion concerning a card which is taken by a fraudster and misused, then replaced and used by the genuine cardholder, and finally taken again by the same fraudster and misused again.[21] He has said that he treats each taking

---

[14]*Section 3.11.*
[15]*Section 3.12. The Code only says that customers can ask. Banks appear to be free to respond as they choose.*
[16]*Section 4.12.*
[17]*Section 4.14.*
[18]*Section 4.15.*
[19]*Section 4.9.*
[20]*Assuming no fraud or gross negligence.*
[21]*As can happen when the fraudster lives in the same home as the cardholder.*

of the card as a separate incident and thus a £50 limit applies to each series of misuses and thus the customer is liable for a total of £100 on these facts.[22]

In an interesting case summary[23] the Banking Ombudsman tells of a Mrs M who forgot to remove her card from an ATM. A fraudster used the card five times each day for ten consecutive days withdrawing £50 each time and he thus obtained £2500. It appears that Mrs M did not report the card missing until after all the withdrawals were made. The Ombudsman found Mrs M grossly negligent but he considered the bank should have monitored the suspicious pattern of withdrawals (and some attempted withdrawals) and that after three days the bank was not acting fairly and reasonably in not taking any action to prevent further withdrawals. He decided the bank could debit Mrs M's account with £1250. By extrapolation, it could be argued that a term which permits a bank to debit a customer's account whenever his card and PIN are used to make a withdrawal is one claiming to render a performance substantially different from that which is reasonably expected of it and thus potentially invalid under the Unfair Contract Terms Act 1977 or is one which, contrary to the requirement of good faith, causes a significant imbalance in the parties' rights and obligations to the consumer's detriment and thus potentially invalid under the Unfair Terms in Consumer Contracts Regulations 1994.[24]

8.4 MACHINE FAILURE OR ERROR

In permitting customers to make ATM cash withdrawals, a bank is providing a service. As with any other service, the bank must perform the service with due care and skill.[25] This implied duty is excludable by express agreement, subject to that being considered reasonable[26] or contrary to the requirement of good faith causing a significant imbalance in the parties' rights to the detriment of the

---

[22]*Banking Ombudsman Scheme Annual Report 1992–93 at p31.*
[23]*Case 10A in the Annual Report 1993–94.*
[24]*Described more fully in 1.1 above.*
[25]*Section 13 of the Supply of Goods and Services Act 1982.*
[26]*The effect of the Unfair Contract Terms Act 1977.*

consumer.[27] More specifically a bank is considered to be under a duty to ensure that its ATMs:

(a) are designed and programmed to respond accurately to the proper commands of cardholders authorised to use the ATMs;
(b) are, as far as is reasonable, maintained in working order; and
(c) provide sufficient information to the bank of completed cash withdrawals to enable cardholders' current accounts to be debited with the right amount on the right date.

Thus an ATM which dispenses the wrong amount of cash renders its bank liable for breach of contract but a customer would be expected to return any excess (or accept that his account can be debited for it) and to seek other nearby machines or human tellers if the ATM failed to dispense the requested cash. Retention of the customer's card by the machine will make it harder for the customer to achieve this. As noted above, the Banking Code states that a bank will refund the amount of a transaction together with interest and charges where faults have occurred in an ATM which were not obvious or subject to a warning message.

[27] *The effect of the Unfair Terms in Consumer Contracts Regulations 1994.*

9   Debit cards

9.1 INTRODUCTION

Debit cards were introduced to replace the cheque as a means of making retail type payments. In 1997, 4.1 million average daily transactions were made by debit card, compared with 8.4 million by cheque. However, debit card usage grew 18.3% from 1996 whilst cheque usage declined 3.7%.[1]

Unlike a credit card transaction, the use of a debit card leads to a debiting of the cardholder's current account with a bank or building society. Most debit card payments are processed electronically and the debit card payment process is known as electronic funds transfer at the point of sale (EFTPOS). In fact there is no transfer of funds. Just as with payment by cheque there is a debiting of the payer's account usually on the day following the transaction and a subsequent crediting of the payee's account with their respective banks. Payment by debit card has the advantage that payment is assured (if the applicable conditions are met) up to any amount so long as authorisation is obtained (if necessary). Payment by cheque is never guaranteed by the paying bank unless a cheque guarantee card is used and even then a maximum limit of £50, £100 or £250 will apply to each single transaction.[2] A further difference is that payment by debit card can be remote (e.g. purchase by telephone or the internet) in exactly the same way as with credit cards. When the debit card is presented personally a payment slip is usually signed to evidence

[1] *APACS Annual Review 1997.*
[2] *See 5.13 above.*

the transaction. In some countries the cardholder keys his PIN into a terminal instead of signing.

Every trader who accepts debit cards will display the logo of the card network he accepts. That trader will deal with a single bank representing the network, which is known as the merchant acquirer. In other words the trader will send all his transaction details to one bank which sends debit details to the various card issuers and sends a credit to the account of the trader. The system normally leads to a debiting of the cardholder's account on day two, mimicking the timing of the debit when payment is made by cheque.[3] The card issuer will normally pay the transaction acquirer on day three by a CHAPS transfer.

Each card issuer issues terms relating to the use of a debit card which form part of the contract between bank and customer. As with ATM cards this contract traditionally made the customer liable for all use of the card but the more modern practice is for the terms of issue to mirror the provisions of the Banking Code and thus make the customer liable for more than £50 only if he has acted fraudulently or with gross negligence.[4]

Each transaction acquirer issues terms relating to the acceptance of debit cards by the traders it acts for. There will also be a written contract between the transaction acquirer and the card scheme representing all the card-issuing banks. The legal relationships arising from use of a debit card depend enormously on the contents of the particular contract in any given case. These written contracts can of course be modified or supplemented by statutory regulation and case law. The rights of the cardholder are especially affected in these ways.

9.2 DEBIT CARDS AND THE CONSUMER CREDIT ACT

The definition of a credit-token and the regulation of a credit-token agreement have been considered in 3.4 above. The main consequences of regulation under the Consumer Credit Act in the case of

[3] *See 6.2 above.*
[4] *Discussed further in 9.3 below.*

debit cards would be documentary requirements, connected lender liability of the issuing bank and limitations on the cardholder's liability for unauthorised transactions on the card.

The relevant parts of section 14 of the Consumer Credit Act 1974 in this case are sub-section (1) which defines a credit-token as

'a card, cheque, voucher, coupon, stamp, form, booklet or other document or thing given to an individual by a person carrying on a consumer credit business, who undertakes:

(a) that on production of it (whether or not some other action is also required) he will supply cash, goods and services (or any of them) on credit; or

(b) that where, on production of it to a third party (whether or not any other action is also required), the third party supplies cash, goods and services (or any of them), he will pay the third party for them (whether or not deducting any discount or commission), in return for payment to him by the individual.

(2) A credit-token agreement is a regulated agreement for the provision of credit in connection with the use of a credit-token.

(3) . . . the person who gives to an individual an undertaking falling within subsection (1)(b) shall be taken to provide him with credit drawn on whenever a third party supplies him with cash, goods or services.'

There seems no real doubt that the use of a debit card to purchase goods or services from a retailer brings the debit card within the definition of a credit-token in (1)(b)[5] and as there is, by subsection (3), deemed to be a providing of credit, it is immaterial whether the cardholder's account is overdrawn. The transaction must constitute a credit-token agreement as defined in subsection (2) because the deemed provision of credit only arises because of the use of the card, it must therefore be credit connected to the use of the card.

If the use of a debit card gives rise to a regulated agreement, that agreement would be classified as 'debtor-creditor-supplier' because of the pre-existing arrangements between the creditor and the sup-

---

[5]*Except in as much as it can be argued that there is no "payment to him by an individual" when the cardholder's current account is debited by his bank, and that account is in credit.*

plier. As a debtor-creditor-supplier agreement, it would come within section 75 which establishes connected lender liability when the cash price of the goods or service being purchased is between £100 and £30,000. Section 187 defines these pre-existing arrangements. Subsection (3A) says arrangements shall be disregarded if they are arrangements for the electronic transfer of funds from a current account at a bank.

It is necessary to consider whether section 187(3A) does in fact apply to debit cards so that their use gives rise to debtor-creditor agreements rather than debtor-creditor-supplier agreements. The typical payment processes set in motion by the use of a debit card are described above. They do not involve a transfer of funds from a current account. There is a debiting of a current account and there is a payment by the bank where the account is held by a transaction acquirer and there is a further payment by the merchant acquirer to the retailer. It would require a liberal (but not overstretched) interpretation of the subsection therefore to conclude that debit card transactions involve arrangements for the electronic transfer of funds from the cardholder's current account.

More difficulty comes from the fact that it seems necessary to imply into section 187(3A) that the arrangements for the transfer of funds from a current account must be between the creditor and the supplier, since it is between these two parties that the pre-existing arrangements must exist in the first place. It is unlikely that there will be any debiting of a current account at a bank when a card issuer pays a retailer since the card issuer is a bank. Furthermore it also follows that the debiting of a current account arrangement between creditor and supplier will be disregarded under section 187(3A) but this leaves open the possibility that there may be other arrangements between them which are not disregarded. In practice there would, of course, be other arrangements between card issuer and retailer, although these often take place through the inter-mediary merchant acquirer. This raises a further argument, i.e. that there are no arrangements between the retailer and card issuer at all when a merchant acquirer is placed between them. This in turn can be countered by arguing that the merchant acquirer is acting as agent of the card issuer when it enters into arrangements with the retailer.

As to documentary requirements, section 74(1)(b)[6] applies to exempt debit cards if they are debtor-creditor agreements enabling the cardholder to overdraw his current account.

As to cardholders' liability for unauthorised transactions, it is generally accepted that sections 83 and 84 do not apply because there is no use of a credit facility by another person.

To summarise the position of debit cards under the Consumer Credit Act:

(a) they are within the definition of credit-token;
(b) they do give rise to regulated credit-token agreements;[7]
(c) they are not within sections 83 and 84 dealing with cardholder's liability for lost cards;
(d) they may give rise to either debtor-creditor or to debtor-creditor-supplier agreements, depending on whether section 187(3A) applies to them;
(e) if they are debtor-creditor agreements, they are exempt from the documentary requirements of the Act to the extent that they constitute an agreement enabling the cardholder to overdraw his account and section 75 does not apply to them;
(f) if they are debtor-creditor-supplier agreements, the documentary requirements apply to them in full and so does section 75.

Section 51 of the Consumer Credit Act prohibits the giving of a credit-token to a person unless a signed request has been made for it or it is a replacement card.

9.3 DEBIT CARDS AND THE BANKING CODE

The Banking Code only applies to personal customers and it is not law except in as much as it may be deemed to form part of the implied terms of the banker-customer contract. It can be enforced by the Banking Ombudsman against banks which belong to that scheme.

---

[6]*And the determination of the Director-General of Fair Trading made under section 74(3) and (3A).*
[7]*Assuming the agreement is not unregulated, or is exempt, for some other reason.*

The Code states that cards will only be sent to customers who request one or as a replacement.[8] On responsibility for losses, the bank will refund the customer the amount of any transaction together with interest and charges where the card was not received by the customer and was misused by another. Otherwise if the card is misused before notification of its loss to the bank, the customer's liability is limited to £50 unless he acted fraudulently or with gross negligence.[9] No specific examples of gross negligence relevant to debit cards are given. The bank has the burden of proving fraud or gross negligence by the customer.[10] It is stated to be essential that the customer notify the bank as soon as he can of any loss of a card[11] but failure to do so does not appear to make the customer liable for transactions on his account over £50.[12]

The Banking Ombudsman has given an opinion concerning a card which is taken by a fraudster and misused, then replaced and used by the genuine cardholder, and finally taken again by the same fraudster and misused again.[13] He has said that he treats each taking of the card as a separate incident and so a £50 limit applies to each series of misuses and thus the customer is liable for a total of £100 on these facts.[14]

Where the terms of issue of a debit card impose liability on a cardholder in the event of misuse, this may be invalid as a term which, contrary to the requirements of good faith, causes a significant imbalance in the parties' rights to the detriment of the consumer.[15] It is also arguable that a failure on the bank's part to monitor the account means it is unreasonably claiming to render

---

[8]*Section 3.9. This mirrors the rule in section 51 of the Consumer Credit Act which is backed by criminal sanctions.*
[9]*Section 4.14.*
[10]*Section 4.15.*
[11]*Section 4.9.*
[12]*Assuming no fraud or gross negligence.*
[13]*As can happen when the fraudster lives in the same home as the cardholder.*
[14]*Banking Ombudsman Scheme Annual Report 1992–93 at p31.*
[15]*The Unfair Terms in Consumer Contracts Regulations 1994.*

a performance substantially different from what is expected of it.[16]

9.4 THE LEGAL CONSEQUENCES OF PAYMENT BY DEBIT CARD

In order to simplify a complex situation, it is assumed here that one contract exists between cardholder and card issuer and another contract exists between card issuer and retailer.[17]

First, a retailer who displays the logo of a card network is making a standing offer to potential customers to settle their liability by using the card displayed. The customer has the right to pay by that card if he wishes.[18] When the cardholder offers his card for payment, this will be to discharge his liability under the contract of sale he has made with the retailer. In the normal case the retailer will be paid by the card issuer (directly or through the merchant acquirer) but if the card issuer has become insolvent he will not receive payment this way. On these facts in Re Charge Card Services Ltd,[19] the court had to consider the nature of payment in relation to a charge card.

It is established law that payment by cheque is a form of conditional payment, i.e. the payee accepts the cheque as payment to him only on the implicit understanding that the cheque is honoured.[20] If it is not honoured, for any reason, he has the right to go back to the drawer and demand a fresh payment. This is the reason for the introduction of cheque guarantee cards and for the practice of writing the drawer's address on the back of a cheque which is not so guaranteed. As explained in 9.1 the nature of debit card payment is such that the retailer, so long as he gets any necessary

---

[16]*The Unfair Contract Terms Act 1977.*
[17]*i.e. missing out the merchant acquirer.*
[18]*Richardson v Worrall [1985] STC 693 at 720.*
[19]*[1987] Ch 150; affirmed [1989] Ch 497 CA.*
[20]*[1987] Ch 150 at 166 and the cases referred to therein.*

authorisation for the transaction, does not have a concern that he will not receive payment.[21]

If a cheque is dishonoured because of insolvency of the paying bank, the drawer is still bound to pay the retailer again. In *Charge Card*, however, it was decided that a charge card transaction which failed because of an insolvent card issuer did not leave the cardholder having to pay again. The argument that a method of payment which involves a risk of non-payment raises a presumption that it is a conditional form of payment which was rejected and it was held that payment by charge card was an unconditional form of payment.

The decision was partly based on the fact that the cardholder was entitled to the benefit of delayed payment when he used a charge card and that if payment was conditional and the retailer was refused payment by the card issuer, the cardholder would have to pay much sooner.[22] On the facts in *Charge Card*, it was clear that the retailer was to assume the risk of non-payment by the card issuer because the card issuer was supposed to have provided a guarantee of its liability to the retailers. It also was held that the features of the charge card transaction where the card issuer effectively held accounts for both the retailer and the cardholder, crediting the former and debiting the latter, supported the case that payment by charge card was an unconditional form of payment. A crucial factor underlying the decision was that if it had been decided that payment was conditional, the cardholder who had already paid the now insolvent card issuer would have had to pay the retailer again. In other words cardholders would pay twice for the same goods. In the case of a cheque which is dishonoured, it seems impossible for this to happen so no injustice to customers is caused by the rule that payment by cheque is a conditional form of payment.

The interesting question is whether payment by debit card is treated like payment by charge card, and is unconditional, or is treated like payment by cheque, and is conditional. The debit cardholder does not benefit from a delayed payment benefit and the

---

[21]*Assuming he is dealing with the genuine cardholder and not an impersonator.*
[22]*[1987] Ch 150 at 191.*

nature of the payment system is somewhat different so the arguments that convinced the court in *Charge Card* that payment by charge card is unconditional do not exist to the same degree with debit cards.

Furthermore, the injustice of the cardholder having to pay twice would not occur in the case of a debit card as it functions in a similar way to payment by cheque. In summary it appears highly questionable that a court would consider payment by debit card to be unconditional. It is settled, however, that payment by credit card or store card constitutes unconditional payment because the payment systems for these types of card are so similar to that by charge card and the court in *Charge Card* expressly spoke of credit cards in the same breath as charge cards.[23]

The decision in *Charge Card* may produce injustice to the retailer beyond his failure to secure payment in the event of the card issuer's insolvency. Card issuers usually include a 'charge-back' clause in their contracts with retailers. This clause permits the card issuer to refuse payment (or reclaim if he has already paid) when the retailer has not obtained any necessary authorisation or when he has accepted payment by presentation of a stolen card. If the retailer is refused payment under this clause, he presumably cannot recover payment from the cardholder where unconditional payment has been made by presentation of the card. Where he was offered a stolen card, he could however recover from the fraudster, as payment by stolen card can hardly constitute any form of payment.

Finally, if the card issuer mistakenly refuses authorisation for a debit card transaction when the cardholder has sufficient funds on his current account, this would be breach of contract by the card issuer and possibly defamation[24] of the cardholder in the same way as if the card issuer had dishonoured a customer's cheque wrongfully.[25]

---

[23]*[1987] Ch 150 at 190.*
[24]*Slander rather than libel if refusal is communicated orally. The refusal would have to be overheard by other people.*
[25]*See 5.12 above.*

10 Insolvency

10.1 INTRODUCTION

The prospect of a customer borrower becoming insolvent is one of the driving forces behind a bank's decision to secure its loan. It is therefore vital to understand the impact that an insolvency would have in any particular case.

Many aspects of insolvency which do not directly affect a security are discussed in chapter 2 and many aspects are discussed under the specific securities in the following chapters. In this chapter the intention is to examine some general principles which will be relevant when security is taken, whatever the asset charged and whether the chargor is an individual or corporate entity.

The first principle to grasp is that there are two quite separate insolvency regimes. One applies to individuals and the other to companies. There are, however, many similarities between them and some rules apply to both regimes.

The governing law is the Insolvency Act 1986 and the Insolvency Rules made pursuant thereto.[1] Individuals are made bankrupt after the making of a 'bankruptcy order', and companies are 'wound up' after a resolution in general meeting or a court order to that effect. 'Insolvency' is a useful umbrella term which can be used to refer to either or both procedures.

---

[1]*See the Insolvency Rules 1986 SI 1986/1925 and the Insolvency Proceedings (Monetary Limits) Order 1986, SI 1986/1996.*

10.2 PRIORITY OF CLAIMS IN AN INSOLVENCY

The law begins by asserting the principle of *pari passu* treatment of creditors. A 'dividend' is declared of x pence in the £, depending on the amount of money available, and the creditors paid accordingly. When a creditor makes a claim against an insolvent debtor, this process is known as 'proving' for his debt.

Insolvency law is very much a matter of some being more equal than others, however, as there are categories of claimant and, by and large, each category must be paid in full before any is paid to the next in order.

The categories for a company are as follows.

(1) Creditors with fixed charges must be paid first from the proceeds of sale of the asset they have a charge over. Thus a bank with a charge over the company's land will receive the proceeds of sale of that land (after the costs of sale have been deducted). If there is insufficient from this source to pay off the bank, it must take what there is and prove in a lower category for the balance.

(2) The expenses of the liquidation.

(3) The preferential creditors. Section 386 and Schedule 6 defines these. They include:

(a) the Inland Revenue for the net amount of PAYE deductions which the company employer was liable to make from employee's wages over the previous 12 months but which have not yet been paid over to the Revenue;

(b) the Department of Social Security for the equivalent Class 1 National Insurance deductions and for the company's own Class 1 liability, also over the previous 12 months;

(c) the Customs and Excise for unpaid Value Added Tax over the previous 6 months and Betting Duties and Car Tax over the previous 12 months;

(d) Occupational Pension Scheme trustees for sums owed under pension contribution obligations;

(e) employees for unpaid wages and salaries, limited to the previous 4 months and to £800 per person and for unpaid accrued holiday pay in respect of any period of employment;

(f) lenders who have lent money which has been used to pay

employees who would otherwise be proving as preferential creditors. This is an example of the subrogation principle. Thus the bank practice of operating a wages account for customers who are employers.[2]

The above time limits on the debts which may be proved as preferential are calculated backwards from the date of the resolution to wind up the company (in a voluntary winding-up) or from the date of the court order winding it up[3] (in a compulsory winding-up) or from the date of the appointment of administrative receivers (in a receivership) or the date of the administration order (in an administration) as the case may be.[4] If the creditor has a claim which is outside the time limit, he may still prove for this debt, but not as a preferential creditor;

(4) The floating chargeholders. If more than one, then in order of priority.
(5) The unsecured creditors, in practice the trade creditors.
(6) For preferential and unsecured creditors, interest on the debt arising since the winding-up commenced (Secured creditors are entitled to claim interest alongside their debt.).
(7) The shareholders can recover the nominal value of their shares and divide any surplus assets among themselves, in the order provided in the company's Memorandum and Articles of Association (preference, ordinary and deferred shares usually rank one after the other). This is only relevant in a member's voluntary winding up, when the company must be solvent.

The categories for an individual debtor are as follows.

(1) Secured creditors. These must of course have fixed charges, as only companies can grant a floating charge.
(2) The expenses of the bankruptcy.
(3) Preferential creditors. These are the same as for company debtors above, *mutatis mutandis*. National Insurance Contribution liab-

---

[2]*See 2.7 above.*
[3]*Interestingly not the date of the petition which is the deemed commencement of the winding-up for other purposes.*
[4]*Section 387 of the Insolvency Act 1986.*

ility extends to include Class 2 and Class 4 contributions. The time limits run back from the date of the bankruptcy order. Again, a bank may be subrogated to an employee's claim if it has advanced money for wages.

(4) Unsecured creditors.

(5) Interest on debts for preferential and unsecured creditors. (Once again, secured creditors are entitled to their interest alongside their debt.)

(6) The bankrupt's spouse for debts owed to him or her.

It should be noted that if there is insufficient to pay a category of preferential or unsecured creditors, a dividend is declared, and each creditor in that category will receive x pence in the pound.

Secured creditors are unable to prove in the bankruptcy unless they release their charge. A bank must also release its charge if it wishes to benefit from a set-off.[5] If the security is inadequate, the asset in question must be sold and proof made as unsecured (or preferential) creditor for the balance. If sale is not convenient, the asset can be valued for this purpose.

Third party security, such as a guarantee, is not affected by this rule. Thus the chargeholder may prove fully in the debtor's bankruptcy at the same time as calling on the guarantor to pay (see chapter 12).

10.3 VOLUNTARY ARRANGEMENTS AND ADMINISTRATION ORDERS

Certain 'schemes of arrangement' and 'compositions' specific to companies may be made under section 425 of the Companies Act 1985. Individuals may execute a 'Deed of Arrangement' under the Deeds of Arrangement Act 1914. All of these, however, are little used in practice and are not discussed here.

A voluntary arrangement under the Insolvency Act 1986[6] involves either a company or an individual making a proposal to creditors, whereby the creditors may agree to accept something less than full

---

[5]*Re Norman Holding Co Ltd [1991] 1 WLR 10.*
[6]*Sections 1–7 and 252–263.*

payment on their claims. They may do so as a voluntary arrangement, which avoids the considerable expense of a full bankruptcy or liquidation, and therefore there will be more funds available to pay the creditors.

The creditors will meet to consider the proposal and a decision is taken on a majority vote, so that some minority creditors may have the scheme forced on them. However, the salient point for present purposes is that this is not true of secured and preferential creditors, who must either be paid in full or individually agree to the scheme. If the scheme is approved, it is implemented by a 'nominee' who must be an insolvency practitioner.

The important matters arising from the Administration Order procedure are discussed in chapter 16.

10.4 PREFERENCES AND TRANSACTIONS AT AN UNDERVALUE

When a company is wound up or an individual is made bankrupt, the liquidator or trustee in bankruptcy has a duty to realise the available assets and to distribute them according to the law. Some implications of the law dealing with exactly what assets are available have been discussed in chapter 2. Some others arise here. For instance, the assets may be swelled by the reclaiming of a preference, or of a transaction at an undervalue and this can involve the relinquishing of a mortgage. Thus a secured creditor may be adversely affected. Note, however, that any adjustment to the debtor's assets in this way can only be made by court order, and in practice a liquidator or trustee in bankruptcy will be reluctant to incur the expense of seeking the order.

The Insolvency Act refers to 'associates' of company and individual debtors and to those 'connected' with a company. Associates include employees and relatives. Connected persons include directors and shadow directors of companies as well as associates of such persons. Companies in a group and their directors and associates are likely to be caught by these provisions.

Preferences

The law on preferences is contained in sections 239 and 340. A preference is an example of the principle of *pari passu* treatment of creditors. It may consist of the debtor paying off a perfectly genuine debt shortly before he becomes insolvent, so that the recipient is better off than other creditors who have not been paid. It occurs when the debtor:

(a) does anything which has the effect of putting a person, who is a creditor or guarantor of the debtor's liabilities, into a position which, in the event of the debtor's bankruptcy or insolvent liquidation, will be better than the position of the creditor or guarantor would otherwise have been; and

(b) was influenced by a desire to produce the effect mentioned in (a) above. This motive is rebuttably presumed if the debtor and creditor were connected persons or associates; and

(c) the preference occurred when the debtor was unable to pay his debts[7] and occurred within the 'relevant time'. This is a six months period prior to the commencement of the insolvency unless the debtor and creditor were connected persons or associates, in which case it is 24 months.

In Re M.C Bacon Ltd,[8] these definitions were judicially considered for the first time. It was emphasised that the cases based on the old law were no longer pertinent. A preference under the current rules will only occur when the debtor positively and subjectively wished to improve the creditor's position in the event of the debtor's insolvency. In addition, this desire must have influenced the debtor's decision to enter into the transaction in question (in this case, granting a charge to a bank). However, it need not have been the decisive factor, merely one of the factors. It was also held that the relevant time (for considering whether there had been a preference) was the time when the decision was made to grant the charge, not the time when the charge was granted.

---

[7] *This is assumed if the transaction preferred an associate or connected person.*
[8] *[1990] BCLC 324.*

The preference rules may affect a bank in the following situations.

(1) A customer repays his unsecured debt to the bank. He later becomes insolvent. On these facts, the necessary desire to prefer on the part of the debtor may be lacking and wanting to 'keep in' with the bank is not considered a desire to prefer so long as the debtor genuinely believes he can escape insolvency.

(2) A debt secured by a guarantee is repaid (by the principal debtor who is influenced by a desire to prefer the bank) and the guarantor is released. The principal debtor becomes insolvent. This is dealt with by a suitable clause in the guarantee form to preserve the guarantor's liability (see chapter 12).

(3) The same circumstances as in (2), except that the intention is held to be to prefer the guarantor. Where the debtor and the guarantor are connected persons, such as companies in a group, this intention is presumed, the time period extends to two years and furthermore there is no need for proof that the debtor was insolvent at the time. The court may order the guarantor to pay or it may order the bank to do so, in which case it may also order that the guarantor's obligation to the bank be revived. However, a bank may be protected from an order by the proviso that the court cannot make an order against a recipient who took in good faith, for value and without notice of the relevant circumstances.[9] Once again, a suitably drafted clause will preserve the bank's claim against the guarantor.

(4) An unsecured debt is secured by a charge taken directly from the debtor, who later becomes insolvent. The bank is now in a better position in the insolvency than it otherwise would have been, and the court may declare the giving of the security to be a preference and has power to void the charge.

(5) The same facts as in (4) except that the bank holds a guarantee from an associate of the debtor which it releases when it receives the direct security from the debtor. The person preferred is now the guarantor, and because of the association with the debtor, the time period extends to two years, there is no requirement to show that the debtor was insolvent when he gave the

[9]*Sections 241(2) and 342(2).*

charge and the intention to prefer is presumed.[10] The same orders are available to the court as are listed in (3) above.

A question which is of interest to bankers is this. By putting pressure on a customer to pay or secure an unsecured debt, and by the customer reluctantly then making payment or granting security, is the customer influenced by a desire to produce the effect of the preference? The Cork Committee Report,[11] which led to the Insolvency Act, considered that putting pressure on a debtor should provide a defence, and the decision in Re M.C. Bacon Ltd[12] affirms that 'a man can choose the lesser of two evils without desiring either'.

Floating charges granted by companies to secure pre-existing debts are subject to a related, but quite different, rule contained in section 245 and are discussed in chapter 16.

Transactions at an undervalue

The rules in sections 238 and 339 are designed to enable the court to order the return of assets given away by the debtor over a fairly long period before the insolvency begins. The definition is:

(a) the debtor makes a gift or enters into a transaction whereby he receives significantly less value than he gives; and

(b) this takes place:

(i) for companies, within two years before the winding-up commences, and at a time when the company was unable to pay its debts, or it became so as a result of the transaction (this is rebuttably presumed if the persons are connected);

(ii) for individuals, within five years before the bankruptcy petition. Inability to pay debts need not be proved if it occurred in the two years before the petition. Otherwise this must be

---

[10]*See on this point Re Fairway Magazines Ltd [1993] BCLC 643.*

[11]*Insolvency Law and Practice (Report of the Review Committee 1981, Cmnd 8558).*

[12]*See above.*

proved, although it is rebuttably presumed if the parties were associates.

No order may be made in respect of a company debtor if it entered into the transaction in good faith and for the purpose of carrying on its business, if at the time there were reasonable grounds for believing the transaction would benefit the company.[13]

Transactions at an undervalue may conceivably affect a bank in the following circumstances:

(1) A bank takes a guarantee to secure the debt of a borrower. The guarantor subsequently becomes insolvent. It would appear that the guarantor received significantly less value than he gave when he entered into the guarantee contract with the bank.[14] In the case of a corporate guarantor (for example with intragroup guarantees) it might be shown that the company entered into the transaction in good faith for the purposes of carrying on its business when there were reasonable grounds for believing it would benefit the company.

(2) A bank makes an unsecured loan to a borrower. The bank later takes a charge from the borrower who subsequently becomes insolvent. The loan cannot be consideration for the charge as it is past consideration. This point was argued unsuccessfully by the liquidator in Re M.C. Bacon Ltd.[15] It was held that the consideration for the charge was the forbearance the bank showed in not calling in the overdraft at that time. Furthermore, the creation of the charge did not deplete the company's assets, but merely appropriated them to a particular creditor.

---

[13]*Section 238(5).*

[14]*Note the consideration for a guarantor's promise in contract law consists of the bank lending the funds to the borrower (see 12.3 below) but the Insolvency Act for the purposes of the transaction at an undervalue seems to look only at what value the guarantor personally receives.*

[15]*See above.*

10.5 TRANSACTIONS DEFRAUDING CREDITORS

Sections 423–425 empower the court to make an order reversing a transaction which amounts to a fraudulent undervalue. This will be more difficult to prove than a transaction at an undervalue as it requires that the debtor made the transaction for the purpose of:

(a) putting assets out of reach of someone who has or will have a claim against him; or
(b) otherwise prejudicing such a person.

The provision is broader than the transaction at an undervalue, however, in that no time limits are set. Indeed, an order can be made even if no insolvency ever occurs.

10.6 EXTORTIONATE CREDIT TRANSACTIONS

Sections 244 and 343 give the court wide powers to reopen a transaction whereby the debtor obtained credit, if this was within three years before the commencement of the winding up or bankruptcy and the transaction was extortionate. The conditions are that either:

(a) it requires grossly exorbitant payments to be made; or
(b) it grossly contravenes ordinary principles of fair dealing.

The court has the power to make a variety of orders, including a forfeiture of security held by a lender.

Under a similar provision contained in the Consumer Credit Act 1974,[16] an interest rate of 48% was held not to be extortionate.[17]

---

[16]*Extortionate credit bargains, discussed in 3.8 above.*
[17]*Ketley v Scott [1981] ICR 241.*

11 Taking security from individuals

11.1 INTRODUCTION

Recent years have seen a considerable increase in the inclination of individuals who have given charges or guarantees to secure loans to dispute the legal validity of such charges and guarantees. A number of cases in this area have reached the appeal courts and there is thus no shortage of relevant judicial dicta. As can happen in an area of law which is flooded with learned judgments, it can be difficult to see the wood for the trees. This chapter represents an attempt to present a fair overview of the essential law without necessarily reaching every detail within it.

A charge and a guarantee are both created by contracts and, like all contracts, both can be rendered void by a number of factors. One such vitiating factor is undue influence. Another is misrepresentation. Strictly, the presence of either of these factors entitles the affected party to void the contract if he so wishes. Thus these factors present the charge-giver or guarantor the opportunity to escape liability.

If a bank takes a guarantee from G to secure the debt of D, the contract of guarantee is between the bank and G and does not directly involve D. If the bank applies undue influence over G or misrepresents facts to him, the guarantee contract will clearly be voidable. Typically, however, G is alleging that it was D who unduly influenced him, not the bank. What then becomes important is the law governing the ways in which the bank can find that its guarantee contract is voidable even though it itself did nothing untoward but because of the actions of D in which the bank is somehow implicated.

This chapter is entitled 'Taking Security From Individuals'. This area of law is in practice limited in this manner but it is worth pointing out that misrepresentation might conceivably be raised by a corporation that had given a charge or guarantee. It is even theoretically arguable that a corporation, through the minds of its human agents, was unduly influenced.

The duty, such as it exists, to advise a potential guarantor of matters concerning the principal debtor's account is discussed in chapter 12.

11.2 UNDUE INFLUENCE

It is a general principle of law that where one party to an agreement has been subject to the strong influence of the other party, so that he does not form an independent judgment as to whether to enter into the agreement, then the transaction becomes voidable for undue influence, i.e. the influenced party may choose to void it if he wishes. This defence is to be distinguished from that of duress, whereby physical force or the threat of it is used to obtain the other party's agreement. The legal effect of duress is also to make the transaction voidable.

It has emerged from decided cases that the law considers that undue influence may be presumed to exist in certain relationships. These have long included parent/child (when it is the child raising undue influence by the parent), doctor/patient, solicitor/client, religious leader/disciple and more recently the relationship between members of a particularly tightly knit immigrant group was added to the list.[1] In these relationships undue influence is presumed to exist but the court will hear evidence which may rebut that presumption. These relationships are known as Class 2A relationships.[2]

The relationships of banker/customer, husband/wife and parent/child (when it is the parent who is raising undue influence) are amongst those capable of being considered ones of presumed undue

---

[1] See the cases listed in M. Hapgood, Paget's Law of Banking, 11th edition 1996 at p 510.

[2] From Bank of Credit and Commerce International SA v Aboody [1990] 1 QB 923 CA and adopted in Barclays Bank v O'Brien [1994] 1 AC 180 HL.

influence if it is shown that in the particular relationship, there is the appropriate degree of trust, confidence or influence. Any cohabiting relationship is included in this category, whether heterosexual or homosexual,[3] as is a non-cohabiting relationship where the couple have a long-standing emotional relationship and have two children.[4] It is also now confirmed that this category includes a husband who claims undue influence by his wife.[5] Such relationships where undue influence is presumed because of the special nature of the relationship are labelled Class 2B.

Whether the relationship of presumed undue influence falls into the Class 2A category or the Class 2B, it is necessary for the claimant to prove that the disputed transaction was manifestly disadvantageous to him or her before a claim for undue influence will be upheld. A number of cases have examined this requirement. In National Westminster Bank plc v Morgan,[6] Mr and Mrs M owned a house which was charged to a building society. The mortgage payments fell into arrears and the society obtained a possession order. The bank was asked by Mr M to provide short-term bridging finance to pay off the society, pending money being raised from other sources. The bank had also made business loans to Mr M. The bank manager visited the M house and Mrs M agreed to sign the charge form so long as the house was not used as security for the business loans. To this the manager agreed, although the charge form included the standard all-monies clause.[7] The bridging loan was defaulted upon and the bank sought a possession order, which was resisted by Mrs M on the grounds of undue influence. Her defence failed, as giving the charge to the bank was not disadvantageous to her. She was about to lose her house in any case when she signed the mortgage deed and the bank did not seek to rely on the all-monies clause in respect of the business debts. Since there

[3]*Barclays Bank v O'Brien [1994] 1 AC 180 HL.*
[4]*Massey v Midland Bank [1995] 1 All ER 929 CA.*
[5]*Barclays Bank v Rivett (10 Feb 1997) described in the Encyclopaedia of Banking Law at C181.*
[6]*[1985] AC 686 HL.*
[7]*See chapter 13 for an explanation of this clause.*

was no manifest disadvantage to Mrs M, she was unable to establish presumed undue influence.

In Lloyds Bank v Bundy,[8] Mr B provided a series of guarantees, backed by charges on his sole property, to secure the bank's business loans to his son. It was a feature of the case that the bank allowed the loan to increase beyond the agreed limit (and the limit on the guarantee) and then approached Mr B to increase his limit. Mr B was elderly, did not understand business matters well and placed a degree of trust in his bank. When the son defaulted, the bank sought a possession order against Mr B which the court refused on the basis that, due to the trust placed in the bank by Mr B, the bank had failed to recognise a conflict of interest. It should have declined to accept the guarantee until Mr B had obtained independent advice. The transaction was manifestly disadvantageous to Mr B and he also had shown that there was the necessary degree of trust in his relationship with the bank.

In Bank of Credit and Commerce International SA v Aboody,[9] Mr A set up a company and persuaded Mrs A to be an officer of it. She took no part in business affairs, however, and signed any document put before her by Mr A. The matrimonial home was in Mrs A's sole name. Mr A arranged a bank loan for the company which was to be secured by a charge on Mrs A's house, and she obediently signed the necessary forms. The company defaulted on the loans and a possession order was sought against Mrs A. The court granted this as it found that, although the marital relationship was sufficiently one of trust and confidence, Mrs A had enjoyed the benefits of the continued existence of the company for some time after the charge was given. There was thus no manifest disadvantage proved.

More recent cases have adopted a narrower definition of what constitutes financial advantage to a spouse in a similar position. In Goode Durrant Administration v Biddulph,[10] the wife's indirect advantage in the potential profit to her husband's company (the loan to which she guaranteed) was not taken into account and her personal 2.5% shareholding in the company was considered too small

[8] *[1975] QB 326 CA.*
[9] *[1990] 1 QB 923 CA.*
[10] *[1994] 2 FLR 551*

to justify the risk she assumed by signing the guarantee. In Bank of Scotland v Bennett,[11] the wife in this case also could show the transactions were not to her advantage when she owned 11.8% of the shares in the company at the time she signed the guarantee and owned 45.1% by the time she charged her house to back up the guarantee. In Barclays Bank v Sumner,[12] however, a wife's 50% holding in the relevant company appears to have been considered sufficient to deny manifest disadvantage.

When the guarantee or charge secures a loan that is made in the joint names of husband and wife, there is on the face of things nothing to indicate disadvantage to the wife, since she is jointly entitled to the borrowed funds. In CIBC Mortgages v Pitt,[13] the husband influenced his wife to jointly mortgage their home to raise funds which the husband used to speculate on the stock market. However, the lender was told the funds were required for the purchase of a holiday home for the couple and the charge was upheld. The mere fact that the loan is made in joint names would not save the lender, however, if he in fact knows that the funds will be used for the exclusive benefit of the husband.[14]

Where a Class 2A or Class 2B relationship of presumed undue influence is established, the presumption is rebuttable. The onus is on the bank to prove that there has not been any undue influence. In order to do this, the bank may be able to point to the fact that the claimant received independent legal advice before entering into the transaction. The law relating to this and other methods of rebutting the presumption is considered below.[15]

If a claimant is unable to establish presumed undue influence, it is open to him or her to try to prove actual undue influence, known as Class 1 undue influence. This requires it to be shown that the other party had the capacity to influence the complainant, that he did so influence him or her, that the influence was undue, and that

---

[11] *[1997] 1 FLR 801.*
[12] *[1996] EGCS 65.*
[13] *[1994] AC 200 HL.*
[14] *Allied Irish Bank v Byrne [1995] 1 FCR 430.*
[15] *In 11.4.*

it caused the complainant to enter into the transaction. It is not necessary for the complainant to show manifest disadvantage.[16]

In Barclays Bank v O'Brien,[17] the defendant wife claimed undue influence had been exerted on her by her husband. The court found that theirs was not the kind of relationship where undue influence was presumed (i.e. it did not fall into Class 2B). The court also held that she had failed to establish evidence of actual undue influence (Class 1). She did, however, establish misrepresentation by her husband; this is discussed in the following section.

11.3 MISREPRESENTATION

This takes the form of some misrepresentation that is made to the provider of the security which induces him to sign, something he would not otherwise have done. The effect is akin to undue influence in that the victim may void the transaction if the other party to the contract is the maker of the misrepresentation or that other party is somehow tainted by the misrepresentation made by another person.

In MacKenzie v Royal Bank of Canada,[18] the plaintiff wife had mortgaged some shares to provide security for loans to her husband's company. She was misled by both her husband and by the defendant as to the effect of the documents she signed, and as the misrepresentation was deemed material, it was held she could void the charge over the shares.

In Barclays Bank v O'Brien,[19] the defendant wife had been told by her husband that the charge over the matrimonial home which she was being asked to sign was limited in value to £60,000 and limited in time to a short period. The charge secured a loan to a company with which her husband was involved and in which she had no direct involvement. It was held that the misrepresentation as to the financial limit (the charge was in fact expressed to be unlimited) had induced the wife to sign and therefore the wife was

[16]*CIBC Mortgages v Pitt [1994] AC 200 HL.*
[17]*[1994] 1 AC 180 HL.*
[18]*[1934] AC 468 PC.*
[19]*[1994] 1 AC 180 HL.*

not liable beyond the limit she had been led to believe existed.[20] It appears the wife had only claimed to limit the charge on the basis of the misrepresentation, and had not sought to invalidate it on this basis. In TSB Bank v Camfield,[21] the court invalidated the charge entirely on the basis of a similar misrepresentation by the husband as to the financial limit of the charge.[22]

It appears that in addition to the kind of misrepresentation described above, which has the effect of voiding the security, there can be a negligent misstatement, the effect of which falls short of influencing the person to sign the document but which does lead him to misunderstand the effect of it. The security will not be voidable but the bank will be liable in negligence if it is the maker of the statement. In Cornish v Midland Bank,[23] a Mr and Mrs H purchased a farm and approached the bank for finance to renovate it. The bank agreed to do so, subject to a limit of £2,000 and to it taking a second mortgage. Mrs H was left with the impression that the bank had agreed not to lend more than the limit, whilst in reality the charge form included the standard 'all-monies' clause. Furthermore, she was unaware that she had executed any form of mortgage. Soon after, Mr and Mrs H separated (to the bank's knowledge), and Mr H alone operated the account until it was overdrawn well beyond the limit. The court held that the mortgage was valid but that the bank had been negligent in misleading Mrs H (now named Cornish) as to the limit, and it was therefore liable to compensate her for her loss resulting from this. It was also suggested that the bank owed her a duty not to allow Mr H to continue to borrow on the account and to notify her if he did. Further suggestions that, as she was also a personal customer, the bank owed her a duty to advise her as to the nature and effect of the document she was about to sign, have since been disapproved in Midland Bank v

---

[20]*Because the bank was tainted by the husband's misrepresentation due to the bank having had constructive notice of it, see below.*
[21]*[1995] 1 WLR 430 CA.*
[22]*Once again the wife succeeded on the basis that the bank had constructive notice of the husband's misrepresentation.*
[23]*[1985] 3 All ER 513 CA.*

Khaira,[24] although the point was not addressed by the House of Lords in Barclays Bank v O'Brien. It has been suggested that a bank owes a customer a duty of care when some special trust or confidence is being placed in the bank by the security-giver.[25]

11.4 HOW A BANK CAN BE AFFECTED BY UNDUE INFLUENCE[26]

A bank's rights against a security-giver can be affected in the following ways:

(a) it exerts the undue influence itself against the security-giver;
(b) it used another person as its agent and that person so exerted undue influence on the security-giver;
(c) it has actual notice that another person so exerted undue influence on him or her;
(d) it has constructive notice that another person did so.

Lloyds Bank v Bundy[27] and MacKenzie v Royal Bank of Canada[28] are two cases where the bank involved itself exerted the undue influence on the security-giver. Such a conclusion may be reached from deeming the banker-customer relationship to be Class 2B presumed undue influence which the bank has failed to rebut or from finding that there is evidence of actual undue influence (Class 1).

In some cases it may be shown that the bank used another person as its agent and that that person exerted undue influence. Prior to the decision in *O'Brien*, this method was successfully used to invalidate charges, for instance by pleading that the bank had given the charge forms to the husband through whom the wife signed them,[29] but in *O'Brien* this was considered artificial. In any case lenders soon learned that security forms should not be handed to

---

[24][1992] 1 WLR 623.
[25]*Midland Bank v Khaira, see above.*
[26]*This section should be read so as to include misrepresentation as well as undue influence.*
[27]*See above.*
[28]*Noted above.*
[29]*e.g. Kings North Trust v Bell [1986] 1 WLR 119 CA.*

intermediaries for conveying to the security-giver. It could still happen that the bank is deemed to use another as an agent such as where the bank has virtually recruited the agent to get the charge forms signed by the security-giver.[30]

In the vast majority of cases, however, the bank is entirely innocent of exerting undue influence, either directly or through an agent, and the security-giver is claiming that another person did so, such as the husband in Barclays Bank v O'Brien.[31] The security-giver may then be able to show that the bank had actual knowledge of the undue influence. This also is rare in practice, it is much more likely that the bank had constructive notice of it. This requires it to be shown that:

(a) there is an emotional relationship between the security-giver and his or her cohabitee or other close person (this appears to be identical to the category of relationships which are capable of constituting ones of Class 2B undue influence[32]); and

(b) the transaction on its face was not to the financial advantage of the security-giver (this is analogous to the requirement in establishing Class 2B undue influence that the transaction was manifestly disadvantageous to the security-giver and the cases discussed above[33] are therefore relevant here also) and that there is a substantial risk a wrong has been committed by the other person in the emotional relationship.

Once the security-giver has shown that he or she was unduly influenced, the burden of proof is on the bank to show that it did not have constructive notice of it.[34]

Usually the bank is aware of the nature of the relationship between the parties so condition (a) is not contentious. Most guarantors are in an emotional relationship with the other party and that is why they are prepared to enter into a disadvantageous transaction.

---

[30]See Shams v United Bank (24 May 1994) described in the Encyclopaedia of Banking Law at C183.
[31]Noted above.
[32]Described above in 11.2.
[33]See 11.2.
[34]Barclays Bank v Boulter [1997] 2 All ER 1002 CA.

Credit Lyonnais Bank Nederland NV v Burch[35] was a rare case where there was no such obvious relationship as the guarantor was an employee of the company whose debt was secured and she denied an emotional relationship with the director of the company. The transaction was so disadvantageous to her that the court was able to find in her favour.

Sometimes the bank does not know enough facts to establish condition (b) but a solicitor involved in the transaction does know these facts. Where the solicitor has not passed on what he knows to the bank, it becomes crucial to the question of constructive notice whether the bank is deemed to know what the solicitor knew. In Midland Bank v Serter,[36] a solicitor acted for a wife and her husband as well as for the bank, who had instructed him to register its charge. The wife claimed the solicitor knew of the undue influence exerted on her by her husband and therefore that the bank was also deemed to know it. It was held that the bank was only deemed to know what the solicitor knew in his capacity of registering the charge and found in favour of the bank. The decision would have been different, it seems, if the bank had instructed the solicitor to advise the wife on whether she should give the security.

In another case[37] the loan was being made to a joint account and thus the transaction was not on its face to the wife's disadvantage. The solicitor involved knew, however, that the loan was really to pay off the husband's debts. It was held the solicitor could not convey this to the lender without the couple's consent. Without such consent, the solicitor should have ceased to act for the lender but given that he continued to do so, his knowledge could not be imputed to the lender unless he was acting fraudulently. On appeal this case upheld the lender's victory but on the grounds of section 199(1)(ii)(b) of the Law of Property Act 1925 which limits what a purchaser of land (and therefore also a legal mortgagee) is deemed to know through his solicitor.

If the necessary conditions are established for a bank to be deemed to have constructive notice, that notice can be negatived by the bank

---

[35]*[1997] 1 All ER 144 CA, see below.*
[36]*[1995] 1 FLR 1034 CA.*
[37]*Halifax Mortgage Services v Stepsky [1996] 2 All ER 277.*

following a procedure laid down by the House of Lords in *O'Brien*. This consists of the bank seeing the wife (or whoever is the security-giver) on her own and explaining:

(a) the extent of her liability; and
(b) the nature of the risk she is incurring by signing the security, e.g. she might lose her home; and
(c) that she should take independent legal advice.

It was said that the above would suffice in the normal case but that if the bank knew facts which made undue influence probable rather than possible, it should go further and insist on her obtaining independent legal advice.

The danger for a bank in adopting this procedure as routine is that the wife may reveal some facts in the meeting which indicate that undue influence is probable or that a misrepresentation has taken place and a bank would then be obliged to see that she receives independent legal advice. The employee who attends the meeting would need to be able to judge this matter accurately. Alternatively, the wife might later claim that she did not understand the explanations given to her at the meeting. Whilst a strict reading of the dicta in O'Brien appear to render it irrelevant whether she understood any of the explanation, a bank might have a weakness on these facts, especially if it was considered that it was clear she did not understand.

In some cases a bank may insist on independent legal advice; in others the wife or other security-giver may obtain it voluntarily. When it is given, other issues arise. Cases discussed above concern whether a bank is struck with the knowledge of the facts that the solicitor had. Another issue is whether the bank need be concerned as to the adequacy of the advice given by the solicitor. In Barclays Bank v Thompson,[38] the husband and wife were told by the bank to take legal advice before granting the charge over their home which was to be security for the husband's debts. The bank itself instructed solicitors to register its charge and it also specifically asked these solicitors to advise the wife. The wife was seen on her own and the solicitors confirmed to the bank that the advice had been given to

---

[38] *[1997] 1 FLR 156 CA.*

her. The wife later claimed that the explanation was inadequate.[39] It appears that a failure to adhere to the suggested procedure laid down by the House of Lords in *O'Brien* (i.e. not seeing the wife on her own) will not matter if the wife does in fact receive independent legal advice. Nor will it matter to the bank if that advice is defective if the solicitor confirms it was given. This has the effect of shifting the risk in transactions where independent advice is given to the solicitor.[40]

In Massey v Midland Bank,[41] the couple in that case were also jointly told by the bank that the wife should be independently advised. She was advised by a solicitor but her partner was present during the meeting. This did not prevent the charge from being upheld. In Banco Exterior Internacional v Mann,[42] the wife was advised by a solicitor who acted for her husband and her husband's company. This also did not prevent the charge from being upheld. In Bank Melli Iran v Samadi-Rad,[43] however, it was suggested that an assurance given by solicitors that the wife would be independently advised was insufficient for the bank to rely on. An undertaking that she had been so advised would, however, be sufficient.

Finally in Credit Lyonnais Bank Nederland NV v Burch,[44] the defendant was a not very highly paid employee of the company whose debt she charged her home to guarantee. The controller of the company persuaded her to sign an unlimited guarantee securing the company's overdraft which had a limit of £270,000. The defendant was advised in a letter from the bank that she should

---

[39]*She also claimed that the bank had notice of facts known to the solicitors it had instructed but this claim also failed for similar reasons to those given in Midland Bank v Serter, noted above.*

[40]*See Wolfson (1997) NLJ 137. Although the overall risk to be borne will be much reduced because presumably in most cases the advice will be properly given.*

[41]*[1995] 1 All ER 929 CA.*

[42]*[1995] 1 All ER 936 CA.*

[43]*[1995] 2 FLR 367 CA.*

[44]*[1997] 1 All ER 144 CA.*

seek independent advice and warning her that the guarantee would be unlimited. She was not told the planned overdraft limit for the company nor that its debts at that time already stood at £163,000. The defendant did not claim to have had an emotional relationship with the controller of the company. The court still felt able to conclude that the bank had constructive notice of a Class 2B type of presumed undue influence on the facts. This was decided on the basis that the bank knew she was only a junior employee of the company, who had no interest in it as director or shareholder and that the transaction was manifestly disadvantageous to her. Two members of the court held it was the category of case where independent legal advice must be obtained if the bank's charge is to be upheld. One member went further and suggested that it would have made no difference even if she had been independently advised.[45]

Under the terms of the Banking Code, a bank must advise a person proposing to act as guarantor or surety that by giving the security he might become liable for another's liabilities and that he should seek independent legal advice before entering into the security. All the charge documents should contain this recommendation as a clear and prominent notice. The person should also be advised of the limit to their liability and it is stated that unlimited guarantees will not be taken.[46] The force of this statement of practice is limited by the fact that it follows from the way it is framed that only guarantees of loans to personal (i.e. non-business) customers are covered by it. Most of the guarantees granted in the reported cases were given to secure business debts. (A similar statement of practice that a bank should recommend to a guarantor that he obtain independent advice is, however, contained in 'Banks and Business: working together. A Statement of Principles,' published by the British

[45]*Millet LJ at 156. In Royal Bank of Scotland v Etridge (1998) The Times, 17th August, the Court of Appeal agreed that if a bank has material information not available to the advising solicitor or if the transaction is one which no competent solicitor could advise the security-giver to enter, independent legal advice would not prevent the bank being fixed with constructive notice.*
[46]*Section 3.14.*

Bankers Association in July 1997.) Furthermore, even where it does apply, it does not have the force of law and the Banking Ombudsman does not have the power to invalidate the security. He can, however, award £100,000 for the complainant's loss, inconvenience or expense.[47]

Finally, it is pertinent to recall that in the Morgan case,[48] Lord Scarman issued a warning to the effect that the law leaves the dividing line, between mere folly on the one hand and unconscionable transactions on the other hand, deliberately uncertain. He said there is no precisely defined law setting limits to the equitable jurisdiction of a court to relieve against undue influence.

11.5 *NON EST FACTUM*

In order to lose the benefit of a security due to undue influence or misrepresentation, the bank must be somehow connected to the wrongdoing, if only by constructive notice of it being exerted by another. Otherwise the security is valid. The defence of *non est factum* is different in that a totally innocent third party can be prejudiced by it.

In effect the signatory of the document is saying that the signing of the document was not his action. To be successful, this will require three elements.

(1) The signatory was unable to read the document, e.g. through blindness or illiteracy. In Saunders v Anglia Building Society,[49] the disability was due to the signatory's glasses being broken.

(2) The document which was signed was fundamentally different from that which the signatory thought he was signing. This will perhaps result from a fraudulent misrepresentation by the person who stands to gain from the security being granted, such as a

---

[47]*Assuming the bank is a member of the scheme, see 1.1 above. It is within the Ombudsman's terms of reference to hear a complaint from a guarantor, paragraph 29(c)(2).*
[48]*See above.*
[49]*[1971] AC 1004 HL.*

principal debtor who is deceiving a relative into signing what is really a guarantee form.

(3) The signatory acted carefully in signing the document. Thus in the ordinary case he should read it. In more exceptional circumstances, he should wait until he has his glasses available and then read it, or (if he is blind or illiterate) he should seek out some trustworthy person to read it to him before he signs it.

It follows that only in the most extreme circumstances will a signatory be able to dispute liability on a document on the basis of *non est factum* but that where he is able to do so as a result of a third party's fraud, a bank cannot defend itself by pointing out that it acted properly.

12 Guarantees

12.1 INTRODUCTION

When banks take guarantees they do so to secure loans they make to customers. The guarantor may typically be a relative of a personal borrower or a director of a company borrower. The previous chapter dealt with a number of cases which involved guarantees, in Barclays Bank v O'Brien,[1] for example, the wife in that case agreed to charge the home which she jointly owned with her husband as security for the debts of a company with which her husband was associated. In other cases a loan is made to one company in a group and cross-guarantees are taken from the other companies in the group.

Guarantees may also be given by a bank in favour of a third party to guarantee payment by the bank's corporate customer of some contingent liability to that third party. A performance bond is an example of such a bank guarantee. We are not concerned with these in this book.

Guarantees are usually executed on standard forms, which the bank prepares and which invariably include a battery of clauses many of which are designed to increase the bank's rights under the guarantee and to reduce the guarantor's rights. Interesting questions arise as to the enforceability of some of these clauses in the light of modern consumer protection legislation.

[1] *[1994] 1 AC 180 HL.*

12.2 GUARANTEES AND INDEMNITIES

The distinction between a guarantee and an indemnity is significant for the following reasons.

(1) A guarantor is agreeing to pay if the principal debtor does not, whereas an indemnifier agrees to pay in any case.[2] This is sometimes referred to as the secondary liability of the guarantor compared to the primary liability of the indemnifier. A bank creditor can demand payment from an indemnifier directly as if he were the principal debtor himself, but it must ask a principal debtor to repay before turning to a guarantor. A bank would have no objection to doing so, but what is more significant is that the bank cannot demand that the guarantor pay if the principal debtor is not liable in law to pay. In Coutts & Co. v Browne-Lecky,[3] a bank had lent money to a minor, taking a guarantee as security. The loan was irrecoverable due to the minor's lack of capacity, and the guarantee was therefore also not enforceable without a clause specifically making the guarantor liable in these circumstances. In fact, section 2 of the Minors Contracts Act 1987 now provides that a guarantor will be liable even if the loan is irrecoverable from a minor. However, a loan made to an organisation acting *ultra vires* its powers can render a guarantee similarly unenforceable.

(2) Section 4 of the Statute of Frauds 1677 requires that, to be enforceable, a guarantee (but not an indemnity) be in writing and signed by the guarantor. Banks are naturally keen to comply with these requirements for evidential purposes in any case. A guarantee (and an indemnity), provided in connection with a credit agreement regulated by the Consumer Credit Act 1974, must be in properly executed written form, otherwise it will be unenforceable without a court order.[4] The Act, and Regulations made pursuant to it,[5] specify in some detail the precise nature

---

[2]*Moschi v LEP Air Services Ltd [1973] AC 331 HL.*
[3]*[1947] KB 104.*
[4]*Section 105 of the Consumer Credit Act 1974.*
[5]*Consumer Credit (Guarantees and Indemnities) Regulations 1983,SI 1983/ 1556.*

of the form to be used. The standard form contracts used by banks (when the loan agreement being secured is regulated by the Consumer Credit Act 1974) are headed 'Guarantee and Indemnity'.

12.3 CONSIDERATION AND CAPACITY

Any contract not 'under seal' requires consideration in order for it to be valid. A guarantor often makes his promise to pay and receives nothing in return. This does not matter, as the law only requires that consideration moves from the promisee. Thus the guarantor makes his promise to the bank which then makes its loan to its customer, the principal debtor. There is a potential problem where the money was lent before the guarantee was taken, as this could mean that the loan amounts to 'past consideration' and is therefore invalid. In this case, the consideration may consist of continuing the account, or even refraining from action to recover the debt, as the requirement for consideration may be satisfied by a forbearance for a reasonable time.[6] It is the practice of banks to state these alternatives on the guarantee form. The legal requirement to state the consideration was abolished in 1854, and it is suggested that the statement achieves nothing if in fact the bank has not provided any consideration. If lack of consideration is ever a problem, the guarantee contract could simply be executed as a deed. A 12.5% stamp duty on such deeds was abolished in 1971.

In some cases the guarantor lacks capacity to enter into the guarantee contract. A guarantee from a minor is void for this reason under the Minors Contracts Act 1987, and a guarantee given by an organisation will be void when it acts beyond its powers. Since the enactment of sections 35 and 35A of the Companies Act 1985,[7] there is less concern over companies acting beyond their powers either as borrowers or as guarantors but the power of local

---

[6]*Fullerton v Provincial Bank of Ireland [1903] AC 309 HL.*
[7]*For these, see 16.2 below.*

authorities to guarantee the debts of others has been successfully challenged.[8]

12.4 DUTY TO A GUARANTOR BEFORE THE GUARANTEE IS SIGNED

It is well established that a guarantee contract is not *uberrimae fidei* (of the utmost good faith) and therefore there is no general duty on the bank to warn a potential guarantor of circumstances about the principal debtor's account that might make the former think better of signing the form.

However, in Hamilton v Watson,[9] it was stated that the bank should disclose 'anything that might not naturally be expected to take place between the . . . debtor and creditor, to the effect that his [the surety's] position shall be different from that which the surety might naturally expect.' In Cooper v National Provincial Bank,[10] the principal debtor's account could be operated by her spouse, who was an undischarged bankrupt. The guarantor knew nothing of this and sought to have the guarantee contract set aside. The court declined to do so. The court considered that the facts were within the category of what might be naturally expected. In Lloyds Bank v Harrison,[11] the court did not consider the bank had acted wrongfully by not disclosing that the principal debtor was in serious financial difficulties at the time the guarantee was taken. But in Levett v Barclays Bank,[12] the court found in favour of a guarantor who had not been told by the bank that it had agreed with the principal debtor that the Treasury stock the guarantor had deposited as security for the debt would be used to pay off the debt directly.

Whilst there is generally no duty of disclosure, a bank which does disclose facts must not give a misleading impression to the

---

[8]*As beyond the powers granted in section 111 of the Local Government Act 1972, see Credit Suisse v Allerdale Borough Council [1996] 2 Lloyd's Rep 241 CA and Credit Suisse v Waltham Forest L.B.C. [1996] 4 All ER 176 CA.*
[9]*(1845) 12 Cl & Fin 109 HL.*
[10]*[1946] KB 1.*
[11]*(1925) 4 Legal Decisions Affecting Bankers 12.*
[12]*[1995] 1 WLR 1260.*

guarantor and if it is asked a specific question by the guarantor it must give a reply which is true and not misleading, assuming it chooses to answer at all.[13] It appears, therefore, that the bank's duty to disclose is limited to extreme circumstances.

The above issue is to be distinguished from the bank's possible duty (such as it exists) to see that the guarantor obtains independent advice and its duty not to misrepresent the effect of the guarantee document, both of which are discussed in chapter 11.

The Banking Code declares that banks should advise intending guarantors that they may become liable as well as or instead of the principal debtor.[14] They should be told the limit of their liability (unlimited guarantees will not be taken) and encouraged to take independent legal advice. It appears that these provisions only apply when the debt of a personal customer is being guaranteed. Furthermore the Code does not have any direct legal effect.[15]

12.5 DEMAND, DETERMINATION AND THE LIMITATION ACT

Once a guarantee is signed, a contingent liability arises for the guarantor. Subject to any financial limit stated on the form, the guarantor will usually not know how much he will eventually be liable for, or when he will have to pay. It is possible that he will never have to pay anything.

The answer to these matters lies in the determination of the guarantee. When the form is signed, unless a temporal limit is stated, a liability is established which might crystallise any time in the future. This occurs when the guarantee is determined, which will commonly be either when the bank makes demand of the guarantor

---

[13]See *Westminster Bank v Cond (1940) 46 Com Cas 60*, this case also tends to support the view that a bank has a duty to answer questions put to it by the guarantor.
[14]Section 3.14, this appears to constitute poor advice since the consequence of signing the form is that the guarantor will become liable in this fashion. The wording in the Code suggests that the guarantor may escape liability when presumably it is meant that demand may not be made.
[15]For further discussion of this point see 11.4 above.

(assuming the form provides for this) or after the guarantor gives notice to determine. He is then liable for whatever the principal debtor owes the bank at that time, which may of course be nothing.

It follows that a contingent guarantee liability can continue for decades before determination. This does not fall foul of the Limitation Act 1980, since it has been held that the statutory time limit for enforcement of contracts (six years) does not begin to run until demand has been made.[16] Where the guarantee contains a clause to the effect that the guarantor is liable as principal debtor, however, it may be that no demand is necessary to render the guarantor liable[17] and this would presumably mean that the guarantor's liability would expire at the same time as that of the principal debtor, irrespective of any demand or lack of demand having been made on the guarantor.[18]

12.6 JOINT GUARANTEES

Bank guarantee forms invariably provide for two or more guarantors of the same debt to be jointly and severally liable; the reasons for extending the liability of guarantors in this way are partly historical, but there is a remaining advantage in that on the death of one guarantor, his estate will assume liability instead of liability terminating on his death.[19]

There are a number of cases which illustrate the principle that the liability of joint (or joint and several) guarantors is mutually dependent. In James Graham & Co. (Timber) Ltd v Southgate Sands,[20] where joint guarantors appear to have all signed but one signature later proves to be forged, all escape liability. In National Provincial Bank v Brackenbury,[21] it was intended that four persons would be joint guarantors; one declined to sign, and the other three (who had signed) were not liable. In Ellesmere Brewery Company v Cooper,[22]

---

[16]*Bradford Old Bank Ltd v Sutcliffe [1918] 2 KB 833 CA.*
[17]*See MS Fashions Ltd v BCCI [1993] Ch 425 CA.*
[18]*See 1.12 above.*
[19]*See 2.6 above for a fuller discussion of this point.*
[20]*[1985] 2 WLR 1044 CA.*
[21]*(1906) 22 TLR 797.*
[22]*[1896] 1 QB 75.*

it was intended that four guarantors would each be liable up to specified limits. One altered his limit to a lower figure after the others had signed, with the result that none of them were liable at all. And in Smith v Wood,[23] the release of one guarantor discharged the others. This will not be so, however, if the form includes a clause permitting release of a guarantor.

The logic underlying the above decisions, which might appear rather harsh for the bank creditor, is based on a co-guarantor's right of contribution.[24] This means that if the co-guarantors each guarantee the same debt, any one can be obliged to pay the creditor (subject to his limit, if any), but if he has then paid more than his share, he has a right to be indemnified pro rata by the others. The appropriate shares will be equal ones, unless the limits vary, in which case the shares are proportionate to the limits.[25]

12.7 STANDARD BANK GUARANTEE TERMS

The common law seeks to protect a guarantor, who often gains nothing from providing his promise to pay another's debt, by conferring on him a number of rights. Under the freedom of contract principle, however, the law recognises his right to give up those rights if he so chooses. Banks have long taken advantage of this principle by drafting standard form contracts which have just this effect, so far as is possible. Common law also provides that any clause in a contract which restricts a guarantor's rights is to be construed in his favour.[26] There is also a possibility that certain clauses may be rendered invalid by statute, namely the Unfair Contract Terms Act 1977 and the Unfair Terms in Consumer Contracts Regulations 1994.[27]

The following standard clauses will not necessarily be found in every agreement, and the list is not exhaustive. Sometimes two or more of the following are combined in a single clause. References

---

[23]*[1929] 1 Ch 14.*
[24]*Scholefield Goodman & Sons Ltd v Zyngier [1985] 3 WLR 953 PC.*
[25]*Ellesmere Brewery Company v Cooper, see above.*
[26]*First National Finance Corporation v Goodman [1983] BCLC 203.*
[27]*Discussed in 1.1 above and in 12.8 below.*

are made below to the Principal Debtor ('PD') and to the Guarantor ('G'):

Consideration

This is discussed in 12.3 above.

Demand

The guarantor's liability to pay is stated to arise from demand being made on him by the bank. This is discussed in 12.5 above. The demand is deemed to have been made the day after it is posted to the guarantor.

'All monies' and the 'whole debt'

A guarantee of a specific debt would be discharged by repayment of that debt, and any further borrowing would not be secured; it is often important for a bank to know that all overdrafts, loans, guarantee liabilities, interest and charges owing by the principal debtor, are covered by the security. The demand clause will specify that the guarantor will be liable for all monies owed to the bank by the principal debtor, and then go on to say the amount recoverable shall not exceed a given limit (if it is a limited guarantee). The purpose of this approach is to negate two common law rights of the guarantor.

First, he would otherwise be entitled to take a proportionate part of any direct security that the bank is holding. Assume the bank had lent £2,000 and had taken a direct security from PD worth £1,000 and a guarantee from G, limited to £1,000. Without the benefit of this clause, when G paid £1,000 to the bank, he would be entitled to £500 worth of the direct mortgage, since he had paid half PD's debt. The bank would then recover a total of £1,500 from its securities. With the benefit of the clause, the bank can refuse to give up any part of the direct mortgage unless it receives the full £2,000 from G. Thus the bank will recover £2,000 from its securities.

The second benefit is illustrated by the facts of Re Sass,[28] G had guaranteed PD's account up to a limit of £300. PD became bankrupt when his account was overdrawn £755. The bank demanded £300 from G. This was paid and placed by the bank in a separate account, whereupon the bank proved in PD's bankruptcy for the full £755. The rule against double-proof prevents the bank from claiming this and G claiming his £300 from PD's trustee.[29] It was held that the effect of the clause was to permit the bank to claim the full £755 and to prevent G from claiming at all, unless he chose to exceed his limit and to pay the full £755. This is beneficial for the bank if a dividend is paid by PD's trustee, so that (for example), if the bank received a dividend of 60p in the pound on its claim of £755, it obtains £453 from that source, which together with the £300 from G, would see it nearly repaid.

Continuing security

Clayton's case[30] would have the effect of discharging a current account debt in an active account, even if it never moved into credit. It is therefore made clear that the guarantee is continuing in nature and secures present and future loans.

Notice to determine

The continuing security clause will go on to say that if the guarantor wishes to determine the guarantee, he must give three months notice to the bank. This negates the common law position whereby a guarantor is entitled to give notice of instant determination.[31] Again, at common law, notice of death of the guarantor will determine the guarantee instantly.[32] However, the bank can include a provision to the effect that notice of death will not determine it, and the personal representatives of the guarantor will have to give three months

---

[28] *[1896] 2 QB 12.*
[29] *ex parte European Bank (1871) 7 Ch App 99.*
[30] *See 1.13 above.*
[31] *Beckett v Addyman (1882) 9 QBD 783 CA.*
[32] *Bradbury v Morgan (1862) 1 H&C 249.*

notice to do so. No attempt is made by banks to require a three month notice period in the event of the guarantor's mental capacity or bankruptcy. It seems unlikely that either would be effective. On the question of whether a bank is entitled to increase its loan to the principal debtor, during the three months period after notice to determine is given, and to hold the guarantor (or his personal representatives) liable for the full amount, the decided cases are not conclusive.[33] It is generally agreed, however, that, in the unlikely event of a bank doing so, this would be within its legal rights.

Variation, release, compounding and granting time

If the bank materially varies its agreement with PD, such as increasing a fixed rate of interest, this will discharge G's liability at common law.[34] If the bank releases other securities it is holding which secure PD's debt (the effect of which may be to prejudice G's position if he loses his right of contribution), then G's liability is reduced by the amount of the lost contribution.[35] If the bank compounds the debt, i.e. accepts less than full payment, G's liability is discharged at common law.[36] Similarly, at common law, G is discharged when the bank grants time to PD.[37] A suitably drafted clause will deal with all of the above so that G remains fully liable if any of the events occur.

Continuation of the principal debtor's account

There is a danger that continuation of the account after determination of the guarantee would lead to a technical repayment by PD under the rule in *Clayton's case*, and thus a discharge of G's liability. The clause declares that subsequent credits into the account will not reduce the liability of G, even if the account is not ruled off.

---

[33]*Coulthart v Clementson (1879) 5 QBD 42 and Lloyd's v Harper (1880) 16 ChD 290 CA.*
[34]*Burnes v Trade Credits Ltd [1981] 1 WLR 805.*
[35]*Wulff v Jay (1872) LR 7 QB 756.*
[36]*Perry v National Provincial Bank of England [1910] 1 Ch 464.*
[37]*Polak v Everett (1876) 1 QBD 669.*

Such a clause was tested, and found effective, in Westminster Bank v Cond.[38]

Restriction on guarantor taking security from principal debtor

If G were free to do this, the bank's claim against PD would be subordinated. However, if G contravenes the clause and does take a charge from PD, it seems the charge is valid. The clause will therefore go on to say that G's liability to the bank in these circumstances will be increased by the amount of the value of the charge. This is helpful if the guarantee is limited.

Independent security

In case a second guarantee from the same guarantor was construed to be a replacement of the earlier, this clause clarifies the position. Equally, any other security for the same debt will not limit the guarantee.

Changes and amalgamations of parties

If the bank changes its name or amalgamates with another, G may be discharged at common law.[39] Where there is a change in the constitution of a partnership, there is a statutory provision[40] which revokes (as to future debts) guarantees given by partnerships and also guarantees given to secure the debts of partnerships, unless the contrary is expressed. Naturally, the clause does so. The clause cannot, however, make a future partner liable, and therefore when a partnership guarantor admits a new partner, a fresh guarantee should be taken.

---

[38](1940) 40 Com Cas 60.
[39]First National Finance Corp v Goodman [1983] BCLC 203.
[40]Section 18 of the Partnership Act 1890.

Conclusive evidence

For procedural convenience, in the event of litigation against G, it is provided that the extent of G's liability can be proved by a bank statement certified as correct by a bank employee of a certain seniority (usually Regional Manager). This would not otherwise be admissible evidence in court but it has been held that the clause is effective, due to the special reputation bankers enjoy for honesty.[41] Also, any admission of liability by, or on behalf of, PD will be stated to be binding on G. This is helpful if PD is insolvent and his trustee, or (if PD is a company) his administrative receiver or liquidator, accepts the bank's proof of PD's debt.

Avoided payments by PD will be ineffective

The preference and '12-month rule' provisions of the Insolvency Act 1986 are explained in 10.4 and 16.6. The concern is that PD will settle his debt with the bank, and the guarantee is then determined with G's liability appearing to be nil. Soon after, PD is made bankrupt (or goes into liquidation), and his trustee (or liquidator) reclaims the payment. The clause proclaims that G's liability will remain in these circumstances and that the bank is entitled to retain the security for a period of 25 months (24 months being the maximum relation back period for preferences). It seems that the bank could in any case claim against G but the clause removes any possible doubt. Were the bank to permit the guarantee document to be destroyed when PD repays, however, it is doubtful whether the clause would assist. Thus as a buttress to the above, it is provided that the guarantee document permanently remains the property of the bank.

Suspense account

A clause will permit the bank to place payments received from G into a suspense account without any obligation to use them to

---

[41]*Bache & Co. (London) Ltd v Banque Vernes et Commerciale de Pans SA [1973] 2 Lloyd's Rep 437 CA.*

reduce the amount owed from PD. If PD is insolvent, the dividend received by the bank will be maximised by the bank being able to claim for the full debt, without taking into account receipts from G. See the comments above on the all-monies and whole debt clause which interrelate to this point.

Indemnity or Principal Debtor

A clause may express that G is liable as principal debtor. This may have the effect of rendering G liable irrespective of the fact that PD is not liable on the debt and it may have the effect of making it unnecessary for the bank to make demand on G in order to make G liable.[42] The decided cases on these points suggest that much depends on the precise wording of each clause and on the precise reason for PD not being liable on the debt.[43]

Expenses and interest

A clause will entitle the bank to add the full costs of enforcing the guarantee to its claim from G. The bank will also be granted the right to charge compound interest from demand until payment.

12.8 THE GUARANTOR'S RIGHTS

The clauses explained above seek to remove many of the guarantor's rights. The guarantor may be able to establish that some of the clauses are ineffective under consumer protection legislation, however. The Unfair Contract Terms Act 1977 has only a limited impact on bank guarantee forms because the bank is not generally seeking in its form to restrict its liability for its breach of contract nor is it claiming to be able to render a service to the guarantor which is substantially different from what could be reasonably expected of it. The Act does have an impact on set-off clauses, however, see

---

[42] See 12.5 above.
[43] See Heald v O'Connor [1971] 1 WLR 497; General Produce Co v United Bank [1979] 2 Lloyd's Rep 255; Credit Suisse v Allerdale Borough Council [1995] 1 Lloyd's Rep 315; MS Fashions Ltd v BCCI [1993] Ch 425.

below. The ambit of the Unfair Terms in Consumer Contract Regulations 1994 extends to any terms in a contract which are not individually negotiated and voids any term which contrary to the requirement of good faith causes a significant imbalance in the parties' rights and obligations, to the detriment of the consumer. All of the clauses in a guarantee form which seek to reduce or remove the rights which a guarantor would otherwise enjoy are vulnerable to this rule. Furthermore it is stated that any ambiguity in the meaning of a term must be resolved in favour of the consumer.[44]

The Regulations will not apply to all guarantees, however. First the guarantor must be a 'consumer'. This is defined as a natural person acting for purposes which are outside his business. Thus all guarantees given by companies and some given by individuals, such as directors giving personal guarantees, are excluded. An argument has been advanced that the Regulations do not apply to any bank guarantees, based on the contention that the bank when entering into a guarantee contract is not acting as a supplier of a service nor for a purpose relating to a supply of a service, and that the making of a loan to a customer is not a supply of a service but a mere transfer of money.[45]

Right to know the extent of his liability

The authority for this is obscure but it is widely accepted that G can at any time and, presumably with any reasonable frequency, insist on knowing the current debt owed by PD to the bank. This seems to be an exception to the bank's duty of secrecy to its customer, PD; presumably as under compulsion of law or implied consent from PD. The bank should not, however, give more information than G needs. Thus if PD's debt is greater than the limit on G's liability, G should simply be told that his liability is fully relied upon, and if PD's account is in credit, G should be told he has no liability at present.

Where the loan agreement is regulated by the Consumer Credit Act 1974, G also has a statutory right to a statement of PD's account

[44]*This overlaps with the common law position, see note 26 above.*
[45]*See M. Hapgood, Paget's Law of Banking, 11th edition, p632.*

(as well as to copies of the security document and the loan agreement) on written request with a fee of £1. The bank may refuse to comply if PD at that time owes nothing, or if a similar request was complied with in the previous month. Otherwise it must respond within 12 days plus one month, failing which it commits an offence.[46]

Right to be indemnified by PD

Assuming PD asked G to provide the guarantee[47] and that G has paid the bank, G can call upon PD to reimburse him (but not prove in PD's insolvency unless he pays the whole debt, see 12.7). Furthermore, if G wishes to take the initiative, he may determine the guarantee without waiting for demand to be made from him by the bank; he may then take legal action to force PD to pay the debt.[48]

Rights of subrogation and contribution

Where G pays off PD's debt, he is entitled by subrogation to the bank's rights. Therefore, he can take any security which the bank is holding from PD. He can take a proportionate part of any security if he has paid off part of the debt up to his limit.[49] But the 'all-monies' and 'whole debt' clause described above will seek to remove this right unless he pays off the whole debt – see 12.7 above. G is also entitled to a rateable share of any security which the bank is holding from other guarantors of PD's debt. In addition, G has a right of rateable contribution from other guarantors.

Right to set-off

G can only be asked to pay what PD owes, and if PD has a good defence to the bank's claim, G may also raise this as a defence.[50]

[46]See Part VIII of the Consumer Credit Act 1974.
[47]See Owen v Tate [1976] QB 402 CA.
[48]Thomas v Nottingham Incorporated Football Club Ltd [1972] 2 WLR 1025.
[49]Section 5 of the Mercantile Law Amendment Act 1856 and see Re Butlers Wharf Ltd [1995] 2 BCLC 43.
[50]Bechervaise v Lewis (1872) 20 WR 726.

However, in The Fedora,[51] it was held that a set-off clause (which denies this right to G) is effective, at least where the defence is not clear cut. The set-off clause is vulnerable to the provisions of the Unfair Contract Terms Act 1977 and this Act applies to all contracts which are on written standard terms, including those where the guarantor is not a consumer. The bank can argue that the clause is reasonable.[52]

12.9 LETTERS OF COMFORT

In the corporate and international sectors of banking, a letter of comfort may be accepted by the lending bank in place of a full-blown guarantee. Such a letter may be provided by a parent company to secure a loan to a subsidiary, or by a central government in respect of a loan to a government agency. In the former case, the letter will normally contain a statement to the effect that the parent agrees to maintain its holding in the borrower, and that it is the parent's policy that the subsidiary's business will remain in a position to meet its liabilities to the bank.

Such a letter of comfort was examined by the courts in Kleinwort Benson Ltd v Malaysian Mining Corp Berhad.[53] It was held that whilst there was a promise by the parent to maintain its holding in the subsidiary, nothing was said which gave rise to any promise that the latter would meet its debts.

Whilst the typical letter of comfort is not actionable, it would be where the wording is sufficient to render the maker liable for the debts of the other party. This would be subject to the parties having intended to create legal relations. A letter of comfort is sometimes given with the express intention, on the part of the giver, that he should not be sued on it.

---

[51]*[1986] 2 Lloyd's Rep 441 CA.*
[52]*See Stewart Gill Ltd v Horatio Myer & Co Ltd [1992] QB 600.*
[53]*[1989] 1 WLR 379 CA.*

13 Land as security

13.1 INTRODUCTION

Land is defined in English law as 'real property', as distinct from all other forms of asset which are 'personal property'. An entirely different set of legal rules applies to real property.

13.2 LEGAL ESTATES AND INTERESTS IN LAND

Under section 1 of the Law of Property Act 1925 the forms of ownership of land are defined as 'estates' in land. There are two:

(1) Freehold. This is more technically referred to as the 'fee simple absolute in possession'.
(2) Leasehold. Or 'a term of years absolute'.

Freehold ownership of land is as close as one can get to absolute title. It will last indefinitely and there is no rent to pay.

Leasehold ownership must expire at some date. A lease grants a right of possession for any period of time – it is common to find periodic tenancies which are as short as one week (although this will usually be repeatedly renewed) or as long as 999 years. There is invariably a rent attached to a lease which the lessee must pay to his lessor or landlord. In commercial properties it is common to find a series of leases on one building, so that the freeholder leases to a head lessee who in turn leases to a sub-lessee and so on. In this case each sub-lease must not expire after the lease above it. When a lease expires, the right of possession will revert to the freeholder (or to the superior leaseholder if it is a sub-lease). Thus freeholds which are subject to tenancies are referred to as 'reversions'. When a lease is granted at a periodic rental which is below market rents, a premium is charged. This is the price which is paid when a flat is 'bought' on a long leasehold subject to a ground rent. The purchaser is buying the right to possession of a flat at a low rental which is fixed for a long period of time.

Freehold or leasehold ownership of land may be subject to a range of legal and equitable interests. These include:

(a) legal and equitable mortgages;
(b) easements, e.g. the right of a landowner to go on to a neighbour's land (a right of way);
(c) restrictive covenants, e.g. the right of a landowner to prevent his neighbour from building on his land.

Leases may also incorporate positive covenants which, for instance, will oblige a lessor and lessee to maintain the structure of a building. Positive covenants (unlike restrictive covenants) on freeholds are not effective against successors in title, and this is the reason why flats are usually sold on long leases rather than freehold. It is commonly believed that the reason for this is that flats are often on an upper floor of a building. In fact there is no obstacle to what is known as a 'flying freehold'.

13.3 REGISTERED AND UNREGISTERED LAND

Land may also be classified as:

(a) registered;
(b) unregistered.

Most of England and Wales now consists of areas of 'compulsory registration'. This means that all freeholds and leases with more than 40 years unexpired must be placed on their District Land Register on the next occasion they are transferred, if they are not already registered. When a property is registered, it is identified by a title number and there are three parts to the Register:

(1) The Property Register. With freehold property this usually con-sists simply of the street address and a reference to an attached

plan of the locality, with a red line drawn around the property in question.

(2) The Proprietorship Register. This states the name or names (the maximum is four) of the persons holding legal title to the property. Their title will normally be described as 'Title Absolute', which is state guaranteed title. This means that if the person named is not the owner, the state will compensate any innocent purchaser. Title may also be described as 'Qualified', 'Possessory' or 'Good Leasehold', each of which does not carry the full state guarantee.

(3) The Charges Register. This will incorporate such matters as legal mortgages and restrictive covenants.

Matters known as 'minor interests' may be entered on the Proprietorship and Charges Registers. These are divided into:

(a) notices;
(b) cautions;
(c) inhibitions;
(d) restrictions.

These can deal with such matters as bankruptcy of the person with legal title, the right of a spouse to occupy residential property and equitable mortgages.

The Registers never leave the District Land Registries. The 'deeds' of registered land consist of a document known as the 'Land Certificate', which is a copy of the register inside an impressive cover. If the land is subject to a legal mortgage the 'deeds' will be a 'Charge Certificate', similarly a copy of the register but also with the original mortgage deed. The mortgagee holds this document. Where two or more legal mortgages are registered on the same title, each mortgagee will be given his own Charge Certificate, incorporating the original of his mortgage and showing, in the copy Charges Register, details of his mortgage and all previously registered mortgages.

Conveyancing of registered land is theoretically simple. The purchaser checks the Register of the property to see that the vendor is the registered owner and that no charges or minor interests affect the title, he pays his money to the vendor and then asks the District Land Registry to amend the Register so that he becomes the registered owner. In practice the Register is searched by reference to the copy in the Land or Charge Certificate, or Office Copies can be obtained from the Registry. In either case a date is stamped on the copy and a Priority Search is then made, which is firstly a request of the Registry whether any entry has been made on the Register since the date the copy was made, and secondly the Registry grants a Priority Period of 30 working days, during which time it will not make any entry on the Register without the permission of the applicant, who must then complete his purchase and lodge the necessary documents with the Registry before this Priority Period expires.[1] If the proper procedure is followed, the system protects the purchaser or mortgagee from everything except for overriding interests.[2]

Conveyancing of unregistered land is based upon the concept of the good root of title. A vendor must produce the conveyance or other document evidencing his acquisition of the legal title to the land. If this was less than 15 years previous,[3] he must also produce earlier conveyances until he has established an unbroken chain of title going back in time at least 15 years. The deeds of unregistered land therefore consist of a collection of previous conveyances; prior mortgages and the discharges of them also form part of the chain. Matters such as bankruptcy of the vendor (dealt with as minor interests in the case of registered land) are this time entered on a special register that is kept for unregistered land – the Land Charges Registry, which must therefore be searched by an intending purchaser or mortgagee. The land is not registered, however, and a search is made against the name of the vendor.

Searches of other registers

LOCAL LAND CHARGES

A purchaser or mortgagee will search this register in order to discover matters which would adversely affect title, such as a

---

[1] *See the Land Registration (Official Searches) Rules 1993.*
[2] *See 13.5 below.*
[3] *If he acquired the land otherwise than by conveyance (i.e. he inherited it or was given it) this period increases to 30 years.*

compulsory purchase order. Standard form enquiries may also be made of the local authority, which would reveal matters such as plans to construct new roads in the local vicinity.

COMPANIES REGISTER

Where the vendor or mortgagor is a corporate entity, the register of the company will reveal any fixed charges over its land and floating charges over the whole of the company's undertaking.

13.4 TYPES OF OWNERSHIP OF LAND

The freehold or leasehold estate may be divided into:

(a) the legal title;
(b) the equitable or beneficial interest.

Where the two categories do not exactly coincide, a form of trust will exist whereby the person with the legal title holds it on trust for one or more persons (possibly including himself). For example, A may own the legal title and A and B may own the equitable title. The person with legal title is then called a trustee. The beneficial interest belongs to the person entitled to the proceeds if the property is sold, for example because he paid some or all of the purchase price.

Legal title may be shared by a maximum of four persons who must all be adults. If five or more jointly own land, this will have to be achieved through a trust. There is no limit to the number that may have beneficial interests. Neither is there any age limit. A holder of the legal title, however, must be an adult.

Where the legal title is shared this will take one of two forms:

(a) a joint tenancy;
(b) a tenancy in common.

The key to the difference lies in the 'right of survivorship'. In a joint tenancy of A and B where A dies, B automatically becomes sole owner of the legal title. If they were tenants in common, A's share would pass according to the terms of his Will or to the rules of intestacy.

Any beneficial interest in land can only exist behind a 'trust of land', which means that a purchaser or mortgagee can safely pay his money to two or more owners of the legal title, and persons with a beneficial interest must claim from those vendors of the legal title (if they can). The purchaser will obtain a good title. This is a principle known as 'overreaching' the claims of the beneficial owners.

Where a purchaser takes his title from a sole legal owner, however, the position is more complex. He can still obtain a good title but only if he has no notice (actual or constructive) of the beneficial interest. Constructive notice consists of matters which the purchaser should be aware of, whether or not he is. These matters relating to beneficial interests are of vital interest to a bank accepting a mortgage of land, since the position of legal mortgagees is comparable to that of purchasers. The precise situation differs, at least in terminology, between registered and unregistered land.

13.5 INTERESTS IN REGISTERED LAND

As observed earlier,[4] the system of registered land conveyancing is geared towards the notion that a purchaser of registered land need only ensure that the entries on the Register are satisfactory and follow the correct procedures. Matters became more complicated in 1980. Under section 70 of the Land Registration Act 1925, a purchaser takes the land subject to any overriding interests over it. These overriding interests are the only matter relating to the land which need not (and indeed cannot) be entered on the Register. An obvious example in residential property is some form of tenancy protected under rent legislation. This would not appear on the register and yet a purchaser of mortgagee's title would be subject to it, whether he knew of it or not. Such a tenancy of a property offered for sale or mortgage could substantially reduce its value. In practice, this has not caused many problems, either because vendors have not attempted this type of fraud or perhaps the true position would always be too evident to the purchaser, irrespective of the lack of notice from the register of the property.

Another category of overriding interest is that held by a person

---

[4] In 13.3.

who has a beneficial interest in the property and who is in actual occupation of it. This suddenly became a serious problem for mortgagees with the decision in Williams and Glyn's Bank v Boland.[5] The legal title was in the sole name of Mr B but Mrs B had contributed to the purchase price. Therefore Mr B held the legal title on trust for the benefit of himself and Mrs B, and of course her interest did not appear on the Register. The bank took its legal mortgage from Mr B, who later defaulted and the bank sought to exercise its power of sale. First it needed possession of the house and, as nobody can be evicted in these circumstances without a Court order, the bank went to court for a possession order. Mrs B resisted this on the grounds that she had an overriding interest, based on her equitable interest and actual occupation coexisting at the time the bank took its mortgage from Mr B. The House of Lords agreed, and the bank found itself not only without possession but also without a valid legal mortgage, since a legal mortgage must be on the whole property and Mr B did not own the whole property. It then had an equitable mortgage on Mr B's share.

In City of London Building Society v Flegg,[6] Mr and Mrs M purchased a house with funds supplied by Mrs M's parents (Mr and Mrs F) and by a mortgage lender. All four of them lived in the house. Later, the mortgage loan was re-financed by the plaintiffs, who took a legal mortgage from the Ms and in ignorance of the beneficial interest of the Fs. The Ms held the legal title on trust for themselves and for the Fs. Following default on this loan, the Building Society sought a possession order which the House of Lords held they were entitled to obtain, since the overriding interest of the Fs was overreached by the mortgaging of the property by two trustee legal owners.[7] This overreaching has since been held to take effect even where no monies are advanced at the time the mortgage is taken.[8]

In order to establish an overriding interest, there must have been actual occupation and a beneficial interest in the property at the

[5][1981] AC 487 HL.
[6][1988] AC 54 HL.
[7]The overreaching principle is contained in section 27(1) of the Law of Property Act 1925 and section 17 of the Trustee Act 1925.
[8]State Bank of India v Sood [1997] 1 All ER 169 CA.

time the mortgage was created. Where the mortgage loan funds the purchase of a property, it will normally be the case that the beneficial interest and the bank's mortgage come into existence at the same instant, since the person claiming the beneficial interest cannot claim to have had a beneficial interest under the legal title of the seller. This instant will be the completion of the sale. For instance, in Abbey National Building Society v Cann,[9] a mother and son purchased a property partly with money put up by the mother and partly with funds raised by a mortgage loan from the plaintiff. The legal title to the property was placed in the sole name of the son. On default and the plaintiff seeking possession, the mother claimed an overriding interest. The court found against her, holding that her beneficial interest did not exist at the time the bank's mortgage came into existence.[10] Of course it is also unlikely that the person with the newly created beneficial interest in the property will have been in actual occupation of it before completion.

Accordingly the risk to a bank of its title being damaged by an overriding interest is non-existent when the mortgage is granted by two or more holders of the legal title (unless the bank actually knew of the beneficial interest) and is minimal in the case of house-purchase mortgages.[11] There remains the mortgage or re-mortgage by a sole existing legal titleholder.[12]

13.6 INTERESTS IN UNREGISTERED LAND

A purchaser of unregistered land must ensure that the vendor can show a good root of legal title, and he must search the Land Charges Register against the name of the vendor. For instance, a wife may protect her right of occupation of a matrimonial home which is solely owned by her husband by registering a Class F Charge in respect of the property against her husband's name at the Land

---

[9]*[1991] 1 AC 56 and discussed in 13.8 below.*
[10]*The court found against her also on the grounds that she was not already sufficiently in occupation and that she knew that the mortgage was being created.*
[11]*A beneficial owner can register a caution to protect his interest.*
[12]*Discussed further in 13.8 below.*

Charges Registry.[13] The same registry will reveal details of any other matters affecting the title such as restrictive covenants, easements, bankruptcy orders or mortgages not protected by possession of the title deeds.

Where there are hidden beneficial owners, i.e. persons who have a beneficial interest in the property but do not have a legal title so do not appear on the deeds, there is a similar risk to a purchaser as confronts the purchaser of registered land. The position will once again depend on whether there are two legal owners transferring the property. If there are two or more, the overreaching principles apply in exactly the same way as for registered land. If there is a sole legal owner, the position depends on whether the purchaser has notice (actual or constructive) of the beneficial interest. Actual notice is simple; if the purchaser knows of the interest at the time he makes the transaction, he does not get good title. The purchaser is deemed to have constructive notice of the interest when the legal owner does not occupy the land and the purchaser fails to make enquiry of whoever does occupy it. Where the legal owner does occupy the land, the case of Caunce v Caunce[14] suggests that the purchaser will have no constructive notice of an interest of any other occupant (in this case a wife), unless the situation should raise some suspicion in his mind. In view of the judicial trend over the last decade or so to bolster the protection for spouses who are not legal owners, there must be some doubt as to whether this decision would be followed today.

13.7 THE MEANING OF OCCUPATION

For someone to have an overriding interest in registered land, occupation of the land is essential. In unregistered land, occupation is a considerable factor in deciding whether a purchaser has constructive notice of a beneficial interest. It is worth considering exactly what constitutes occupation. In Kingsnorth Finance Co. Ltd v Tizard,[15] an ex-wife, who had left the matrimonial home but who visited every

---

[13]*Under the terms of the Matrimonial Homes Act 1983.*
[14]*[1969] 1 WLR 286.*
[15]*[1986] 1 WLR 783.*

afternoon and stayed one night in every fortnight, was held to be in occupation.

In Abbey National Building Society v Cann,[16] the person claiming an overriding interest had never lived in the house and was in Holland at the time the mortgagee took its charge. Some personal belongings were moved in to the newly acquired house some 35 minutes before the mortgage was completed. This was considered to be insufficient for actual occupation. In Lloyds Bank v Rosset,[17] a wife was held to be in occupation of a semi-derelict house by her actions of supervising building works on it.

13.8 THE RISKS FOR A MORTGAGEE

Where a bank is offered a mortgage of land there is a danger that some person or persons other than the legal owner may have an overriding interest (if registered land), or the bank will later be deemed to have had constructive notice of a beneficial interest (if unregistered land). If so, the bank will be left with an equitable mortgage of the legal owner's beneficial share of the property (if any).

Registered land

Since occupation is a pre-requisite of an overriding interest, the obvious approach is to discover who is in occupation and ask each if he has a beneficial interest, the Land Registration Act lays down that if enquiry is made of a person with an overriding interest and he fails to disclose it then the mortgagee gets good title.[18]

Asking the legal owner whether others have an overriding interest does not provide any protection against claims from those others. The danger is that the bank will not discover some person who occupies, especially where the broadest interpretation of that word is used and a visit to the property would not reveal that person's existence. So far the main concern has centred on spouses (usually

[16]*[1991] 1 AC 56 HL.*
[17]*[1991] 1 AC 107 HL.*
[18]*Section 70(1)(g).*

wives), but any person who satisfies the criteria will have an overriding interest. Where the property is occupied by non-legal owners the usual practice is to have them sign a deed of postponement. This procedure is not effective in the case of tenants, however, as their overriding interest cannot be postponed behind the mortgagee's interests, as the tenants' rights under the Rent Act 1977 cannot be derogated.[19] There is no minimum age limit for a person to hold a beneficial interest, but fortunately for lenders it appears that a child cannot have an overriding interest.[20]

Abbey National Building Society v Cann reassured lenders in a number of ways.[21] The son told the plaintiff he intended to live alone in the house. In fact he intended to live there with his mother, and she acquired a beneficial interest in the new house since first, she had a beneficial share in the previous house and second, had agreed to vacate the previous house on condition that she was allowed to live in the new one. The mother's claim to have an overriding interest in priority to the plaintiff's mortgage failed for three reasons. First, her beneficial interest did not come into existence until the moment of completion of the mortgage, which was held to be contemporaneous with the completion of the purchase. Since the plaintiff had advanced its mortgage monies to the son's solicitor a few days prior to completion, it had acquired an equitable charge before, and therefore in priority to, the mother's beneficial interest. Second, she was not considered to be in actual occupation at the time the mortgage was completed. An argument that the relevant time to consider occupation was the time of registering the mortgage (always some time after purchase), was dismissed. Third, she knew that her son had insufficient funds to purchase the house without a mortgage loan, and she was therefore taken to have impliedly authorised him to mortgage the house to the plaintiff, even though she knew nothing of that mortgage.

There is clearly an express authorisation when there is actual knowledge of the mortgage.[22] There was also deemed to be an

[19]*Woolwich Building Society v Dickman [1996] 3 All ER 204 CA.*
[20]*Hypo-Mortgage Services Ltd v Robinson (1977) The Times, 2nd Jan, CA.*
[21]*See 13.5 above.*
[22]*Bristol and West Building Society v Henning [1985] 1 WLR 778.*

implied consent to the mortgage where the holder of a beneficial interest in a property actually consented to the original mortgage and later the property was re-mortgaged to a new lender by the registered owner without the other's knowledge or consent. If the debt on the new mortgage is greater than that on the original, however, the other's liability is limited to the amount that had been owed on the original mortgage debt.[23]

Unregistered land

Occupation is again important and whilst the bank may acquire good title where a person with a beneficial interest occupies the property, the vagaries of the suspicious circumstances test are such that it is clearly good policy to apply the same procedure as that followed in the case of registered land.

The foolproof approach for both types of land would be to take the mortgage from two legal owners, and therefore to enjoy the protection of the overreaching principle. Where the land is owned by a sole legal owner, the bank could require him to convey to a fellow trustee as joint tenants. Even this approach may not suffice if the bank knows of the beneficial interest, as the overreaching principle requires good faith on the part of the mortgagee. Similarly, it would not assist where the mortgage monies did not accrue to both trustee legal owners but only to one of them.

13.9 THE MATRIMONIAL HOMES ACT 1983

Parliament has recognised the social problem of one spouse (usually the husband), who owns the matrimonial home as sole legal owner, secretly selling to an innocent third party and disappearing with the proceeds. In this situation, the non-owning spouse now has a right to occupy the matrimonial home (whether or not he or she does in fact occupy it), but this right must be registered to have any effect on a purchaser or mortgagee.[24] Only spouses have this right,

---

[23]*Equity and Law Home Loans Ltd v Prestidge [1992] 1 WLR 137 CA.*
[24]*See 13.6 above.*

which does not extend to non-married partners. The right to occupy is not dependent on the spouse having any beneficial interest in the property.

13.10 TYPES OF MORTGAGE OVER LAND

The two types are:

(1) Legal.
(2) Equitable.

Legal mortgage

The Law of Property Act 1925 permits two alternative methods of creating a legal mortgage over land. First, it may be by demise, which means by granting a long lease to the mortgagee. Second, it may be a charge by deed expressed to be by way of legal mortgage. The latter is universal but the legal consequences are similar whichever is used. The latter may be preferable in the case of mortgages of leasehold interests. The legal mortgage must be by deed and the mortgagor's signature must be witnessed. Section 1 of the Law of Property (Miscellaneous Provisions) Act 1989 provides that a document is a deed if it is clearly intended to be a deed. Seals are no longer necessary.[25]

Equitable mortgage

Common law requires a minimum only of an intention by the owner to grant a security right in return for value given, such as a loan. In the case of land, section 2 of the Law of Property (Miscellaneous Provisions) Act 1989 requires any contract for the future disposition of an interest in land to be in writing, signed by both parties, and to incorporate all the terms expressly agreed by the parties. An equitable mortgage over a legal interest in land constitutes an agreement to give a legal mortgage and will be within section 2, thus a

---

[25]*See 16.3 below for the means by which companies execute documents.*

mere deposit of the title deeds to land will not create a valid charge.[26] The mortgagee must sign the mortgage, as well as the mortgagor.

In practice, banks now require the title deeds to be deposited, a memorandum of deposit to be signed by the mortgagor and by the bank, and inclusion of all agreed terms in the memorandum. Note that the section does not apply to a legal mortgage, since this constitutes an actual disposition of an interest in land, not a contract to do so.[27]

In the case of registered land, the equitable mortgage cannot be registered as such but a notice or caution can be put on the register.[28] This is good protection against a subsequent legal mortgage. With unregistered land, the mortgage only has to be registered as a Land Charge if the title deeds are not held.

If the mortgage (legal or equitable) is to secure a granting of credit which is regulated by the Consumer Credit Act 1974, a special procedure must be followed which includes a 'cooling-off' period, failing which the charge will be void.[29]

The Mortgage Code (second edition, 1998), applies to a bank dealing with a 'personal customer' who is considering taking out a mortgage loan (other than to secure an overdraft) that is secured on a home that the customer will own and occupy. It does not apply to loans regulated by the Consumer Credit Act. The lender can advise the customer at any of three levels and must inform the customer at the outset which it is offering. An 'advice and recommendation' must take account of the customer's particular requirements and on prevailing market conditions and written reasons for the recommendations must be given. 'Information on the different types of mortgage product' is restricted to the products offered by that lender, and 'information on a single mortgage product only' can be given where the lender only offers one product or the customer has already made up his mind.

[26]*United Bank of Kuwait v Sahib [1996] 3 WLR 372 CA.*
[27]*Note that section 40 of the Law of Property Act 1925 is now repealed.*
[28]*As mere deposit of the title deeds is no longer effective, a Notice of Deposit of the Land Certificate can no longer be registered (nor can Notice of Intended Deposit), Land Registration Rules 1995.*
[29]*See 3.6 above.*

In all cases the lender must provide certain information, including an explanation of the main repayment methods and in the case of interest-only mortgages the repayment vehicles which may be used, a description of the types of interest rates available, a description of fees payable, an illustration of future potential repayments at the end of any discounted fixed or discounted period, whether any insurance must be arranged and if so whether it must be arranged by the lender, and explanations of the effects of early repayment of the loan, early surrender of an insurance policy, and long-term sickness or relationship breakdown.

Registration and priority – registered land

A priority search of a title at HM Land Registry will give the searcher 30 working days during which nobody else can register an entry against that title. Where two or more mortgages have been granted over the same piece of registered land, their priority ranks in order of registration on the Charges Register for the title to that land.

However, a subsequent mortgagee can only be fully registered with the consent of every prior mortgagee, since the Land Registry will not register the subsequent charge unless the existing Charge Certificates are all returned to the Land Registry for updating. This will give a prior, registered mortgagee the option to refuse to allow registration of the later charge or to agree the terms of a suitable priority document. This latter option will be important if the prior mortgagee wishes to continue lending on the security of his mortgage.

If a second mortgagee of registered land does not wish to, or cannot, obtain the consent of a prior mortgagee for registration of the later charge, the second mortgagee can protect his security by registering a caution. This will give only limited protection but will at least give notice of his interest as mortgagee. His mortgage, being equitable (even if it is created by deed and expressed to be a legal mortgage), will rank after all legal, registered mortgages and should rank against other equitable mortgages in order of registration, whether they have been registered by a caution or notice.

Registration and priority – unregistered land

A search against the titleholder's name at the Land Charges Registry will again produce a 30 working-day period during which nobody except the searcher can register an entry against the name of the person searched against.

The first mortgagee in time, whether his mortgage is legal or equitable, is entitled to hold the title deeds to the property and, if he does so, he need not register his mortgage at the Land Charges Registry – in fact, he will not be able to register. A second mortgagee is deemed to have constructive notice of the first charge by virtue of the mortgagor not being able to produce the title deeds.

A mortgage over unregistered land, unless protected by deposit of deeds, will be void against subsequent mortgages if it is not registered at the Land Charges Registry.[30] A legal charge can be registered as a Class C(i) puisne mortgage, and an equitable charge as a Class C(iii) general equitable charge.

By virtue of section 97 Law of Property Act 1925, mortgages over unregistered land rank in order of date of registration at the Land Charges Registry, regardless of whether they are legal or equitable mortgages, save only that the first mortgagee in time who holds the title deeds will rank ahead of all subsequently created mortgages.

If the first mortgagee does not take the title deeds, he must register his security as a *puisne* charge in order that he will be protected by registration constituting notice to subsequent mortgagees.[31] A subsequent mortgagee taking possession of the title deeds should give notice to the first mortgagee but he cannot register his subsequent charge at the Land Charges Registry. If the first mortgagee holds the title deeds but subsequently releases them and they are deposited with another mortgagee who is ignorant of the first mortgage (and innocent of any fraud on the first mortgagee), the first mortgagee may lose his priority.[32]

Any unregistered charges will rank after all registered charges and will be void against a purchaser for value. However, they will

---

[30] *Section 4(5) of the Land Charges Act 1972.*
[31] *Section 198 of the Law of Property Act 1925.*
[32] *Agra Bank Ltd v Barry (1874) LR 7 HL 135.*

be valid against the mortgagor who will therefore have to account for the sale proceeds to unregistered mortgagees.

13.11 STANDARD BANK MORTGAGE TERMS

These include:

(a) exclusions of sections 93 and 103 of the Law of Property Act 1925, permitting the bank to consolidate two or more mortgages it holds from the same customer and removing the waiting periods following default;

(b) exclusion of the mortgagor's power to grant leases or sub-leases. Any such lease will therefore be invalid. This provision is not totally effective in the case of agricultural property;

(c) a promise by the mortgagor to keep the property in good repair and insured. Banks very sensibly take other steps to verify that the property is insured, e.g. by demanding receipts;

(d) a continuing security clause to cover further advances and to protect against the effects of *Clayton's case*. Even so, if notice of second mortgage is received the bank will not enjoy first priority for further lending. Furthermore, in Deeley v Lloyds Bank,[33] a current account secured by a first mortgage was not ruled off when notice of second mortgage was received, and the bank lost priority due to the effect of *Clayton's case*, even though there was no real new lending;

(e) a power to grant leases at a premium. This may be a more useful remedy than a simple sale in a case such as a mortgage of a developer's newly constructed freehold block of flats.

The equitable mortgage memorandum of deposit

This will incorporate:

(a) a continuing security clause;

(b) a promise by the mortgagor to grant a legal mortgage to the bank if requested to do so. If the mortgagor agrees to such a request the bank will acquire a power of sale. If he will not agree, the

[33] *[1912] AC 756 HL.*

bank may seek an order for specific performance from the court, which should be granted as this relates to a contract for the conveyance of an interest in land;[34]

(c) the bank may be granted an irrevocable power of attorney by the mortgagor. In this event, as the bank holds the title deeds, it will enjoy automatic power of sale, assuming the equitable mortgage itself was executed as a deed.[35]

13.12 REALISING THE MORTGAGE

A legal mortgagee has the following options:

(a) to exercise his power of sale;
(b) to appoint a Receiver;
(c) to foreclose;
(d) to enter into possession of the property;
(e) to sue on the mortgagor's covenant to repay the debt.

13.13 THE MORTGAGEE'S POWER OF SALE

A sale frequently permits a bank to obtain a large sum which can repay the customer's debt, and it is therefore the most popular remedy. Once the mortgagor is in default, a mortgage by deed carries a statutory power of sale under section 101 of the Law of Property Act 1925. This will include all legal mortgages, as well as equitable mortgages executed under seal or in accordance with section 1 of the Law of Property (Miscellaneous Provisions) Act 1989. The property may be sold whole or in parts. For commercial reasons, the bank will invariably wish to offer the property for sale without the customer in occupation and, unless the latter has abandoned the property, a court order should be obtained in case an offence under the Protection from Eviction Act 1977 is committed by the bank.

---

[34]*Because of this, the memorandum of deposit must be signed by both the mortgagor and the mortgagee, section 2 Law of Property (Miscellaneous Provisions) Act 1989.*
[35]*Re White Rose Cottage [1965] Ch 940CA. Powers of attorney are explained in 2.2 above.*

An order is always necessary in the case of residential property, unless it has been abandoned. The court has power to adjourn the proceedings or to suspend the order for possession if it appears likely that the mortgagor can pay off the arrears within a reasonable period[36] and this can extend to the whole of the remaining term.[37] In the case of an instalment mortgage, this means that the mortgagor must pay the normal instalments and a fixed proportion of the arrears each month until the arrears are repaid.[38] If he misses a payment, the order will automatically become effective without the need for a further application to court. Where the mortgage is to secure an overdraft with no repayment by instalment, the court may only suspend its order if it is likely that the mortgagor can repay the whole debt. Where the order is not suspended, it will usually grant possession 28 days hence.

The court may agree to grant the mortgagor time to sell the property if thereby a full repayment can be achieved within a reasonable time.[39] The court may also be willing to order a sale on the mortgagor's application (and against the mortgagee's wishes) where he is otherwise unable to sell because of negative equity.[40] In deciding whether or not to order a sale, the court can take into account non-financial matters.[41]

A spouse who has registered a right to occupy under the Matrimonial Homes Act will not be able to resist possession unless the registration was in place before the bank took its charge.

The Mortgage Code (second edition, 1998) applies to a bank dealing with a 'personal customer' who took out a mortgage loan (other than to secure an overdraft) that is secured on a home that the customer owns and occupies. It does not apply to loans regulated by the Consumer Credit Act. It provides that lenders will consider

---

[36]Section 36 of the Administration of Justice Act 1970.
[37]Cheltenham and Gloucester Building Society v Norgan [1996] 1 WLR 343 CA which also offers guidance on the exercise of the court's discretion.
[38]A default clause (which renders the entire debt immediately repayable when an instalment is missed) is disregarded.
[39]Target Home Loans v Clothier [1994] 1 All ER 439.
[40]Palk v Mortgage Services Funding [1993] Ch 330 CA.
[41]Polonski v Lloyds Bank Mortgages (1997) The Times, 6th May.

cases of mortgage arrears sympathetically and positively and will follow the general principles of the 'Statement of Practice on Handling Arrears and Possessions' issued by the Council of Mortgage Lenders, including developing a plan for dealing with the arrears which is consistent with both the lender's interests and those of the customer. It states that possession of the property will only be sought as a last resort when attempts to reach alternative arrangements with the customer have been unsuccessful.

Mortgagee's duty to obtain a proper price

In strictly commercial terms, the mortgagee will not have an interest in obtaining a price for the property that is any higher than the debt owed to him. The law is therefore careful to protect the interest of the mortgagor, and imposes a duty on the mortgagee to act in good faith and to take reasonable care to sell at a proper price.[42] He is not, however, obliged to delay a sale in the expectation of a rising market. It has recently been suggested that he may sell the property to himself.[43] In Bishop v Bonham,[44] it was expressly agreed in a mortgage of shares that the mortgagee had wide powers of sale and would not be liable for any loss arising from a sale. The court held this did not exclude the mortgagee's duty to take reasonable care to obtain a proper price. Since Standard Chartered Bank v Walker,[45] it cannot be regarded as safe simply to offer the property at auction having no regard to the location and advertising of the auction, or to the price obtained. The preferred practice is now to instruct professional agents to value the property and to sell at or near the valuation price. If the courts do regard the price to be improper, the mortgagee is still liable but he has a right to pursue a claim by way of indemnity against the valuer.

The law relating to claims against valuers has recently been given a thorough airing by a substantial number of cases flowing from

[42]*Cuckmere Brick Co. Ltd v Mutual Finance Ltd [1971] Ch 949 and Downsview Nominees Ltd v First City Corpn Ltd [1993] AC 295 PC.*
[43]*Palk v Mortgage Services Funding, see n39.*
[44]*[1988] 1 WLR 742 CA.*
[45]*[1982] 1 WLR 1410 CA.*

property price deflation in the early 1990s. This caused many secured properties to be sold at less than the value of the loan secured on them and lenders could sometimes establish that the valuer had been negligent in placing an over optimistic value on the property. The cornerstone decision is now that of the House of Lords in South Australia Asset Management v York Montague.[46] It holds that where the valuer was negligent, the lender's claim against him in damages will normally amount to a figure which is the *lesser* of (i) the lender's total loss and (ii) the amount of the overvaluation plus interest. For example, if a property is valued at £100,000 (at a time when its true value is £80,000) and the lender lends £90,000 on it and it realises £75,000 net of costs on a forced sale one year later, the lender's total loss will be £15,000. The amount of the overvaluation will be £20,000, to which figure a year's interest would be added. Thus in this example, the damages payable would be £15,000 (taking the lesser of the two figures).

The courts are prepared to find contributory negligence on the part of a lender who should have suspected that the valuation was too high or who lent on a very high ratio to the valuation figure.[47]

Lenders have also made claims against solicitors who acted in the transaction, for instance on the grounds that the solicitor (acting for both mortgagor and mortgagee) knew about a mortgagor's poor past borrowing record and failed to inform the lender of this before the mortgage was taken. On these facts it was held that the solicitors were not under a duty to inform the lender if no specific instructions had been issued for them to do so.[48]

Equity protects a guarantor as well as the mortgagor. This was established in Standard Chartered Bank v Walker[49] but the creditor can choose the timing of the sale. In China and South Sea Bank v Tan,[50] F Ltd borrowed from the plaintiff bank, offering shares in

---

[46][1997] AC 191 HL.

[47]Platform Home Loans v Oyston Shipways (1998) The Times, 15th January, CA.

[48]National Home Loans Corporation v Giffen Couch and Archer [1998] 1 WLR 207 CA.

[49]See n45 above.

[50][1990] 1 AC 536 PC.

another company as security, and a guarantee was also taken from T. The shares were at one time adequate security but they eventually became worthless, and a claim was made against T for the HK$33 million then owing. T argued that the bank owed him a duty to exercise care in timing its sale of the shares. This was rejected. A creditor may choose the timing of its sale, but when he does sell he must take care to obtain the best price. There are other duties, however, such as a duty to perfect the direct security (e.g. by registering it properly), and not to surrender it. These duties, and the extent to which they may be lessened by agreement between the parties, are discussed in chapter 12.

In Parker-Tweedale v Dunbar Bank[51] the matrimonial home of Mr and Mrs P was in Mrs P's sole name but Mr P had a beneficial interest. On default, D Bank, with Mrs P's consent, exercised their power of sale. Mr P objected that the sale price was too low. It was held that, as mere beneficiary under the trust for sale of the house, he had no grounds to object to the sale price, but only had a claim against Mrs P for breach of trust.

Applying the proceeds of sale

Assuming the mortgagee has a first charge, the order is:

(a) proper expenses of the sale;
(b) his claim including costs;
(c) a second mortgagee (if one exists), or otherwise to the mortgagor, unless he is bankrupt, in which case to the trustee in bankruptcy.

If there are insufficient funds to repay junior mortgagees, their mortgages are discharged by the sale in any case.

In the unlikely event of a sale by a junior mortgagee, the senior mortgagee must be repaid first. If there is insufficient to repay that senior mortgagee, the purchaser acquires the property encumbered by that mortgage.

[51][1991] Ch 12 CA.

13.14 OTHER REMEDIES OF THE MORTGAGEE

Appoint a receiver

Under the terms of a standard mortgage, a receiver may be appointed when the debt has become due, which will be when demand is made. The appointment must be in writing and is effective from the moment the receiver accepts his appointment. The receiver is the agent of the mortgagor[52] and the mortgagee is therefore not responsible for his acts or omissions. However, in Standard Chartered Bank v Walker[53] the bank was liable for the receiver's negligence, as it had been directing him. It is common practice in any event for the receiver, when he is appointed, to seek an indemnity for any liability in negligence from the mortgagee.

The receiver is most commonly appointed when the mortgaged property is income-producing, such as the freehold of a block of flats which is let at market rents. The proceeds must then be applied according to section 109(8) of the Law of Property Act:

(1) Payment of certain expenses of the property.
(2) Paying prior mortgagees (if any).
(3) Paying his commission, insurance premiums and proper repairs.
(4) Paying interest to the mortgagee.
(5) Paying principal to the mortgagee.

Foreclosure

In its true legal meaning this term refers to a process of applying for a court order of foreclosure, the effect of which is to render the mortgagee the owner of the mortgaged property, and to discharge the debt irrespective of the value of the property and the size of the debt. This remedy is nowadays rarely obtained since the court would order a sale instead; the term has become used to describe the process of obtaining possession and exercising power of sale.

---

[52]*Law of Property Act 1925 section 109(2).*
[53]*[1982] 1 WLR 1410 CA.*

Entering into possession

As discussed in 13.13 above, this process frequently precedes the exercising of the mortgagee's power of sale. In fact, most mortgagors would be surprised to learn that any legal mortgagee has the right to go into possession of the mortgaged property even if there is no default. The original legal concept of a mortgage being a transfer of the mortgaged property to the mortgagee means that it is the mortgagee, not the mortgagor, who is primarily entitled to possession. The mortgage will provide for the mortgagor to be entitled to possession while he complies with the terms of the mortgage. Taking possession by the mortgagee is, therefore, no more than the assertion of his common law right. In practice, possession may take place where the mortgagee wishes to let the property, and the acceptance by the mortgagee of rent will constitute taking possession. The mortgagee will be liable to the mortgagor for any damage, or for devaluing the property (e.g. by letting to a Rent Act tenant), or for rent received, or for rent which should have been received. He is allowed, however, to keep the property empty pending a sale without being liable for rent.[54]

A mortgagee in possession of empty property will be liable to third parties who go onto the property, or who own land adjacent to it, and who have a claim under the Occupiers Liability Act 1957 or in private nuisance. For these reasons, the mortgagee will prefer to appoint a receiver to act on his behalf, but as the agent of the mortgagor, thus avoiding being deemed at law to have taken possession himself.

A mortgage will usually provide that the mortgagor cannot grant leases. The mortgagee will thus be entitled to possession as against a tenant whose lease was not agreed by the mortgagee, unless the lease was granted before the mortgage was executed.

Sueing on the covenant to repay

The mortgagee will, of course, be entitled to sue the borrower for repayment under the loan agreement which is secured by the mort-

---

[54]*Shepard v Jones (1882) 21 ChD 469.*

gage. However, if the mortgage contains a covenant to repay, the mortgagee will have the additional right to sue the mortgagor for repayment under the terms of the mortgage. Where the mortgage secures lending to someone other than the mortgagor, the covenant to repay will, in effect, be a guarantee and will give the mortgagee the right to sue two parties (the borrower and the mortgagor) for repayment.

If the mortgage is a deed, the mortgagee will be entitled to sue on the covenant to repay for up to 12 years after demand has been made under the mortgage, and this period may start running some time after demand has been made under the loan agreement. An action for repayment under the loan agreement must usually be commenced within six years of demand, since the loan agreement will usually be under hand, not executed as a deed.

In Bank of Baroda v Dhillon,[55] the bank had taken a legal mortgage over the matrimonial home, the legal title to which was in the husband's sole name. The wife successfully claimed an overriding interest in the property. The bank claimed on the basis of its charge which was still valid against the husband's share of the property and the court granted an order for sale under section 30 of the Law of Property Act 1925.[56] There was a bankruptcy order against the husband but as the bank was claiming under its charge, it was paid first from the share of the proceeds which arose from his share in the property. In Re Zanfarid, BCCI v Zanfarid,[57] Mr and Mrs Z had given the bank a charge over their home to secure a loan to a company with which Mr Z was associated. Mrs Z's liability on the charge was in doubt due to the effect of the Barclays Bank v O'Brien case.[58] The bank surrendered its charge over the property and petitioned for Mr Z's bankruptcy. It was then open to the trustee in bankruptcy to seek a sale order of the house. The proceeds relating to the husband's share in the house would then be paid to the

---

[55]*(1997) The Times, 4th Nov, CA.*
[56]*Section 30 was repealed by the Trusts of Land and Appointment of Trustees Act 1996, under which applications are now made.*
[57]*[1996] 1 WLR 1420.*
[58]*See Chapter 11.*

husband's creditors generally but in this case there were no significant creditors apart from the bank.

Remedies of an equitable mortgagee

SALE

A power of sale will only be available to an equitable mortgagee 'under seal'. This requires both that the equitable mortgage is executed as a deed and that an accompanying deed such as an irrevocable power of attorney is also executed. Otherwise an application must be made for a court order.[59]

POSSESSION

An equitable mortgagee has no inherent right to possession of the mortgaged property but may apply to the court for possession.

SPECIFIC PERFORMANCE OF THE AGREEMENT TO GRANT A LEGAL MORTGAGE

The memorandum of deposit usually contains a promise by the mortgagor to grant a legal mortgage over the property if asked by the mortgagee. Specific performance of this promise is available from the court as it relates to land.[60] Once obtained, the mortgagee has all the rights enjoyed by a legal mortgagee.

RECEIVER

The equitable mortgagee has no right to appoint a receiver unless the mortgage is under seal and specifically grants this right. Otherwise the court may grant an order to appoint a receiver.

---

[59]*Section 91 of the Law of Property Act 1925.*
[60]*This is the effective result of section 90(1) of the Law of Property Act 1925.*

FORECLOSURE

This right is in theory available to any equitable mortgagee who has the right to demand a legal mortgage but, as explained above, this remedy is, to all practical purposes, defunct.

SUEING ON THE COVENANT TO REPAY

The position is the same as for a legal mortgage. The limitation period would be six years if the mortgage was not executed as a deed.

Where the mortgage (legal or equitable) secures the grant of credit which is regulated by the Consumer Credit Act, a court order under that Act must be obtained before any enforcement takes place.[61]

13.15 MORTGAGES OF LEASEHOLD PROPERTY

It will frequently be commercially attractive to lend against the value of leasehold property, as this may have a very high resale value. Clearly the value is likely to diminish over time as the lease shortens but this will not be a concern with long leases, and can in any case be taken into account when deciding the extent of the loan. There are several other matters, however, which are peculiar to mortgages of leaseholds.

(1) There is a possibility that the lessor may forfeit the lease, with the result that the lease vanishes and renders worthless any charge on it. Forfeiture may result from failure to pay rent or from persistent breaches of covenants in the lease. The law requires the lessor to follow a lengthy procedure in order to obtain forfeiture, and the court has power to grant relief against forfeiture, which it will give on any reasonable application by the lessee, but the mortgagee of the lease will not necessarily hear of the forfeiture proceedings until it is too late. The lessee would not normally sit idly by while a valuable lease is forfeited but he may not act if it is overmortgaged and he has no equity

---

[61] *Section 126 of the Consumer Credit Act 1974.*

in it. If the mortgagee applies for relief from forfeiture, the court will commonly require him to rectify or pay the mortgagor's breach and to guarantee against future breaches, or take over the lease in the mortgagee's name as tenant. Some leases contain a clause which provides for automatic forfeiture in the event of the lessee's bankruptcy. Such a lease is obviously not suitable security for a mortgagee. In such a case the lessor would have to be approached to execute a Deed of Variation to the lease, in order to remove the clause.

(2) The lease may contain some restriction (absolute or conditional on the lessor's consent) on mortgaging or assigning the lease. If there is a restriction on mortgaging, a bank can decline to accept the lease as security unless the lease is varied or the lessor's consent obtained. In the case of a restriction on assigning, a mortgage will be effective if the charge by way of legal mortgage is used, as opposed to the charge by demise. A problem may later arise if the mortgagee wishes to exercise his power of sale, which will require an assignment of the lease to a purchaser. Where the restriction is conditional, the lessor's consent may not be unreasonably refused.[62] Where the restriction is absolute, the mortgagee would be well advised to have the lease varied before accepting it as security.

(3) The lease will commonly contain repair covenants, to deal with repair and maintenance of the building and contributions to the costs of these by the lessees. The lease may also contain easements to permit passage of services such as water, gas, drainage etc. through parts of the building demised to other lessees. These provisions are notoriously complex to draft, and care must be taken in each case to tailor them to the precise design of the building in question. It is false economy to avoid the expense of having a lawyer scrutinise the covenants and easements in the lease. Even when this precaution is taken, it can happen that a matter has been overlooked and a purchaser refuses to buy the lease as it stands, and the lease is therefore heavily devalued unless it can be varied. If an independent lawyer was employed

---

[62]*Section 89(1) of the Law of Property Act 1925.*

to examine the lease, an action should lie against him in these circumstances.

13.16 DISCHARGE OF A MORTGAGE

This is usually by redemption, i.e. the mortgagor repays the full debt. Any provision in the mortgage which prevents redemption will be void,[63] unless the mortgagor is a company granting a debenture. The mortgagee may refuse to release its charge if the loan has been repaid but contingent liabilities are outstanding which may give rise to a debt at a later date, e.g. liability under a guarantee.[64]

Registered land

Discharge of a legal mortgage is by Form DF1, signed by the mortgagee and sent to the District Land Registry with the Charge Certificate. The Registry delete the entry on the Charges Register and return the Land Certificate to the mortgagor, unless there are other legal mortgages outstanding.

Discharge of an equitable mortgage will involve notice to the Land Registry by the mortgagee that any Notice or Caution should be deleted. The mortgagee will return the Land Certificate to the mortgagor and cancel any Memorandum of Deposit or Deed (if 'under seal').

Unregistered land

Discharge of a legal mortgage is by signed receipt, usually on the back of the mortgage deed itself. This receipt now forms part of the title deeds and must be preserved with them. The title deeds are returned to the mortgagor unless notice of second mortgage has been received. There is no duty to search for second mortgages[65] but it is good practice to do so in case an earlier notice has been misfiled.

---

[63]*As a clog on the equity of redemption.*
[64]*Re Rudd & Son Ltd [1986] BCC 98, 955.*
[65]*Law of Property Amendment Act 1926, section 7 and Schedule.*

Any registered land charge should be vacated by notice to the Land Charges Registry.

Discharge of an equitable mortgage involves return of the title deeds (subject to notice of second mortgage), and cancellation of the memorandum of deposit and any deed. Any land charge should be vacated.

13.17 RISKS FOR A LENDER

To summarise:

(a) some defect in the mortgagor's title, which may not be clear from search of the Land Register or Land Charges Register and Local Land Charges Register. This may be an overriding interest accruing to another in the case of registered land, or a beneficial interest in the case of unregistered land;

(b) a forged signature on the mortgage deed. The charge will then be void. If there are two co-owners and the signature of one is forged, the mortgagee has an equitable mortgage over the share of the property beneficially owned by the genuine signatory;[66]

(c) the various pitfalls which present themselves in the case of mortgages of leaseholds (discussed in 13.15 above);

(d) a claim of undue influence or *non est factum* by one of the mortgagors (see chapter 11).

[66]*First National Securities Ltd v Hegarty [1984] 3 WLR 769.*

14 Shares as security

14.1 INTRODUCTION

Types of stocks and shares

This book is concerned primarily with two types:

(a) registered shares in companies registered under the Companies Acts, whether listed on the Stock Exchange or not;
(b) British Government Stocks, e.g. 'gilts'.

Securities may also be offered in the form of debenture stock issued by companies, bearer shares, shares issued by foreign companies, certificates of deposit issued by banks, commercial paper and Euronotes and Eurobonds issued by companies, savings certificates and bonds issued by the UK or foreign governments, to name only some of the possibilities. To a large extent the principles that follow will apply irrespective of the type of security, bearing in mind (i) that title to a bearer instrument will be transferred by mere delivery, (ii) title to negotiable securities can be perfected when title to non-negotiable securities would not be, and (iii) conflict of laws issues arise when shares in a foreign company are mortgaged.

Basis of lending

Any quoted security may be easily valued. However, this value is likely to be far more volatile than in the case of life policies and land. Valuation of unquoted shares is basically an exercise in balance sheet interpretation, with strong reference to the value of overall control of a company. Attention also needs to be paid to the possibility of an impediment to transfer of an unquoted company's shares; this may be found in the company's Articles of Association.

14.2 TYPES OF MORTGAGE

The mortgage may be:

(a) a legal mortgage; or
(b) an equitable mortgage.

Legal mortgage

This is effected by transferring title to the security from customer to the bank, in much the same way as if the bank had purchased it. The bank mortgagee thus becomes the registered holder of shares which are mortgaged to it. Assuming the mortgage is of company shares, the bank will take from the customer:

(a) the Share Certificate;
(b) a signed and completed share transfer form.

The transfer will have to be stamped but Stamp Duty is applied at a flat rate of 50 pence when the transfer is by way of mortgage. The two documents are sent to the Registrar of the Company concerned, who will issue and send to the mortgagee a Share Certificate in his name. For the sake of convenience, most banks maintain nominee companies for the purpose of holding shares that have been transferred by way of legal mortgage.

The above documents are sufficient to create a valid legal mortgage and there is no requirement for any further mortgage form, nor for any documents to be executed as deeds. However, it is invariably bank practice to take a memorandum of deposit from the customer incorporating various protective clauses and confirming that the shares are transferred by way of security rather than sale.

Equitable mortgage

In law this requires a minimum only of an intention for the bank to assume an equitable interest in the shares, in return for some valuable consideration provided to the customer. Unless clearly deposited by way of safe custody, the mere deposit of a Share Certificate will create an equitable mortgage over the shares.[1] In practice, the bank will require deposit of the Share Certificate and a signed memorandum of deposit in order to clarify the terms of the mortgage (see 14.3). A transfer form signed by the customer but otherwise left blank is often taken and whilst in this case legal title to the shares remains with the mortgagor until the form is completed and submitted for transfer, for purposes of determining priority over other equitable interests, the relevant time is when the mortgagee advances funds (see 14.5).

14.3 THE MEMORANDUM OF DEPOSIT

This will incorporate (among other terms):

(a) a continuing security clause to cover further advances and to exclude *Clayton's case*;
(b) a clause excluding the waiting periods after default, which would otherwise apply under section 103 of the Law of Property Act 1925;
(c) a statement that dividends from the shares will form part of the security;
(d) a statement that the bank holds the shares as security. Otherwise, it might be argued in the case of an equitable mortgage that the customer had merely deposited the shares under safe deposit arrangements, or in the case of a legal mortgage that the bank had purchased the shares;
(e) in an equitable mortgage, the customer agrees to execute any transfer which the bank requests him to complete.

14.4 REALISING THE MORTGAGE

Legal mortgages

Once the customer is in default, the bank has a power of sale of the shares, which it can easily exercise since the shares are registered

[1] Harrold v Plenty [1901] 2 Ch 314.

in its name. See 13.12 for a discussion of the mortgagee's duty to take reasonable care to obtain a proper price.

Equitable mortgages

A court order would be required for the bank to sell the shares. However, the bank normally holds a blank, signed transfer form which it may complete and thereby effect a sale. Alternatively, a sale will be possible if the equitable mortgage is under seal and the bank holds irrevocable power of attorney granted by the customer.[2] Otherwise the bank can seek to enforce the clause in the memorandum of deposit by which the mortgagor promises to grant a legal mortgage if so requested.

14.5 RISKS FOR THE LENDER

Legal mortgages

Shares in a private limited company may be difficult to transfer or to sell at a satisfactory price. The company's Articles of Association may prohibit registration of a transfer of shares save in the directors' absolute discretion. Alternatively, the Articles may require a selling shareholder to offer his shares to existing members of the company.

There is no system of registering equitable or beneficial interests in shares[3], and therefore any such interest will only bind a legal mortgagee if he has notice of it. Such notice must be actual or constructive, in the sense that it is clear from the situation that a beneficial interest may exist. In other words, when a customer presents a genuine share certificate in his name, this proves that he holds the legal title to the shares. It is quite possible that he holds the legal title as trustee, so that some other person has a beneficial interest. However, it is only if the bank knows or ought to surmise from the situation that this is a nominee holding (and knows this at the time it takes its legal mortgage), that its title is defective.

[2] *Powers of attorney are explained in 2.2 above.*
[3] *A notice of trust in respect of a shareholding cannot be entered on the company's register, Companies Act 1985, section 360.*

There is, however, a risk from a forged transfer document, and it will not assist if the shares have since been registered in the bank's name or even if the shares have been sold. In Sheffield Corporation v Barclay,[4] a genuine but stolen share certificate was presented to the bank with a forged transfer document. The bank sent these in for registration and obtained a share certificate in its own name. Later the shares were sold by the bank to an innocent purchaser. When the original owner realised his loss, he sued the company. Naturally, the company had two innocent persons claiming ownership of the same block of shares, and had to recognise both. The bank was held liable to the company for having misrepresented the situation by submitting a forged transfer. It was considered irrelevant whether or not the bank had been negligent. In the event of the share certificate also being forged, the company will presumably bear at least part of the responsibility if it completes the transfer.

Where the shares are partly paid, the bank holding a legal mortgage will be liable for further calls from the company. However, demand may be made of the customer at this time and the shares sold if a default occurs. It could only involve the bank in a loss if the company were in insolvent liquidation.

As legal owner of the shares, the bank will receive dividends, bonus and rights issues, the memorandum of deposit typically provides that these accrue to the bank in partial discharge of the mortgagor's debt.

A variety of consequences may flow from the legal mortgage for the company whose shares are mortgaged to the bank. If the bank's holding in the company exceeds 50%, the company may be considered a subsidiary of the bank for certain purposes, and thus the company will cease to be a member of its original group. Thus a company's Value Added Tax grouping may be jeopardised and there may also be complications in connection with group accounting. Of interest to the bank is the consideration that much smaller holdings may come within the disclosure of interests rules. A solution to these problems can be found if the bank mortgagee disclaims all voting rights in the company whose shares are mortgaged to it until the bank makes demand.

[4][1905] AC 392 HL.

Equitable mortgages

Unlike a legal mortgagee, the equitable mortgagee takes subject to prior equitable interests of which he has no notice, actual or constructive (such interests are very possible with shares because it is so common for shares to be held by a nominee or trustee). Contrast this with the legal mortgagee whose title defeats prior equitable interests unless he had actual or constructive notice of them at the time he took his legal mortgage. It is now the position that a mortgagee who advances funds on the security of a share certificate and a blank signed transfer, since he has it within his power to become a legal mortgagee, enjoys the same priority as an actual legal mortgagee. This was held in Macmillan Inc v Bishopsgate Investment Trust,[5] where shares in a U.S. company which beneficially belonged to the plaintiff were mortgaged by companies in the Maxwell group as security for loans. Since the mortgagees had no notice, actual or constructive, of the equitable interest at the time they advanced the funds and since at that time they held the share certificates and a blank signed transfer, they took priority over the equitable interest. It was also held in this case that when shares in a foreign company are mortgaged, the matter of priority is governed by the law of the place of incorporation of the company. That law also determines what formalities are necessary to perfect a transfer of title.[6]

A different risk is that a fraudulent customer may deposit the share certificate with an equitable mortgagee, and then claim to the company that the certificate is lost, obtain a new certificate and sell the shares. The bank's title will be inferior to that of an innocent purchaser. There is a procedure whereby the equitable mortgagee may utilise the Rules of the Supreme Court Order 50 to serve a 'Stop Notice' on the company, which will then be obliged to give the mortgagee 14 days notice before registering any transfer of ownership. In this time the bank can seek an injunction from the court to stop its customer from selling the shares. This procedure is not appropriate as a matter of routine, however, and if there is any

[5] *[1995] 1 WLR 978.*
[6] *See also [1996] 1 All ER 585 CA where this point was considered on appeal.*

concern about fraud on the part of the customer, it would be far simpler to take a legal mortgage from the start.

As the bank does not hold legal title to the shares, any dividend or rights or bonus issue will go to the mortgagor, although the bank can require that these be mandated to his account with the bank. Rights and bonus issues, of course, may dilute the equity, making the block of shares held under the bank's charge less valuable. The memorandum of deposit can specify that the mortgagor agrees to charge these to the bank if requested to do so.

15 Life assurance policies as security

15.1 INTRODUCTION

Life assurance policies may take one of three different forms.

(1) Whole life policy. This matures on death of the life assured.
(2) Endowment policy. This matures on expiration of a fixed term or on earlier death of the life assured. Endowment policies may be either low-cost or full-cost. The former is commonly used in conjunction with a house-purchase mortgage loan. During the term of the mortgage loan, interest only is paid to the lender, and at the end of the term the endowment policy matures in order to repay the principal.
(3) Term policy. This provides cover against death of the life assured during a fixed term. If the life assured survives this term, no monies are paid.

In the first two types of policy there will inevitably be a claim at some stage. In the third there will not necessarily be a claim, and consequently this type of policy has no surrender value.

Basis of lending

When a lender is using a life policy as security for a loan, it is a simple matter to discover the present surrender value of the policy, i.e. what it can be cashed in for. Assuming premiums are paid, the surrender value should increase as time passes. A policy with no surrender value, such as a term policy or a newly enacted policy, may still be assigned in order to protect the lender against death of the borrower.

Parties involved in a life policy contract

(a) the Insurer, i.e. the Life Company;
(b) the Policyholder, usually he takes out cover on his own life for his own benefit (or for the benefit of his beneficiaries on his death);
(c) the Life Assured. It may be that the policyholder takes out cover on the life of another (see discussion on insurable interest below);
(d) the Beneficiary. It may be that the policyholder has declared that some other person will receive payment when the policy matures. This is a policy written in trust, and includes settlement policies made under the provisions of the Married Women's Property Act 1882.

15.2 TYPES OF MORTGAGE ON LIFE POLICIES

Mortgages of life policies are truly assignments of the debt owed by the Insurer. There are two types:

(a) Legal Assignment;
(b) Equitable Assignment.

In both types, the policyholder (or such other beneficiary as may exist) assigns to the lender the benefit he is entitled to receive at some future date from the Insurer. The Assignee can only receive as good an interest as the Assignor holds; life policies are not negotiable instruments.

Legal assignment

This is usually effected under the Policies of Assurance Act 1867. The procedure under the Act requires:

(a) a written assignment. It need not be executed as a deed;
(b) the assignor's signature must be witnessed; and
(c) written notice of the assignment must be given to the Insurer.

If a written request is made to the Insurer, the Act requires him to issue a written acknowledgement of notice. For this service the

Insurer is entitled to charge a sum not exceeding five shillings (now 25 pence).

Once the legal assignment has been perfected, the assignee acquires the right to receive payment (subject to prior assignments) and can give a good discharge to the Insurer.

A legal assignment may also be effected under the general provision relating to assignments in section 136 of the Law of Property Act 1925, which requires:

(a) an assignment of the whole debt;
(b) an assignment in writing (not necessarily as a deed);
(c) written notice is given to the debtor (the Insurer). There is no provision for acknowledgement of notice.

Equitable assignments

The law only requires that the parties intend that the equitable rights of the policyholder pass to the assignee, supported by valuable consideration. As with Share Certificates, the deposit of a life policy otherwise than for safe custody will create an equitable mortgage.[1] It is bank practice, however, to bolster its position by having a memorandum of deposit signed by the customer assignor and by giving notice of assignment to the Insurer, for the reasons explained below. Power of sale without reference to the court can be achieved by taking an irrevocable power of attorney alongside the equitable assignment.[2]

15.3 PRIORITIES BETWEEN DIFFERENT ASSIGNEES

This is determined by the rule in Dearle v Hall[3], which provides that the first to give notice to the Insurer has first priority, irrespective of whether the assignments are legal or equitable. However, Spencer v

---

[1]*Spencer v Clarke (1878) 9 ChD 137.*
[2]*See 2.2 above.*
[3]*(1828) 3 Russ 1.*

Clarke[4] establishes that non-production by the policyholder of the original policy may be constructive notice to the assignee of prior assignment, even if the first assignee did not give notice to the Insurer.

It follows from the above that an assignee who takes the original policy and is the first to give notice of assignment to the Insurer, will enjoy first priority whether his assignment is legal or equitable.

15.4 STANDARD TERMS

(a) a continuing security clause to counteract the effect of the rule in *Clayton's case*;

(b) a promise by the assignor to pay the premiums and his agreement to the bank paying them for him, and to the bank debiting his account accordingly;

(c) in a legal assignment, the bank has the right to sell and surrender the policy, and the statutory waiting periods in section 103 of the Law of Property Act 1925 are excluded;

(d) section 93 of the Law of Property Act 1925, which would prevent the assignee from consolidating, is also excluded;

(e) in an equitable assignment, the bank can require the assignor to provide a legal assignment on demand by the bank.

15.5 REMEDIES OF THE ASSIGNEE

(1) The legal assignee may surrender the policy to the Insurer and is entitled to receive the full surrender value. Alternatively, he may sell the policy to a third party. After deducting his loan, interest and expenses he will pass on the balance to the policyholder. A higher figure may be obtained by sale of the policy to an investor, and it may be that the assignee is under a duty to do so in order to obtain the best possible price, as laid down in Cuckmere Brick Co Ltd v Mutual Finance Ltd.[5] If the policy has matured, the assignee is entitled to the full capital value from the Insurer, subject to the same duty to pass on the balance;

---

[4] *(1878) 1 ChD 137.*
[5] *[1971] Ch 949. Also see 13.13 above.*

(2) An equitable assignee's rights depend on whether his assignment is under hand or 'under seal'.[6] If under hand, a sale can only occur with a court order. If under seal, the accompanying irrevocable power of attorney in favour of the assignee will permit a sale by him.

15.6 POTENTIAL RISKS FOR THE LENDER

Beneficiaries

The assignment must always be taken from the person entitled to receive payment on maturity of the policy, and this may be someone other than the policyholder or his personal representatives. If so, the lender must ensure:

(a) none of the beneficiaries are under 18 when making the assignment, as it would then be ineffective;
(b) the beneficiary must be named. If a policy in favour of 'the wife of X' is assigned, this would not bind a later (different) wife;
(c) the lender must be conscious of the possibility of the beneficiary raising undue influence when the security is realised, particularly when all the benefit of the loan accrues to another.

Insurable interest

It is possible for a policyholder to insure the life of another but, under the Life Assurance Act 1774, which was passed to prevent '... a mischievous kind of gaming', this is restricted to certain relationships. Apart from one's own life, one can insure the life of one's spouse.[7] The life of a parent, that of an employee[8] and that

---

[6]*i.e. executed as a deed. Seals are no longer necessary, Law of Property (Miscellaneous Provisions) Act 1989, section 2.*
[7]*Note it is not necessary for the spouse to know that a policy of insurance has been taken out on his or her life. The crime pages of the newspapers reveal this to be a not infrequent inducement to matrimonial homicide.*
[8]*This permits a company to take out a life assurance policy, the so-called 'key man' type of policy.*

of a debtor (among others) may be insured but only to a limited extent.

Where insurable interest is lacking, the Act declares the life insurance contract null and void. Therefore the Insurer may refuse to pay on maturity of the policy and may refuse to return premiums. However, in Hughes v Liverpool Victoria Friendly Society,[9] an agent of the Insurer had told the policyholder that the policies were valid; the court considered this to be fraud and the premiums had to be returned. Insurers on occasions do issue policies where it is doubtful whether any insurable interest exists.

Where the policy has been assigned, there is no requirement that the assignee has an insurable interest. Also where an insurable interest has ceased to exist, e.g. due to divorce, this will not affect the policy.

Non-disclosure and misrepresentation

Insurers are protected by the *uberrima fides* rule, which requires the proposer to disclose all facts which would be material to the Insurer when deciding whether to issue cover, or how much premium to charge for doing so. Therefore, the proposer is under a duty to disclose material facts, even if he is not asked the relevant question, and he must honestly answer all questions he is asked.

Where the policyholder has failed in this duty, the Insurer is entitled to void the policy and therefore to refuse to pay on a claim. Premiums are returnable unless the policyholder acted fraudulently.

Suicide

A policyholder, who is also the life assured, may seek to bring about maturity of the policy by committing suicide. Most Insurers include a clause excluding liability to pay if death is caused in this manner during the first year of the policy. Such a clause will be effective, but it was held in Beresford v Royal Insurance Co Ltd[10] that it raises an implication that the Insurer agrees to pay where suicide occurs

[9] *[1916] 2 KB 482.*
[10] *[1938] AC 586 HL.*

after the initial period. The clause usually goes on to say that if death is caused by suicide during the first year, the Insurer will pay any assignee of the policy.

In the *Beresford* case, a 'sane' suicide occurred after the initial period. It was held that normally the Insurer would not be obliged to pay, as the policyholder should not be able to deliberately cause the insured event to occur and cause the insurance monies to be paid, in the same way as an Insurer could not be forced to pay on a buildings policy if the policyholder burned his own house. However, the effect of the clause was held to be that the Insurer had impliedly agreed to pay if suicide occurred after the initial period. Nevertheless, the Insurer won the Beresford case as suicide was at that time illegal and the court refused to enforce the contract on public policy grounds. The Suicide Act 1961 'legalised' suicide, and on the same facts the Insurer would now be obliged to pay.

Where no suicide clause is included in the policy, the basic rule applies, and any 'sane' suicide will not produce a valid claim. An 'insane' suicide, however, will do so. This is because it is not a deliberate act.

Where the Insurer is entitled to refuse to pay, he is not obliged to return premiums as he has been on risk until the suicide, when death might have been caused by other means.

Murder and unlawful killing

Where the life assured is murdered either by the policyholder, the beneficiary or by anyone entitled indirectly to the insurance monies through the deceased's will or under the rules of intestacy, the Insurer is not obliged to pay. It seems likely that the same applies to a manslaughter killing. The Insurer would not be obliged to return premiums.

Non-payment of premiums

In practice a bank will wish to monitor payment of premiums by establishing a direct debit from the policyholder's account. An Insurer to whom notice of assignment has been given may warn a bank when a policy is about to lapse due to non-payment of premiums. Where the bank is aware that the policy is about to lapse, its mortgage will normally give it the right to pay the premiums itself, to convert the policy into a paid-up state or to surrender the policy.

Where the bank has not taken any action, the position will depend on the terms in the policy. Frequently the Insurer will use the surrender value of the policy to pay premiums, and after a given time convert it into a paid-up state. In the absence of such provisions, however, there has to be a risk that the policy will lapse with no return of premiums.

16 Taking security from companies

16.1 INTRODUCTION

If a secured loan is made to a registered company, the legal position is often similar to that pertaining when the security is taken from an individual. If the asset charged is land, the same considerations of registration apply. If it concerns a life or other insurance policy, the same doctrine of notice applies.

As a general rule, it is fair to say that when a fixed charge is granted by a company, all the law which applies in the 'individual' case applies but there may be extra considerations due to a company being involved. One must also be aware that companies are able to create a special type of charge known as a floating charge. When a bank lends to a corporate customer, any security it takes is likely to be in the form of a 'debenture'. This has no connection with loan stock debentures which may be traded on the Stock Exchange, it is simply a practice term used to describe the typical form of charge taken by a bank from a company customer. This debenture will incorporate a fixed charge over the book debts and the fixed assets of any value which the company owns, and a floating charge on the company's assets in general.

The law relating to companies is contained chiefly in a consolidating enactment, namely the Companies Act 1985. This has been amended and supplemented by the Companies Act 1989. Matters relating to liquidation and receivership are contained in the Insolvency Act 1986.

16.2 CORPORATE CAPACITY

The long-established *ultra vires* rule was abolished by the Companies Act 1989. A new section 35 is inserted into the Companies Act 1985, which declares that the validity of an act done by a company shall not be called into question on the ground of lack of capacity by reason of anything in the company's memorandum. A company therefore will continue to have a memorandum setting out the objects of the company but a third party will not be affected by it whether or not he knows of the contents of the company's 'objects clause'.

A new section 35A provides that in favour of a person dealing with a company in good faith, the power of the board of directors to bind the company shall be deemed to be free of any limitation under the company's constitution. It is expressly provided that a person shall not be regarded as acting in bad faith, by reason only of his knowing that an act is beyond the powers of the directors.

In section 35B it is stated that a party entering into a transaction with a company is not bound to enquire as to whether the transaction is within the company's memorandum or whether it is within the powers of the directors acting on behalf of the company.

Under these rules, a bank lending to a company need not be concerned to look at the company's memorandum and articles of association to determine whether the company or its agents are acting properly. Nor will it be put on notice of lack of capacity by having seen these documents. In order to be free from doubt as to whether the persons representing the company have authority to do so, however, it is necessary that the bank deals with the board of directors or some other person authorised by the board.

The *ultra vires* rule still applies in some situations. For example, where the directors exceed their powers and the other party to the transaction includes a director of the company.[1] A bank may have to be careful if, for instance, it lends to a company under a loan agreement containing a directors' guarantee.

[1] *Section 322A.*

16.3 EXECUTION OF DOCUMENTS BY A COMPANY

These rules affect the form of documents whereby a company grants security to a bank.

Section 36A declares that a company need no longer have its own company seal. Whether it has one or not, a document signed by two directors, or by one director and the company secretary, has the same effect as if it had the company's seal on it. If it is clear from the document's face that it is intended to be a deed, then it takes effect as a deed. The company's seal is not necessary.[2] A document such as an equitable mortgage which must be in writing but need not be 'under seal' may be signed on the company's behalf by anyone having the company's express or implied authority to do so.[3]

16.4 THE FLOATING CHARGE

When a fixed charge is taken over the assets of an individual or of a company, the chargee has the comfort of knowing that he enjoys first priority over the asset (assuming it is a first charge and is perfected) and that the chargor is not able to validly dispose of the asset without his permission. Thus a first fixed charge over an asset which is unlikely to decline in value (such as some types of land and insurance policies) is a good security. Fixed charges over assets which will decline in value (such as some types of plant and machinery which will have to be replaced after a few years), are good security only in the early years. The replacement asset will not automatically be covered by the charge, although the customer can be asked to provide a new charge.

It is possible to take fixed charges over current assets (such as stock in trade) but it is likely to be highly inconvenient, for both bank and customer, for permission to have to be sought each time the asset is disposed of and for a fresh charge to be granted to cover the replacement items. Fortunately this is not a problem with one form of current asset, namely book debts. The law does permit

[2]*Similar rules apply to Scottish companies.*
[3]*Section 36.*

a fixed charge to be taken which covers future book debts (see chapter 18).

The floating charge therefore has two great advantages over the fixed charge:

(a) it can conveniently cover the stock in trade of a business customer; and
(b) it can automatically cover all assets which are acquired in the future.

An effective floating charge cannot be created by a non-corporate entity, as non-possessory charges created by individuals must be registered under the Bills of Sale Act, with details entered of all the specific items covered by the charge. An exception to this rule is a form of agricultural floating charge which may be created under the Agricultural Credits Act 1928 (see chapter 19).

The floating charge may in theory be expressed to be over certain classes of asset but in practice it is invariably expressed to be over all of the assets of the company chargor. In this case it is an equitable charge which 'hovers' until some event crystallises the charge, at which time it becomes a fixed equitable charge on the assets which the company happens to own at that time.[4] The crystallising events would typically be either the company going into liquidation or the chargeholder appointing administrative receivers, following a default by the company.

16.5 STANDARD DEBENTURE TERMS

(1) The company agrees to pay on written demand all monies owing, and demand may be made at the company's registered office.
(2) The company grants fixed charges over the assets listed in a schedule and a floating charge over all the assets present and future.
(3) A promise by the company not to grant any charge which would rank equally with or ahead of the bank's floating charge,

---

[4]Re Yorkshire Woolcombers Association Ltd [1903] 2 Ch 284 CA.

and a promise not to dispose of assets except in the ordinary course of business.

(4) The company, on the bank's written demand, will grant a legal mortgage to the bank of any land it acquires in the future.

(5) A 'continuing security' clause (see 13.11 above).

(6) Power for the bank to appoint receivers (or administrative receivers) and managers at any time after the bank has made demand, or if the company so requests, or a petition has been presented to the court under section 9 of the Insolvency Act 1986 for the making of an administration order in respect of the company.[5] The receiver is to be the agent of the company and is granted specific powers, including sale of company property and to carry on its business. Irrevocable power is granted to the bank and to the receiver to execute deeds on the company's behalf. The bank may determine the remuneration of the receiver.

(7) Exclusion of sections 93 and 103 of the Law of Property Act 1925.[6]

(8) A promise by the company not to assign its book debts to third parties and to pay those debts into its account with the bank when they are received (see 18.2 for an explanation of the considerable importance of this clause).

(9) To provide copies of the annual accounts of the company.

(10) To keep its assets in good repair and insured.

16.6 FIXED AND FLOATING CHARGES COMPARED

(1) The company is free to buy and sell those assets which are covered only by the floating charge. The danger for the bank is that the company will run down the level of its assets, so that when the charge crystallises, it fixes onto very few assets. This may constitute a breach of clause (3) above (see 16.5) but if the company is insolvent, this will not assist.

---

[5] *See 16.10 below.*
[6] *See 13.11 above.*

(2) Nothing can subordinate a first fixed perfected charge. However, the floating charge is subordinated to a subsequent fixed charge.[7] If a company does grant a fixed charge to a different creditor after giving a bank the standard debenture, it will contravene clause (3) above but this in itself would not invalidate the charge unless the chargee had notice of the clause. Such notice may be constructive in the form of registration of particulars of the clause.[8] A floating charge may also, in effect, be subordinated by an unsecured creditor who obtains a court judgment against the company and enforces the judgment (e.g. by bailiffs seizing stock) before the charge crystallises.[9]

(3) Holders of a first fixed charge will have first priority to the proceeds of sale of the asset they have a charge over, after sale expenses have been met. The floating charge enjoys no such first priority claim against any of the assets it covers and indeed it is subordinated to preferential creditors, as defined in section 386 and Schedule 6 of the Insolvency Act 1986,[10] who must be paid in full before any payment is made under the floating charge.

(4) Any charge which is granted to secure a previously unsecured debt is potentially vulnerable as a preference under section 239 of the Insolvency Act 1986, if the company commences winding-up within the next six months (24 months if the parties are 'connected persons') and the company was influenced by a desire to prefer the bank over other creditors. There is in fact little risk of this rule entitling a liquidator to void a charge unless the debt is also secured by a guarantor who is connected to the company.[11] Floating charges, however, are additionally vulnerable under section 245, which provides that such charges which are granted to secure a pre-existing debt will be invalid

---

[7] *Wheatley v Silkstone and Haigh Moor Coal Co. (1885) 29 ChD 715.*
[8] *Section 199(1) of the Law of Property Act 1925 and see the registration of charges in 16.11 below.*
[9] *Re Opera Ltd (1891) 3 Ch 260 CA.*
[10] *See 10.2 above.*
[11] *See 10.4 above.*

if the company commences winding-up[12] within the following 12 months (24 months if the parties are connected), if it can be proved that the company was insolvent at the time the charge was given or became insolvent as a result of giving it.[13] Significantly, a desire to prefer does not have to be proved. Because the rule is aimed at charges which secure a previously unsecured debt, a charge will be valid to the extent that money is provided at the time the charge is given or after it is given.

The fact that the charge is valid in respect of money advanced at the same time or afterwards leads to a linkage with the rule in *Clayton's case* which can be beneficial to banks. In Re Yeovil Glove Co Ltd,[14] the company already had an overdraft of £67,500 when the bank took a floating charge from it. The overdraft balance subsequently remained at a similar figure but it was an active account and around £110,000 was paid in and out over the next few months. Within 12 months of the charge being taken, winding-up of the company commenced. The liquidator claimed the charge was void but the court held that the effect of *Clayton's case* was to bring forward the effective date of the debt so that it post-dated the creation of the charge, which was therefore fully valid.

However, if there is no genuine activity on the account and the court considers the later debits on the account do not represent fresh payments to the company, the *Clayton's case* rule will not be applied.[15]

(5) The stock covered by the floating charge may not belong to the company at all, due to a 'retention of title' clause in the contract of sale which operates for the benefit of the supplier of the stock. If, as a result, the stock never became the property of the company in the first place, no chargeholder or other creditor can

[12]*Meaning the winding-up petition in a compulsory winding-up and the resolution to wind-up in a voluntary winding-up.*
[13]*To be solvent the company must be able to pay its debts as they fall due and have an excess of assets over liabilities. There is no requirement to prove insolvency when the creditor is a connected person to the company.*
[14]*[1965] Ch 148 CA.*
[15]*Re Destone Fabrics Ltd [1941] Ch 319.*

receive the proceeds of its sale. This naturally is more likely to prejudice a floating charge than a fixed charge.[16]

(6) The holder of a floating charge is able to prevent the making of an administration order by the court under section 9 of the Insolvency Act 1986.[17] A fixed charge holder does not have this ability. In practice this is a powerful reason for a bank to take a floating charge on every occasion it takes company security.

16.7 CRYSTALLISATION OF A FLOATING CHARGE

This is the process by which the charge becomes a fixed one over the assets which the company owns at the relevant time. This will occur when the bank appoints a receiver pursuant to its powers in the debenture,[18] or if the company commences winding-up (whether or not the company is in default),[19] or if the company completely ceases to carry on business.[20] The appointment of an administrator may also automatically crystallise a floating charge, although this is not certain, and most floating charges will make express provision for administration to crystallise the security. Such a provision may be one of several in a floating charge which specify particular events which will cause the security to crystallise. For instance, the floating charge may provide that the mortgagee can crystallise the security at any time simply by giving notice to the company.[21] However, the attraction of these procedures has been greatly reduced since 1986 as preferential creditors now have priority over assets subject to a charge which was created as a floating charge,[22] and the date of crystallisation is thus immaterial to priority.[23]

[16]*See 16.9 below for a fuller discussion of retention of title clauses.*
[17]*See 16.10 below for details of administration orders.*
[18]*Governments Stocks and Other Securities Investment Co. Ltd v Manila Railway Co. Ltd [1897] AC 81 HL.*
[19]*Hodson v Tea Company (1880) 14 ChD 859.*
[20]*Re Woodroffes (Musical Instruments) Ltd [1986] Ch 366.*
[21]*Re Brightlife Ltd [1987] Ch 200.*
[22]*Companies Act 1985 section 196(1), as amended.*
[23]*Section 410 of the Companies Act 1985 (as amended) provides that regulations may be introduced which require registration of crystallisation within a certain time period.*

16.8 ADMINISTRATIVE RECEIVERS

'Administrative receiver' is the term used in the Insolvency Act 1986 for a receiver appointed under a floating charge, to distinguish him from receivers appointed by the court and receivers of rent appointed under the Law of Property Act 1925.

The following discussion of the law relating to receivers is from a banker's point of view, in that much law which would not always concern the appointing bank (but which would concern a receiver) is excluded. Also it is assumed that a standard form debenture has been executed.

Appointment of receiver

Standard debenture terms will permit a bank to appoint administrative receivers where it has made demand on the company and payment has not been forthcoming, or following some other default by the company. Where the bank has become concerned about a company account, in practice the bank may suggest that the directors invite the bank to appoint a receiver. An appointment at the directors' invitation will avoid the receiver being a trespasser on the company's property, even if his appointment is invalid. If they decline, the bank may appoint in any case, and assuming the appointment is legally valid and *bona fide*, the appointment cannot be challenged.[24]

A fixed chargeholder will appoint a receiver, as explained in 13.14. A floating chargeholder will appoint administrative receivers. A bank normally appoints the latter. The appointment must be in writing,[25] but it need not be 'under seal'.[26] The appointed administrative receiver must be an insolvency practitioner, authorised to act as such. Companies are not permitted to act as administrative receivers. It is common practice for two receivers to be appointed

[24]*Shamji v Johnson Matthey Bankers Ltd [1986] BCLC 278.*
[25]*Section 109(1) of the Law of Property Act 1925 and the standard debenture so provide.*
[26]*Windsor Refrigerator Co. Ltd v Branch Nominees Ltd [1961] Ch 375.*

jointly, to minimise possible succession problems if one retires or dies.

Administrative receivers will not be displaced by a subsequent liquidation of the company, and they may be appointed even after the winding-up has commenced.[27] Under the Insolvency Act 1986, after being appointed, the receivers must publish the appointment, notify the company, notify creditors and notice of it must appear on company stationery. The bank must notify the Registrar of Companies within seven days and the appointment will appear on the company's charges register.[28]

If time is of the essence, e.g. because a judgment creditor is about to have the company's assets seized, the bank can move very quickly to appoint a receiver. For instance, in R.A. Cripps & Son Ltd v Wickenden,[29] demand was effectively made to the company at 10.45 a.m. No monies having been forthcoming, the receiver was appointed at 12.30 p.m. on the same day. This was held to have allowed sufficient time for the company to comply with the demand, since the law only recognised the need to physically move the money to the bank, and not the need to negotiate the raising of the necessary funds from another source.

Receivers are expressed to be agents of the company in the debenture. This is a strange form of agency since the receiver, for obvious reasons, does not take instructions from the company and he is personally liable on contracts he makes for the company, unless the contrary is stated in each contract. As he is agent of the company, however, the bank that appointed him cannot be held liable for his negligence. In practice, the receiver will demand an indemnity from the bank before accepting. Furthermore, the bank's interventions may negate the written terms of the debenture. In Standard Chartered Bank Ltd v Walker,[30] the bank had taken a standard debenture from JW Ltd and also had personal guarantees from Mr and Mrs W. A receiver was appointed (as agent of the company) and, responding

---

[27]*Re Stubbs (Joshua) Ltd, Barney v Stubbs (Joshua) Ltd [1891] 1 Ch 475. They may not be appointed after an administrator has been appointed.*
[28]*Companies Act 1985, section 405.*
[29]*[1973] 1 WLR 944.*
[30]*[1982] 1 WLR 1410 CA.*

to pressure from the bank, put the company's plant and machinery in an unsuitable auction sale. The bank also called on Mr and Mrs W to pay but the defence was that if a proper price had been obtained for the assets, there would have been a lower claim under the guarantee. The bank was unable to deny liability for the receiver's negligence, as it had chosen to instruct the receiver to make an early sale of the assets and thus make him its agent, regardless of the terms of the debenture.

The amount of a receiver's remuneration may be determined by the bank if the debenture so specifies. The default rate is 5% of gross receipts.[31]

Obligations of the administrative receiver

After the appointment, the Companies Act 1985 and the Insolvency Act 1986 require the directors of the company to prepare a statement of affairs for the receiver who must, in turn, send a copy of it to the Registrar of Companies. Thereafter he must prepare annual (and final) accounts of his receipts and payments for the Registrar, and keep sufficient records for the company's accounts to be prepared.

The receiver must pay off the preferential creditors before the floating chargeholder, although inasmuch as the bank has fixed charges, the proceeds of sale of these assets will go to the bank before the preferential creditors.

It has been seen[32] that a bank may become a preferential creditor by having advanced money for the payment of the company employees' wages. Where the bank's claim against a company in liquidation is partly preferential and partly non-preferential and it holds some fixed and floating charges, it is entitled to set the proceeds of sale from the assets subject to the fixed charge against the non-preferential element, permitting the bank to claim as a preferential creditor for the balance still owing after realisation of the fixed charges.[33]

---

[31] *Section 109(6) of the Law of Property Act 1925.*
[32] *In 2.7 above.*
[33] *Re William Hall (Contractors) Ltd [1967] 1 WLR 948.*

Powers of the administrative receiver

The debenture will grant considerable power to sell assets and manage the company's business. Schedule 1 to the Insolvency Act 1986 grants wide powers in any case. The receiver may petition the court for a winding-up order if this may lead to preservation of the assets of the company.[34] In any case where the court orders a winding-up, a receiver who was appointed before the liquidator may continue to sell assets.[35] One appointed after the liquidator may not.[36] In a voluntary winding-up, the receiver may sell assets after the liquidator is appointed, even if the receiver was appointed later.

16.9 RETENTION OF TITLE OR '*ROMALPA*' CLAUSES

As explained above,[37] the value of a floating charge may be diminished by the effect of these clauses. It is vexing for a supplier of goods to see goods he has just delivered to a company purchaser and which have not yet been paid for, being sold off to pay the company's preferential creditors and floating charge holder while, as an unsecured creditor, he receives nothing. It is unsurprising, therefore, that he will do his best to improve his position, which can in fact be achieved by the simple expedient of inserting a clause into his standard form of conditions of sale. Such an approach may or may not assist a supplier depending on the exact clause used and the exact circumstances of the case. The law relating to these clauses is regrettably complex.

Under the Sale of Goods Act 1979, the parties to a sale of goods contract are free to express the time when the title to the goods being sold will pass. The seller of the goods will therefore prefer to express that title will pass at the time when the goods are fully paid for. In Aluminium Industrie Vaasen BV v Romalpa Aluminium Ltd,[38] the

---

[34]*Re Emmadart Ltd [1979] 2 WLR 868.*
[35]*Sowman v David Samuel Trust Ltd [1978] 1 WLR 22.*
[36]*Re Henry Pound, Son & Hutchins Ltd (1889) 42 ChD 402.*
[37]*In 16.6.*
[38]*[1976] 1 WLR 676 CA.*

seller supplied foil to the buyer on terms that legal and beneficial ownership was to remain with the seller until the foil was fully paid for. Meanwhile the buyer agreed to keep the foil separate from other goods in its possession and, at the seller's request, to assign to the seller the proceeds of any sale of the foil to a subpurchaser. The buyer had borrowed from a bank against the security of a floating charge. At the time the bank appointed a receiver, there was a large amount of foil in the buyer's possession which had been supplied by the seller, which was unpaid for, and which had been kept separate. Also there was a sum of money which the buyer had obtained from sub-purchasers of foil, for which the seller was unpaid. The seller successfully claimed both the foil and the proceeds of sale in priority to the bank's floating charge. It was held that the contract made the buyer a bailee of the foil until it was paid for, and therefore the foil in the buyer's possession was still the property of the seller, and that the foil which had been sold on to sub-purchasers had been sold by the buyer as the seller's agent, and the seller was therefore able to trace the proceeds of sale from the buyer's bank account.

A series of subsequent cases[39] has failed to extend significantly the parameters of the *Romalpa* decision. In particular, it seems it is not possible to reclaim goods if they have simply been mixed with other (similar) goods from other suppliers, such as oil or other liquid goods stored in a vat so that it is impossible to identify precisely the supplier's goods. If the goods have been mixed with other products in a manufacturing process, any right to trace the goods into the finished product seems to be fraught with problems, and to trace the proceeds of sale of the finished product is impossible. Any other form of clause (such as one which permits the purchaser to acquire the legal title to the goods and the right to use them in a manufacturing process but yet reserving an equitable right over them) can only be effective as a charge over the goods which requires registration under section 395 of the Companies Act 1985, and if it is not so registered within 21 days of the contract being made, it is

---

[39]e.g. *Re Bond Worth Ltd [1980] Ch 228; Borden (UK) Ltd v Scottish Timber Products Ltd [1981] Ch 25; Clough Mill Ltd v Martin [1985] 1 WLR 111 CA; Re Andrabell Ltd [1984] 3 All ER 407.*

void against a liquidator of the purchasing company. It is clearly not practical for suppliers to register a charge on each occasion they supply goods to a company but it may be that where a supplier and a purchaser have made a specific agreement to insert a retention of title clause into all their contracts, one registration of this agreement will suffice.

16.10 ADMINISTRATION ORDERS

It has been seen[40] that a floating chargeholder's rights are largely unaffected by the commencement of a company's winding-up and the appointment of a liquidator. This is not true, however, of an administration order and the appointment of an administrator. Section 8 of the Insolvency Act 1986 provides that the court may make an administration order where:

(a) the company is, or is likely to become, unable to pay its debts; and

(b) the making of an order is likely to achieve either:

   (i) a more advantageous realisation of the company's assets than would a liquidation;
      or

   (ii) the survival of at least part of the company's business.

If the order is made and an administrator appointed, then from that moment no chargeholder may realise his security. Fixed charge-holders may not sell assets and floating chargeholders may not appoint receivers. Assets subject to a fixed charge may be sold by agreement between the administrator and the chargeholder or, failing this, by court order. The chargeholder must receive the proceeds of sale of the asset in the usual way when it is sold, although meanwhile interest may have built up or the asset may have depreciated in value.

The floating chargeholder, however, will lose priority to the expenses of the administration and to the trade debts incurred during the administration. Furthermore, the administrator has com-

---

[40]*In 16.8 above.*

plete control over the timing of sales of assets subject to the floating charge. The administrator cannot, however, profit from the company's assets in disregard of third-party interests in them, and third parties may apply for a court order to protect their position.

It is provided in section 9 that once a petition is made to the court for the making of an administration order, the court must give notice of this petition to any floating chargeholder (assuming he has a charge over substantially the whole of the company's assets, which a standard bank debenture will grant). It is further provided that the court is unable to make the order if administrative receivers are in place. The effect of this is that a floating chargeholder is always able to prevent the making of an administration order if he so wishes (by appointing administrative receivers before the court makes the administration order), but that a fixed chargeholder does not have this power. Accordingly, it is now bank practice to take fixed and floating charges in all cases.

If an administrator is appointed, a creditor holding a fixed charge may apply to the court for leave to sell the charged asset if the adminstrator will not agree to it. In deciding whether to grant leave, the court must balance the interests of this creditor and the interests of the creditors in general in seeing a successful administration. In Re Atlantic Computers Ltd,[41] the court was prepared to take into consideration that rental payments to the chargeholder were in arrears and that a delay in selling the charged assets was likely to increase the chargeholder's loss. Similarly, it is open to the adminstrator to apply to the court for leave to sell a charged asset when the chargeholder will not agree to it.

16.11 PRIORITY OF CHARGES AND REGISTRATION

Substantial changes to these rules were introduced by Part IV of the Companies Act 1989. However, the new law has not come into force, and the existing law is described here.

[41] *[1992] Ch 505.*

Charges requiring registration

Section 395 of the Companies Act 1985 requires that certain types of charge created by companies must be registered with the Registrar of Companies at Companies House within 21 days of the creation of the charge. Section 396 lists the charges which must be registered and these include:

(a) a floating charge;
(b) a charge on land, or any interest in land;
(c) a charge on goodwill, intellectual property, book debts or uncalled share capital;
(d) a non-possessory charge on goods.

Clearly the standard bank debenture does require registration as it incorporates a floating charge.

Registration consists of supplying the prescribed particulars of the charge in the prescribed form to the Registrar of Companies, normally including the original document of charge. It is advantageous to include specific details of the term in the debenture which prohibits the company from granting subsequent charges to other lenders which would rank *pari passu* with, or ahead of, the debenture.[42] This is because a subsequent chargee is deemed to have notice of any matters which he would come to know from such enquiries as he reasonably ought to make.[43] Searching the company's register is an enquiry he ought to make and therefore if in doing so he would see details of the *pari passu* clause, he is deemed to know of it, whether he actually searched the register or not.[44] The practice of specifically noting the inclusion of the *pari passu* clause is so prevalent that it has been argued that a failure to note it would entitle a subsequent chargeholder to assume that the previous charge did not include such a clause.[45]

---

[42] *See 16.6 above.*
[43] *Section 199(1) of the Law of Property Act 1925.*
[44] *Section 416 of the Companies Act 1985 (which has not come into force) states that a person taking a charge is deemed to have notice of any matter requiring registration and disclosed on the register at the time he takes his charge.*
[45] *Encyclopaedia of Banking Law at E1114.*

It is the company's duty to register a charge it creates and it commits an offence if the charge is not registered. However, any person interested in the charge may register it and banks prefer to do so for obvious reasons.

The Registrar must provide a certificate stating the date on which the particulars of the charge were registered. This certificate is conclusive evidence that the statutory requirements of registration have been complied with.[46] It cannot be overriden even if it is shown that it was issued following an error, for instance that the date on the particulars was wrongly stated so that the charge appeared to be in date when in fact it was not.[47]

Consequence of failing to register

The requirement is to register the charge within 21 days of the creation of the charge, failing which it becomes void against:

(a) any liquidator or administrator of the company;
(b) any person who for value acquires an interest in the property subject to the charge (such as a purchaser of the property or a second mortgagee of it).

A charge is created when it is executed by the company, irrespective of when monies are advanced by the chargee.[48] This means that a bank which holds an executed but undated company charge risks losing its security by waiting before dating and registering it. If a certificate of registration is issued, however, the charge is unchallengeable, as explained above. A creditor whose charge is unregistered becomes an unsecured creditor in a liquidation. Note, however, that the charge is valid when created but becomes void on the 22nd day after its creation, if it is not registered by then. Even then, the charge will still be valid against the company itself, and can be enforced so long as the company is not in liquidation.

[46]*Section 401(2).*
[47]*Re C.L. Nye Ltd [1971] Ch 442 CA.*
[48]*Esberger & Son Ltd v Capital and Counties Bank Ltd [1913] 2 Ch 366.*

Late registration[49]

If the 21 day period has passed, an application to the court may be made for an order extending the period for registration. This can be granted merely on evidence of accident or inadvertence,[50] but not if the company is in liquidation or winding-up is imminent.[51] The court order will usually safeguard the rights of other creditors acquired after the 21 day period expired. This leads to potentially complex priority issues between different chargees.[52]

[49]Under the registration rules not in force, where the charge is registered after 21 days have passed, the charge will still be valid, although the rights of creditors who have registered charges in the meantime are protected. In addition, a late registered charge will be void against a liquidator or administrator of the company if the company was unable to pay its debts at the time the charge was registered and insolvency proceedings begin within six months of the charge being registered (12 months in the case of a floating charge) (section 400).

[50]Section 404.

[51]Re Eric Holmes (Property) Ltd [1965] Ch 1052; Re Ashpurton Estates Ltd [1983] Ch 110 CA.

[52]See for instance Watson v Duff, Morgan and Vermont (Holdings) Ltd [1974] 1 WLR 450.

17 Charges over bank balances

17.1 INTRODUCTION

In practice it is quite common for a bank to wish to use a customer's credit balance as a form of security for some liability which the customer owes or might in the future owe to the bank.

The concepts of combination of accounts and set-off have been discussed in 1.14 above. These will normally permit, for example, a bank which has lent money on current account to set this off against a credit balance held on a current account in the same name, and thus provide an ideal form of security for the bank since no formal procedures are involved such as application to the court; the bank can simply combine the accounts. Nor is any advance documentation necessary. In the event of insolvency of the customer, the statutory set-off rules in the Insolvency Act 1986 apply, with the same effect.

A simple reliance on common law and statutory set-off will not always be sufficient, however. For instance, the customer may be able to withdraw the funds from the credit balance because the debt owed on the other account is not yet due, or he may assign the credit balance to some third party, or the bank may wish to look to the deposit as security for the debt of a third party, or may wish it to secure a contingent liability (such as liability under a guarantee, which will only become operative if the principal debtor defaults). In these events the right of set-off may not be available to the bank.

There is a clear commercial need, therefore, for a simple and effective form of charging a bank deposit to the bank where it is deposited, in the same way that other property of the customer, such as shares, can be charged. Much the same need arises in the insurance industry, where companies lend money to their policyholders against the security of the life policy issued by themselves. Unfortunately, the law has struggled to meet these needs and something which ought in theory to be quite simple becomes labyrinthine in practice.

The following discussion assumes that a bank wishes (in effect) to take a charge over a credit balance, so that it may prevent the customer from withdrawing it and so that it will be a good security in the event of the customer's insolvency. There are three recognised means of attempting to do so, and in true belt and braces fashion, banks commonly adopt all three in combination (a device known as the 'triple cocktail').

The key to understanding what follows is to remember that when a customer has 'money in a bank account', the law analyses this as the bank owning the money but owing a debt to the customer, who therefore owns the right to receive that debt from the bank (called a chose in action).[1]

17.2 CONTRACTUALLY EXTENDING THE RIGHT OF SET-OFF

As explained earlier,[2] the rights of combination and set-off prior to insolvency are based on common law and, subsequent to insolvency, on statute. Common law will not permit (without documentation) a contingent liability, an unmatured liability nor a third party liability to be set off against a cash balance. Furthermore, the bank may at any time receive notice that the benefit of the credit balance has been assigned to some third party[3] or attached under a garnishee order of the court, and this will prevent a set-off of contingent or subsequent liabilities when they mature or crystallize. Common law is also prepared to perceive an implied agreement between bank

---

[1] *See 1.4 above.*

[2] *In 1.14.*

[3] *Although notice of assignment will be ineffective if the bank and depositor have agreed that the deposit is not assignable, Linden Gardens Trust v Lenesta Sludge Disposals Ltd [1994] AC 85 HL.*

and customer not to set off, for instance when the debit balance is on a loan account[4] but not in the case of a frozen current account.[5]

A properly drafted deposit agreement or letter of set-off will deal with all of the above concerns, with the possible exceptions that it may not permit future and contingent debts to be unaffected by notice of garnishee,[6] (once a bank has received notice of the garnishee order, set-off could not of course be extended to further debts not covered by the original set-off agreement). The agreement should precisely specify which deposits and which liabilities are to be the basis of the set-off (including contingent and future liabilities). The bank will be granted irrevocable authority to debit the credit balance with the debts, and the depositor will be restrained from drawing from the account. If the depositor's credit balance is to be set-off against a debt owed by a different legal entity, a guarantee must also be taken.

On the onset of the depositor's insolvency, garnishee orders will not be a concern as judgment debts cannot be pursued. The chief concern for the bank at that time, therefore, is whether set-off is available in respect of unmatured and contingent debts of the customer. Statutory set-off under section 323 of the Insolvency Act 1986 will apply (for insolvent companies the Insolvency Rules 1986, rule 4.90 has similar effect). This provides for the setting off of mutual credits and debts. Any unmatured debts are accelerated and contingent liabilities may also be set off.[7] This is helpful since any contractual provision which seeks to improve the position of an unsecured creditor in the event of insolvency is void.[8]

In summary, a well-drafted letter of set-off will cover the various pre-insolvency risks (such as assignment of the deposit by the

---

[4]*Buckingham v London & Midland Bank Ltd (1895) 12 TLR 70.*

[5]*Halesowen Presswork and Assemblies Ltd v Westminster Bank [1972] AC 785 HL.*

[6]*See Business Computers Ltd v Anglo-African Leasing Ltd [1977] 1 WLR 578. The agreement will prohibit assignments by the depositor.*

[7]*Stein v Blake [1996] 1 AC 243 HL. Although not contingent debts* owed to the depositor.

[8]*British Eagle International Airlines Ltd v Compagnie Nationale Air France [1975] 1 WLR 758 HL.*

customer) and extend the prevailing right to combine and set-off to future and contingent debts as well as to third party debts. On insolvency of the customer, the mandatory statutory set-off will replace the terms of the set-off agreement (and serve the bank equally well).[9]

Notwithstanding the prevailing assumption that a letter of set-off does not create a charge, it is conceivable that a court might analyse it as such. If this occurred with a corporate customer then there might be a requirement to register the 'charge' under the terms of sections 395 and 396 of the Companies Act 1985, and failure to do so within 21 days of its creation would render it void as against a liquidator and other creditors.[10] As it would be far too late to register when the case came to court, it may seem a sensible precaution to register all set-off agreements as charges within 21 days of their being made.

The set-off agreement, if it is a charge, is one that requires registration if the credit balance constitutes a 'segregated fund'[11] which seems to apply if the money is held in a separate account.

17.3 TAKING A CHARGE OVER THE CREDIT BALANCE

In Morris v Rayners Enterprises, the House of Lords recently held that it is possible to take a charge over a credit balance.[12] Prior to this, it was stated in Halesowen Presswork and Assemblies Ltd v Westminster Bank[13] that a bank could not take a lien over a deposit with it, and this was applied in the first instance decision of Re Charge Card Services Ltd[14] to conclude that a debtor could not take

---

[9]*Whilst any agreement to extend the right of set-off is void following insolvency, a guarantee taken from the customer to secure the debts of a third party is of course valid and liability under it will constitute a contingent liability which is included in the statutory set-off.*

[10]*See 16.11 above.*

[11]*Swiss Bank Corporation v Lloyds Bank Ltd [1982] AC 584 HL.*

[12]*[1998] 3 WLR 909. Also see R. Calnan (1998) 4 JIBFL 125.*

[13]*[1972] AC 785 HL.*

[14]*[1987] Ch 150.*

a charge over a debt owed to itself since this would involve the debt owed by the bank being appropriated to itself, and the bank could not sue itself.

In Morris v Rayners Enterprises,[15] Lord Hoffman distinguished between a lien and the broader concept of proprietary interests. He revisited the well-established law that a deposit with a bank is a form of property known as a chose in action,[16] and he declared that an equitable charge is a form of proprietary interest which is granted by way of security and as such it 'entitles the holder to resort to the property only for the purpose of satisfying some liability due to him . . . and the owner of the property retains an equity of redemption to have the property restored to him when the liability has been discharged . . . A charge is a security interest created without any transfer of title or possession to the beneficiary.' He noted that it is accepted that a charge over a bank deposit can validly be given to a third party and he held that if a charge by a bank over a deposit with it were taken 'there would be no merger of interests because the depositor would retain title to the deposit subject only to the bank's charge. The creation of the charge would be consensual and not require any formal assignment or vesting of title in the bank. If all these features can exist despite the fact that the beneficiary of the charge is the debtor, I cannot see why it cannot properly be said that the debtor has a proprietary interest by way of charge over the debt.'

The application of this conclusion had an interesting effect on the facts in Morris. A company had borrowed from BCCI and a depositor with BCCI had charged his deposit as security for the company's borrowing. The depositor had not given a guarantee. BCCI went into insolvent liquidation and its liquidator sought to recover the loan from the company leaving the depositor to claim for his deposit from the insolvent bank (which claim would of course only be partially met). The depositor, on the other hand, argued that insolvent set-off applied with the effect that his deposit would be lost but the liquidator would not reclaim the loan from the company. The depositor's main argument was that since charging

---

[15] See above.
[16] i.e. the debt owed by the bank to the depositor.

his deposit to the bank was legally impossible, the effect of the document he signed had to be to make him personally liable for the company's debt, which would have led to a set-off. The decision went with the liquidator.

If a charge is taken over the credit balance, the question arises as to whether it requires registration as a charge over a book debt under section 395 of the Companies Act 1985, if the chargor is a company. Once again, there is some doubt as to whether the law does require registration, this time because it is not clear whether the credit balance constitutes a 'book debt'. In Morris, Lord Hoffman expressed no view on the matter but he recorded the view of Lord Hutton in Northern Bank v Ross[17] that an obligation to register is unlikely to arise.

It is open to a bank to register a charge and to be valid this must be within 21 days.[18] It is current practice of the Companies Registration Office to accept applications for registration of charges of credit balances. Where the charge is granted by a non-corporate customer, it appears that registration as a bill of sale is not required.

17.4 THE FLAWED ASSET

In the event that a set-off of a deposit is not available and that a charge taken is not effective, a backstop is provided by an agreement between bank and customer. This is part of the contract of deposit, and restricts the ability of the customer to withdraw his funds until his liability to the bank has been discharged or can no longer arise (if it is contingent), such as a guarantee being determined with no debt due from the principal debtor and thus no liability on the part of the guarantor. Another variation is an agreement that the deposit will not be repaid until the debts of a third party are fully repaid.[19]

There must be some concern that the flawed asset agreement would not survive an insolvency of the customer, due to the *pari passu* principle enacted in section 107 of the Insolvency Act 1986.

---

[17] *[1990] BCC 883.*
[18] *See 16.11 above.*
[19] *This was the form used in Morris v Rayners Enterprises, see above, and there held to be effective as a form of security.*

18 Charges over book debts

18.1 INTRODUCTION

As explained in chapter 16, charges over a company's assets may be either fixed or floating, and fixed charges enjoy a considerable advantage over floating charges in that they rank higher in a company's liquidation. Floating charges, on the other hand, have the advantage of easily being attached to future property, i.e. property which the company will acquire after the charge is taken.

The item 'current debtors' is frequently an important asset on a trading company's balance sheet. If a charge is taken over the company's assets and one year later the company goes into liquidation, the 'current debtors' asset is likely to be made up of entirely different debts owed to the company after this one year. Clearly a floating charge will encompass the new debts but it is also possible for a bank to take a fixed charge over these future debts, although this can only be an equitable fixed charge.[1]

18.2 PROCEDURE FOR TAKING THE CHARGE

A charge over a company's book debts is one of the categories of charges which must be registered within 21 days.[2] A number of complications arise, however, with equitable fixed charges over future book debts, such as the requirement that the charge takes the correct form and that certain details of it be registered. For instance,

---

[1] *Tailby v Official Receiver (1888) 13 App Cas 523 HL.*
[2] *Section 396 of the Companies Act 1985.*

in Siebe Gorman & Co Ltd v Barclays Bank,[3] the bank took a debenture from a company, which included a fixed charge over future book debts. Under the terms of the debenture, the company was legally obliged to pay the proceeds of the debts, when received, into its account with the bank, and was prohibited from assigning the debts to other parties. The bank registered the debenture but the above terms were not noted on the register. The company subsequently did assign the debts to the plaintiff in payment of a debt that it owed to the plaintiff, and the bank was given notice of this assignment. The bank continued to operate the company's current account. The court held that a valid fixed charge had been created over the debts as they came into existence. It further held that the registration of the debenture did not give notice to the plaintiff of the specific terms relating to the charge over the debts. At the moment the bank received notice of assignment of the debts, it enjoyed priority but that (due to the lack of notice of the terms of the debenture) further advances would rank after the plaintiff's claim. Since the bank's loan to the company was on current account and the account was not broken, *Clayton's case*[4] operated to discharge the earlier debt which enjoyed priority, to be replaced by a later debt which did not.

In Re Brightlife Ltd,[5] a non-bank creditor took a fixed charge over a company's future book debts but the company was legally entitled to pay the cheques it received from its debtors into its bank account and to withdraw the proceeds. The charge was held to be merely a floating charge because the chargee could not show that it was capable of exercising effective control over the company's debts.

On the terms of the charge used in Re New Bullas Trading Ltd,[6] the debts received into the company's bank account were subject only to a floating charge (and thus lost priority to preferential creditors) up to the time that administrative receivers were appointed. Debts received into the account thereafter were subject to the fixed charge.

[3] *[1979] 2 Lloyd's Rep 142.*
[4] *See 1.13 above.*
[5] *[1987] Ch 200.*
[6] *[1994] BCLC 485 CA; J.Naccarato and P.Street [1994] JIBFL 109.*

Conclusions

It follows from the above that:

(1) It is not enough to simply describe the charge on future book debts as fixed; the terms of the charge must legally oblige the company to pay the debts into its account with the bank, and to (effectively or specifically) entitle the bank to refuse withdrawals against these credits. It is therefore problematic for a non-bank to take an effective fixed charge over future book debts.

(2) The terms of the charge must also prohibit assignments of the book debts, and details of this and of the obligations in (1) above must be entered on the company's register when the charge itself is registered which must be within 21 days of its creation.

(3) Alternatively to the specific noting of the obligations of (1) on the company's register when the charge is registered, no further advances should be made to the company and current accounts should be ruled off, when notice of assignment is received.

(4) It should be noted that if the company does not comply with its obligation to pay the proceeds of the debts into its bank account, the bank may have no recourse other than to the company itself. This is because the debtors paying the debts can get a good discharge by paying the company and therefore cannot be held liable to the bank which has a charge on the debts. This may be different if the debtors have notice of the charge but they presumably cannot be deemed to know of the charge simply because it is registered.

19 Agricultural charges

19.1 INTRODUCTION

It is always possible for agricultural land to be mortgaged in the same manner as any land, and a land mortgage will normally include fixtures attached to the land. However, some farmers are tenants and thus do not own an interest in the land which is mortgageable, and in any case the assets of a farm will consist of considerably more than the land it occupies.

Corporate farmers may grant a floating charge. A non-corporate farmer will be able to grant a non-possessory chattel mortgage by executing a bill of sale but this procedure has a number of drawbacks, and thus special forms of agricultural charge were established by the Agricultural Credits Act 1928.

The Act defines a farmer as an individual owner or tenant of an agricultural holding. The Act permits a farmer to charge any of his 'farming stock and other agricultural assets'. These are widely defined to include crops and horticultural produce (growing or harvested), livestock (including bees) and the produce and progeny thereof, seeds, manures, agricultural plant and machinery and rights to compensation. Charges may be fixed or floating.

19.2 FIXED CHARGES

A bank with a fixed agricultural charge has a statutory power to take possession of and sell[1] the charged assets following default as

---

[1]*At auction, after five clear days, section 6 of the Agricultural Credits Act 1928.*

defined in the charge. The standard charge will specify the charged assets, and it will include the progeny of charged livestock born after the date of the charge and also any plant which is acquired to replace that charged. The charge will permit the bank to appoint a receiver of the property, or to sell it immediately at auction or by private sale, if the chargor fails to pay on the bank's demand, or on the occurrence of other events such as a judgment creditor enforcing against any of the property, the chargor's death, bankruptcy or arrangement with creditors.

Unlike a normal fixed charge, the chargor is free to sell the assets but is obliged to pay the proceeds of sale to the bank. If he fails to do so with intention to defraud the bank, he commits a criminal offence.

The standard form charge will give the bank power to inspect the charged property. It will also oblige the chargor to keep the property in good repair and insured. Any money received from an insurance claim in respect of the property must be paid to the bank.

19.3 FLOATING CHARGES

Somewhat similar in its nature to the company floating charge, this covers 'the farming stock and other agricultural assets from time to time belonging to the farmer'. Unlike the company floating charge, he must pay over to the bank the proceeds of sale of any of the property covered by the charge, except for money he spends on farming stock which will be subject to the charge.

The charge crystallises[2] automatically on the chargor's death or bankruptcy, or on dissolution of a partnership where the charged property is partnership property. The bank may give written notice to fix the charge, and the standard form will permit this on failure to repay on demand. On crystallisation, the bank enjoys the same statutory right of sale as it has under a fixed charge and it will also have whatever additional rights it has included in the charge. These will normally be the same as granted under the fixed charge, i.e. to appoint a receiver and sell immediately by auction or private sale.

---

[2]*i.e. becomes a fixed charge.*

19.4 REGISTRATION AND PRIORITY

The charge must be registered within seven clear working days of its creation, failing which it becomes void (except against the chargor). There is a procedure for applying for a court extension of this period, however, if the omission to register was accidental or inadvertent. It is registered at the Agricultural Credits Department of the Land Registry under the name of the chargor. Registration constitutes notice to the world at large but when a charge expressly secures a current account or further lending (as bank charges do), the chargee is not deemed to have notice of a later charge if it is registered after he last searched.

It is possible, and clearly desirable, to search the Register before taking the charge. The bank will be deemed to have notice of charges already on the register.

Priority between charges is determined by the order in which they are registered. Once a floating charge is registered, a subsequent fixed charge will be void as respects property covered by the earlier floating charge. Agricultural charges of crops attached to the land take priority over mortgages of that land, in respect of the crops, even if the land mortgage was created first. Claims for rent and taxes normally take priority to fixed and floating agricultural charges.

There is a preference rule for all agricultural charges[3] which is analogous to the 12-month rule for company floating charges under section 245 of the Insolvency Act 1986.[4] If a bankruptcy order is made against a chargor, and the charge was created within three months prior to the petition being presented, then unless it can be proved that the chargor was solvent when he created the charge, the amount secured by the charge will be reduced by the sum owed to the bank prior to the creation of the charge.

For example, say F owes the bank £10,000 unsecured on 1st March when an agricultural charge is taken. On 1st May, when the bank is owed £15,000, a petition is presented against F and the court makes the bankruptcy order on 1st July. The charge is vulnerable because the petition was presented within three months of the

[3] *Section 8(5) of the Agricultural Credits Act 1928.*
[4] *See 16.6 above.*

creation of the charge (although the bankruptcy order was not), and the amount covered by it must therefore be reduced by the sum owed to the bank immediately before the creation of the charge. Thus the charge is good security for £5,000. Note that the provision is worded differently from section 245 and the bank cannot obtain the benefit of the operation of *Clayton's case* when the loan is made on current account.

Appendix 1
Relevant statutory provisions

Bills of Exchange Act 1882
Sections 2, 3, 20, 23–26, 59, 60, 73–81 and 90.

Cheques Act 1957
Sections 1–5.

Law of Property (Miscellaneous Provisions) Act 1989
Sections 1 and 2.

Companies Act 1985
Sections 35, 35A, 35B, 36, 36A, 36C.

Insolvency Act 1986
Sections 122, 123, 213, 214, 238–240, 245, 249, 251 ('shadow director' definition only), 284, 323.

Consumer Credit Act 1974
Sections 8–14, 48–51, 60, 61, 65, 75, 83, 84, 126 and 127.

BILLS OF EXCHANGE ACT 1882

2 Interpretation of terms In this Act, unless the context otherwise requires.

'Acceptance' means an acceptance completed by delivery or notification.

'Action' includes counter claim and set off.

'Banker' includes a body of persons whether incorporated or not who carry on the business of banking.

'Bankrupt' includes any person whose estate is vested in a trustee or assignee under the law for the time being in force relating to bankruptcy.

'Bearer' means the person in possession of a bill or note which is payable to bearer.

'Bill' means bill of exchange, and 'note' means promissory note.

'Delivery' means transfer of possession, actual or constructive, from one person to another.

'Holder' means the payee or indorsee of a bill or note who is in possession of it, or the bearer thereof.

'Indorsement' means an indorsement completed by delivery.

'Issue' means the first delivery of a bid or note, complete in form to a person who takes it as a holder.

'Person' includes a body of persons whether incorporated or not. 'Value' means valuable consideration.

'Written' includes printed, and 'writing' includes print.

3 Bill of exchange defined (1) A bill of exchange is an unconditional order in writing, addressed by one person to another, signed by the person giving it, requiring the person to whom it is addressed to pay on demand or at a fixed or determinable future time a sum certain in money to or to the order of a specified person, or to bearer.

(2) An instrument which does not comply with these conditions, or which orders any act to be done in addition to the payment of money, is not a bill of exchange.

(3) An order to pay out of a particular fund is not unconditional within the meaning of this section; but an unqualified order to pay, coupled with (a) an indication of a particular fund out of which the drawee is to reimburse himself or a particular account to be debited with the amount, or (b) a statement of the transaction which gives rise to the bill, is unconditional.

(4) A bill is not invalid by reason:

(a) that it is not dated;

(b) that it does not specify the value given, or that any value has been given therefor;

(c) that it does not specify the place where it is drawn or the place where it is payable.

20 Inchoate instruments (1) Where a simple signature on a blank . . . paper is delivered by the signer in order that it may be converted into a bill, it operates as a prima facie authority to fill it up as a complete bill for any amount . . . using the signature for that of the drawer, or the acceptor, or an indorser; and, in like manner, when a bill is wanting in any material particular, the person in possession of it has a prima facie authority to fill up the omission in any way he thinks fit.

(2) In order that any such instrument when completed may be enforceable against any person who became a party thereto prior to its completion, it must be filled up within a reasonable time, and strictly in accordance with the authority given. Reasonable time for this purpose is a question of fact.

Provided that if any such instrument after completion is negotiated to a holder in due course it shall be valid and effectual for all purposes in his hands, and he may enforce it as if it had been filled up within a reasonable time and strictly in accordance with the authority given.

23 Signature essential to liability. No person is liable as drawer, indorser, or acceptor of a bill who has not signed it as such: Provided that:

(1) Where a person signs a bill in a trade or assumed name, he is liable thereon as if he had signed it in his own name;

(2) The signature of the name of a firm is equivalent to the signature by the person so signing of the names of all persons liable as partners in that firm.

24 Forged or unauthorised signature. Subject to the provisions of this Act, where a signature on a bill is forged or placed thereon without the authority of the person whose signature it purports to be, the forged or unauthorised signature is wholly inoperative, and no right to retain the bill or to give a discharge therefore or to enforce payment thereof against any party thereto can be acquired through or under that signature, unless the party against whom it is sought to retain or enforce payment of the bill is precluded from setting up the forgery or want of authority. Provided that nothing in this section shall affect the ratification of an unauthorised signature not amounting to a forgery.

25 Procuration signatures. A signature by procuration operates as notice that the agent has but a limited authority to sign, and the principal is only bound by such signature if the agent in so signing was acting within the actual limits of his authority.

26 Person signing as agent or in representative capacity (1) Where a person signs a bill as drawer, indorser, or acceptor, and adds words to his signature indicating that he signs for or on behalf of a principal, or in a representative character, he is not personally liable thereon; but the mere addition to his signature of words describing him as an agent, or as filling a representative character, does not exempt him from personal liability.

(2) In determining whether a signature on a bill is that of the principal or that of the agent by whose hand it is written, the construction most favourable to the validity of the instrument shall be adopted.

59 Payment in due course (1) A bill is discharged by payment in due course by or on behalf of the drawee or acceptor.

'Payment in due course' means payment made at or after the maturity of the bill to the holder thereof in good faith and without notice that his title to the bill is defective.

(2) Subject to the provisions herein-after contained, when a bill is paid by the drawer or an indorser it is not discharged, but

(a) where a bill payable to, or to the order of, a third party is paid by the drawer the drawer may enforce payment thereof against the acceptor, but may not re-issue the bill;

(b) where a bill is paid by an indorser, or where a bill payable to drawer's order is paid by the drawer, the party paying it is remitted to his former rights as regards the acceptor or antecedent parties, and he may, if he thinks fit, strike out his own and subsequent indorsements, and again negotiate the bill.

(3) Where an accommodation bill is paid in due course by the party accommodated the bill is discharged.

60 Banker paying demand draft whereon indorsement is forged. When a bill payable to order on demand is drawn on a banker, and the banker on whom it is drawn pays the bill in good faith and in the ordinary course of business, it is not incumbent on the banker to show that the indorsement of the payee or any subsequent indorsement was made by or under the authority of the person whose indorsement it purports to be, and the banker is deemed to have paid the bill in due course, although such indorsement has been forged or made without authority.

73 Cheque defined. A cheque is a bill of exchange drawn on a banker payable on demand.

Except as otherwise provided in this Part, the provisions of this Act applicable to a bill of exchange payable on demand apply to a cheque.

74 Presentment of cheque for payment Subject to the provisions of this Act:

(1) Where a cheque is not presented for payment within a reasonable time of its issue, and the drawer or the person on whose account it is drawn had the right at the time of such presentment as between him and the banker to have the cheque paid and suffers actual damage through the delay, he is discharged to the extent of such damage, that is to say, to the extent to which such drawer or person is a creditor of such banker to a larger amount than he would have been had such cheque been paid.

(2) In determining what is a reasonable time regard shall be had to the nature of the instrument, the usage of trade and of bankers, and the facts of the particular case.

(3) The holder of such cheque as to which such drawer or person is discharged shall be a creditor, in lieu of such drawer or person, of such banker to the extent of such discharge, and entitled to recover the amount from him.

74A Presentment of cheque for payment: alternative place of presentment. Where the banker on whom a cheque is drawn:

(a) has by notice published in the London, Edinburgh and Belfast Gazettes specified an address at which cheques drawn on him may be presented, and

(b) has not by notice so published cancelled the specification of that address,

the cheque is also presented at the proper place if it is presented there.

74B Presentment of cheque for payment: alternative means of presentment by banker:

(1) A banker may present a cheque for payment to the banker on whom it is drawn by notifying him of its essential features by electronic means or otherwise, instead of presenting the cheque itself.

(2) If a cheque is presented for payment under this section, presentment need not be made at the proper place or at a reasonable hour on a business day.

(3) If, before the close of business on the next business day following presentment of a cheque under this section, the banker on whom the cheque is drawn requests the banker by whom the cheque was presented to present the cheque itself.

(a) the presentment under this section shall be disregarded, and

(b) this section shall not apply in relation to the subsequent presentment of the cheque.

(4) A request under subsection (3) above for the presentment of a cheque shall not constitute dishonour of the cheque by non-payment.

(5) Where presentment of a cheque is made under this section, the banker who presented the cheque and the banker on whom it is drawn shall be subject to the same duties in relation to the collection and payment of the cheque as if the cheque itself had been presented for payment.

(6) For the purposes of this section, the essential features of a cheque are;

(a) the serial number of the cheque,

   (b) the code which identifies the banker on whom the cheque is drawn,

   (c) the account number of the drawer of the cheque, and

   (d) the amount of the cheque as entered by the drawer of the cheque.

74C Cheques presented for payment under section 74B: disapplication of section 52(4) Section 52(4) above:

(a) so far as relating to presenting a bill of exchange for payment, shall not apply to presenting a cheque for payment under section 74B above, and

(b) so far as relating to a bill which is paid, shall not apply to a cheque which is paid following presentment under that section.

75 Revocation of banker's authority. The duty and authority of a banker to pay a cheque drawn on him by his customer are determined by:

(1) Countermand of payment.

(2) Notice of the customer's death.

76 General and special crossings defined (1) Where a cheque bears across its face an addition of:

(a) the words 'and company' or any abbreviation thereof between two parallel transverse lines, either with or without the words 'not negotiable';
    or

(b) two parallel transverse lines simply, either with or without the words 'not negotiable':

that addition constitutes a crossing, and the cheque is crossed generally.

(2) Where a cheque bears across its face an addition of the name of a banker either with or without the words 'not negotiable', that addition constitutes a crossing, and the cheque is crossed specially and to that banker.

77 Crossing by drawer or after issue:

(1) A cheque may be crossed generally or specially by the drawer.

(2) Where a cheque is uncrossed, the holder may cross it generally or specially.

(3) Where a cheque is crossed generally the holder may cross it specially.

(4) Where a cheque is crossed generally or specially, the holder may add the words 'not negotiable'.

(5) Where a cheque is crossed specially, the banker to whom it is crossed may again cross it specially to another banker for collection.

(6) Where an uncrossed cheque, or a cheque crossed generally, is sent to a banker for collection, he may cross it specially to himself.

78 Crossing a material part of cheque. A crossing authorised by this Act is a material part of the cheque; it shall not be lawful for any person to obliterate or, except as authorised by this Act, to add to or alter the crossing.

79 Duties of banker as to crossed cheques (1) Where a cheque is crossed specially to more than one banker except when crossed to an agent for collection being a banker, the banker on whom it is drawn shall refuse payment thereof.

(2) Where the banker on whom a cheque is drawn which is so crossed nevertheless pays the same, or pays a cheque crossed generally otherwise than to a banker, or if crossed specially otherwise than to the banker to whom it is crossed, or his agent for collection being a banker, he is liable to the true owner of the cheque for any loss he may sustain owing to the cheque having been so paid. Provided that where a cheque is presented for payment which does not at the time of presentment appear to be crossed, or to have had a crossing which has been obliterated, or to have been added to or altered otherwise than as authorised by this Act, the banker paying the cheque in good faith and without negligence shall not be responsible or incur any liability, nor shall the payment be questioned by reason of the cheque having been crossed, or of the crossing having been obliterated or having been added to or altered otherwise than as authorised by this Act, and of payment having been made otherwise than to a banker or to the banker to whom the cheque is or was crossed, or to his agent for collection being a banker, as the case may be.

80 Protection to banker and drawer where cheque is crossed
Where the banker, on whom a crossed cheque (including a cheque which under section 81A below or otherwise is not transferable) is drawn, in good faith and without negligence pays it, if crossed generally, to a banker, and if crossed specially, to the banker to whom it is crossed, or his agent for collection being a banker, the banker paying the cheque, and, if the cheque has come into the hands of the payee, the drawer, shall respectively be entitled to the same rights and be placed in the same position as if payment of the cheque had been made to the true owner thereof.

81 Effect of crossing on holder. Where a person takes a crossed cheque which bears on it the words 'not negotiable', he shall not have and shall not be capable of giving a better title to the cheque than that which the person from whom he took it had.

81 A Non-transferable cheque (1) Where a cheque is crossed and bears across its face the words 'account payee' or 'a/c payee', either with or without the word 'only', the cheque shall not be transferable, but shall only be valid as between the parties thereto.

(2) A banker is not to be treated for the purposes of section 80 above as having been negligent by reason only of his failure to concern himself with any purported indorsement of a cheque which under subsection (1) above or otherwise is not transferable.

90 Good faith. A thing is deemed to be done in good faith, within the meaning of this Act, where it is in fact done honestly, whether it is done negligently or not.

CHEQUES ACT 1957

1 Protection of bankers paying unindorsed or irregularly indorsed cheques, etc (1) Where a banker in good faith and in the ordinary course of business pays a cheque drawn on him which is not indorsed or is irregularly indorsed, he does not, in doing so, incur any liability by reason only of the absence of, or irregularity in, indorsement, and he is deemed to have paid it in due course.

(2) Where a banker in good faith and in the ordinary course of business pays any such instrument as the following, namely:

(a) a document issued by a customer of his which, though not a bill of exchange, is intended to enable a person to obtain payment from him of the sum mentioned in the document,

(b) a draft payable on demand drawn by him upon himself, whether payable at the head office or some other office of his bank,

he does not, in doing so, incur any liability by reason only of the absence of, or irregularity in, indorsement, and the payment discharges the instrument.

2 Rights of bankers collecting cheques not indorsed by holders. A banker who gives value for, or has a lien on, a cheque payable to order which the holder delivers to him for collection without indorsing it, has such (if any) rights as he would have had if, upon delivery, the holder had indorsed it in blank.

3 Unindorsed cheques as evidence of payment:

(1) An unindorsed cheque which appears to have been paid by the banker on whom it is drawn is evidence of the receipt by the payee of the sum payable by the cheque.

(2) For the purposes of subsection (1) above, a copy of a cheque to which that subsection applies is evidence of the cheque if:

(a) the copy is made by the banker in whose possession the cheque is after presentment, and

(b) it is certified by him to be a true copy of the original.

4 Protection of bankers collecting payment of cheques, etc (1) Where a banker, in good faith and without negligence:

(a) receives payment for a customer of an instrument to which this section applies, or

(b) having credited a customer's account with the amount of such an instrument, receives payment thereof for himself,

and the customer has no title, or a defective title, to the instrument, the banker does not incur any liability to the true owner of the instrument by reason only of having received payment thereof.

(2) This section applies to the following instruments, namely;

(a) cheques (including cheques which are under section 81A(1) of the Bills of Exchange Act 1882 or otherwise are not transferable),

(b) any document issued by a customer of a banker which, though not a bill of exchange, is intended to enable a person to obtain payment from that banker of the sum mentioned in the document,

(c) any document issued by a public officer which is intended to enable a person to obtain payment from the Paymaster General or the Queen's and Lord Treasurer's Remembrancer of the sum mentioned in the document but is not a bill of exchange,

(d) any draft payable on demand drawn by a banker upon himself, whether payable at the head office or some other office of his bank.

(3) A banker is not to be treated for the purposes of this section as having been negligent by reason only of his failure to concern himself with absence of, or irregularity in, indorsement of an instrument.

5 Application of certain provisions of Bills of Exchange Act 1882 to instruments not being bills of exchange. The provisions of the Bills of Exchange Act 1882 relating to crossed cheques shall, so far as applicable, have effect in relation to instruments (other than cheques) to which the last foregoing section applies as they have effect in relation to cheques.

LAW OF PROPERTY (MISCELLANEOUS PROVISIONS) ACT 1989

1 Deeds and their execution

(1) Any rule of law which –

(a) restricts the substances on which a deed may be written,

(b) requires a seal for the valid execution of an instrument as a deed by an individual, or

(c) requires authority by one person to another to deliver an instrument as a deed on his behalf to be given by deed is abolished.

(2) An instrument shall not be a deed unless –

(a) it makes it clear on its face that it is intended to be a deed by the person making it or, as the case may be, by the parties to it (whether by describing itself as a deed or expressing itself to be executed or signed as a deed or otherwise), and

(b) it is validly executed as a deed by that person or, as the case may be, one or more of those parties.

(3) An instrument is validly executed as a deed by an individual if, and only if –

(a) it is signed –
  (i) by him in the presence of a witness who attests the signature, or
  (ii) at his direction and in his presence and the presence of two witnesses who each attest the signature, and

(b) it is delivered as a deed by him or a person authorised to do so on his behalf.

(4) In subsections (2) and (3) above 'sign', in relation to an instrument, includes making one's mark on the instrument and 'signature' is to be construed accordingly.

(5) Where a solicitor or licensed conveyancer, or an agent or employee of a solicitor or licensed conveyancer, in the course of or in connection with a transaction involving the disposition or creation of an interest in land, purports to deliver an instrument as a deed on behalf of a party to the instrument, it shall be conclusively presumed in favour of a purchaser that he is authorised so to deliver the instrument.

(6) In subsection (5) above –

'disposition' and 'purchaser' have the same meanings as in the Law of Property Act 1925, and

'interest in land' means any estate, interest or charge in or over land or in or over the proceeds of sale of land.

(7) Where an instrument under seal that constitutes a deed is required for the purposes of an Act passed before this section comes into force, this section shall have effect as to signing, sealing or delivery of an instrument by an individual in place of any provision of that Act as to signing, sealing or delivery.

2 Contracts for sale etc. of land to be made by signed writing.

(1) A contract for the sale or other disposition of an interest in land can only be made in writing and only by incorporating all the terms which the parties have expressly agreed in one document or, where contracts are exchanged, in each.

(2) The terms may be incorporated in a document either by being set out in it or by reference to some other document.

(3) The document incorporating the terms or, where contracts are exchanged, one of the documents incorporating them (but not necessarily the same one) must be signed by or on behalf of each party to the contract.

(4) Where a contract for the sale or other disposition of an interest in land satisfies the conditions of this section by reason only of the rectification of one or more documents in pursuance of an order of a court, the contract shall come into being, or be deemed to have come into being, at such time as may be specified in the order.

(5) This section does not apply in relation to:

(a) a contract to grant such a lease as is mentioned in section 54(2) of the Law of Property Act 1926 (short leases),

(b) a contract made in the course of a public auction, or

(c) a contract regulated under the Financial Services Act 1986, and nothing in this section affects the creation or operation of resulting, implied or constructive trusts.

(6) In this section –

'disposition' has the same meaning as in the Law of Property Act 1925,

'interest in land' means any estate, interest or charge in or over land or in or over the proceeds of sale of land.

(7) Nothing in this section shall apply in relation to contracts made before this section comes into force.

(8) Section 40 of the Law of Property Act 1925 (which is superseded by this section) shall cease to have effect.

COMPANIES ACT 1985

35 A company's capacity not limited by its memorandum (1) The validity of an act done by a company shall not be called into question on the ground of lack of capacity by reason of anything in the company's memorandum.

(2) A member of a company may bring proceedings to restrain the doing of an act which but for subsection (1) would be beyond the company's capacity – but no such proceedings shall lie in respect of an act to be done in fulfilment of a legal obligation arising from a previous act of the company.
(3) It remains the duty of the directors to observe any limitations on their powers flowing from the company's memorandum; and action by the directors which but for subsection (1) would be beyond the company's capacity may only be ratified by the company by special resolution.

A resolution ratifying such action shall not affect any liability incurred by the directors or any other person; relief from any such liability must be agreed to separately by special resolution.

(4) The operation of this section is restricted by section 30B(1) of the Charities Act 1960 and section 112(3) of the Companies Act 1989 in relation to companies which are charities; and section 322A below (invalidity of certain transactions to which directors or their associates are parties) has effect notwithstanding this section.

35A Power of directors to bind the company (1) In favour of a person dealing with a company in good faith, the power of the board of directors to bind the company, or authorise others to do so, shall be deemed to be free of any limitation under the company's constitution.

(2) For this purpose –
(a) a person 'deals with' a company if he is a party to any transaction or other act to which the company is a party,
(b) a person shall not be regarded as acting in bad faith by reason only of his knowing that an act is beyond the powers of the directors under the company's constitution, and
(c) a person shall be presumed to have acted in good faith unless the contrary is proved.

(3) The references above to limitations on the directors' powers under the company's constitution include limitations deriving,

(a) from a resolution of the company in general meeting or a meeting of any class of shareholders, or

(b) from any agreement between the members of the company or of any class of shareholders.

(4) Subsection (1) does not affect any right of a member of the company to bring proceedings to restrain the doing of an act which is beyond the powers of the directors; but no such proceedings shall lie in respect of an act to be done in fulfilment of a legal obligation arising from a previous act of the company.

(5) Nor does that subsection affect any liability incurred by the directors, or any other person, by reason of the directors' exceeding their powers.

(6) The operation of this section is restricted by section 30B(1) of the Charities Act 1960 and section 112(3) of the Companies Act 1989 in relation to companies which are charities; and section 322A below (invalidity of certain transactions to which directors or their associates are parties) has effect notwithstanding this section.

35B No duty to enquire as to capacity of company authority of directors. A party to a transaction with a company is not bound to enquire as to whether it is permitted by the company's memorandum or as to any limitation on the powers of the board of directors to bind the company or authorise others to do so.

36 Company contracts: England and Wales. Under the law of England and Wales a contract may be made –

(a) by a company, by writing under its common seal, or

(b) on behalf of a company, by any person acting under its authority, express or implied,

and any formalities required by law in the case of a contract made by an individual also apply, unless a contrary intention appears, to a contract made by or on behalf of a company.'

36A Execution of documents: England and Wales (1) Under the law of England and Wales the following provisions have effect with respect to the execution of documents by a company.

(2) A document is executed by a company by the affixing of its common seal.

(3) A company need not have a common seal, however, and the following subsections apply whether it does or not.

(4) A document signed by a director and the secretary of a company, or by two directors of a company, and expressed (in whatever form of words) to be executed by the company has the same effect as if executed under the common seal of the company.

(5) A document executed by a company which makes it clear on its face that it is intended by the person or persons making it to be a deed has effect, upon delivery, as a deed; and it shall be presumed, unless a contrary intention is proved, to be delivered upon its being so executed.

(6) In favour of a purchaser a document shall be deemed to have been duly executed by a company if it purports to be signed by a director and the secretary of the company, or by two directors of the company, and, where it makes it clear on its face that it is intended by the person or persons making it to be a deed, to have been delivered upon its being executed.

A 'purchaser' means a purchaser in good faith for valuable consideration and includes a lessee, mortgagee or other person who for valuable consideration acquires an interest in property.'

36C Pre-incorporation contracts, deeds and obligations (1) A contract which purports to be made by or on behalf of a company at a time when the company has not been formed has effect, subject to any agreement to the contrary, as one made with the person purporting to act for the company or as agent for it, and he is personally liable on the contract accordingly.

(2) Subsection (1) applies:
(a) to the making of a deed under the law of England and Wales, and (b) to the undertaking of an obligation under the law of Scotland, as it applies to the making of a contract.'

INSOLVENCY ACT 1986

122 Circumstances in which a company may be wound up by the court (1) A company may be wound up by the court if –

(a) the company has by special resolution resolved that the company be wound up by the court,

(b) being a public company which was registered as such on its original incorporation, the company has not been issued with a certificate under section 117 of the Companies Act (public company share capital requirements) and more than a year has expired since it was so registered,

(c) it is an old public company, within the meaning of the Consequential Provisions Act,

(d) the company does not commence its business within a year from its incorporation or suspends its business for a whole year,

(e) the number of members is reduced below 2,

(f) the company is unable to pay its debts,

(g) the court is of the opinion that it is just and equitable that the company should be wound up.

(2) In Scotland, a company which the Court of Session has jurisdiction to wind up may be wound up by the Court if there is subsisting a floating charge over property comprised in the company's property and undertaking, and the court is satisfied that the security of the creditor entitled to the benefit of the floating charge is in jeopardy. For this purpose a creditor's security is deemed to be in jeopardy if the Court is satisfied that events have occurred or are about to occur which render it unreasonable in the creditor's interests that the company should retain power to dispose of the property which is subject to the floating charge.

123 Definition of inability to pay debts (1) A company is deemed unable to pay its debts –

(a) if a creditor (by assignment or other vise) to whom the company is indebted in a sum exceeding £750 then due has served on the company, by leaving it at the company's registered office, a written demand (in the prescribed form) requiring the company to pay the sum so due and the company has for 3 weeks thereafter neglected to pay the sum or to secure or compound for it to the reasonable satisfaction of the creditor, or

(b) if, in England and Wales, execution or other process issued on a judgment, decree or order of any court in favour of a creditor of the company is returned unsatisfied in whole or in part, or

(c) if, in Scotland, the induciae of a charge for payment on an extract decree, or an extracted registered bond, or an extract registered protest, have expired without payment being made; or

(d) if, in Northern Ireland, a certificate of unenforceability has been granted in respect of a judgment against the company, or

(e) if it is proved to the satisfaction of the court that the company is unable to pay its debts as they fall due.

(2) A company is also deemed unable to pay its debts if it is proved to the satisfaction of the court that the value of the company's assets is less than the amount of its liabilities, taking into account its contingent and prospective liabilities.

(3) The money sum for the time being specified in subsection (1)(a) is subject to increase or reduction by order under section 416 in Part XV.

213 Fraudulent trading (1) If in the course of the winding up of a company it appears that any business of the company has been carried on with intent to defraud creditors of the company or creditors of any other person, or for any fraudulent purpose, the following has effect.

(2) The court, on the application of the liquidator may declare that any persons who were knowingly parties to the carrying on of the business in the manner above-mentioned are to be liable to make such contributions (if any) to the company's assets as the court thinks proper.

214 Wrongful trading (1) Subject to subsection (3) below, if in the course of the winding up of a company it appears that subsection (2) of this section applies in relation to a person who is or has been a director of the company, the court, on the application of the liquidator, may declare that person is to be liable to make such contribution (if any) to the company's assets as the court thinks proper.

(2) This subsection applies in relation to a person if –

(a) the company has gone into insolvent liquidation,

(b) at some time before the commencement of the winding up of the company, that person knew or ought to have concluded that there was no reasonable prospect that the company would avoid going into insolvent liquidation, and

(c) that person was a director of the company at that time,

but the court shall not make a declaration under this section in any case where the time mentioned in paragraph (b) above was before 28th April 1986.

(3) The court shall not make a declaration under this section with respect to any person if it is satisfied that after the condition specified in subsection (2)(b) was first satisfied in relation to him that person took every step with a view to minimising the potential loss of the company's creditors as (assuming him to have known that there was no reasonable prospect that the company would avoid going into insolvent liquidation) he ought to have taken.

(4) For the purposes of subsections (2) and (3), the facts which a director of a company ought to know or ascertain, the conclusions which he ought to reach and the steps which he ought to take are those which would be known or ascertained, or reached or taken, by a reasonably diligent person having both –

(a) the general knowledge, skill and experience that may reasonably be expected of a person carrying out the same functions as are carried out by that director in relation to the company, and

(b) the general knowledge, skill and experience that that director has.

(5) The reference in subsection (4) to the functions carried out in relation to a company by a director of the company includes any functions which he does not carry out but which have been entrusted to him.

(6) For the purposes of this section a company goes into insolvent liquidation if it goes into liquidation at a time when its assets are insufficient for the payment of its debts and other liabilities and the expenses of the winding up.

(7) In this section 'director' includes a shadow director.

(8) This section is without prejudice to section 213.

238 Transactions at an undervalue (England and Wales) (1) This section applies in the case of a company where –

(a) an administration order is made in relation to the company; or

(b) the company goes into liquidation;

and 'the office-holder' means the administrator or the liquidator, as the case may be.

(2) Where the company has at a relevant time (defined in section 240) entered into a transaction with any person at an undervalue, the office-holder may apply to the court for an order under this section.

(3) Subject as follows, the court shall, on such an application, make such order as it thinks fit for restoring the position to what it would have been if the company had not entered into that transaction.

(4) For the purposes of this section and section 241, a company enters into a transaction with a person at an undervalue if –

(a) the company makes a gift to that person or otherwise enters into a transaction with that person on terms that provide for the company to receive no consideration, or

(b) the company enters into a transaction with that person for a consideration the value of which, in money or money's worth is significantly less than the value, in money or money's worth, of the consideration provided by the company.

(5) The court shall not make an order under this section in respect of a transaction at an undervalue if it is satisfied –

(a) that the company which entered into the transaction did so in good faith and for the purpose of carrying on its business, and

(b) that at the time it did so there were reasonable grounds for believing that the transaction would benefit the company.

239 Preferences (England and Wales) (1) This section applies as does section 238.

(2) Where the company has at a relevant time (defined in the next section) given a preference to any person, the office-holder may apply to the court for an order under this section.

(3) Subject as follows, the court shall, on such an application, make such order as it thinks fit for restoring the position to what it would have been if the company had not given that preference.

(4) For the purposes of this section and section 241, a company gives a preference to a person if –

(a) that person is one of the company's creditors or a surety or guarantor for any of the company's debts or other liabilities, and
(b) the company does anything or suffers anything to be done which (in either case) has the effect of putting that person into a position which, in the event of the company going into insolvent liquidation, will be better than the position he would have been in if that thing had not been done.

(5) The court shall not make an order under this section in respect of a preference given to any person unless the company which gave the preference was influenced in deciding to give it by a desire to produce in relation to that person the effect mentioned in subsection (4)(b).

(6) A company which has given a preference to a person connected with the company (otherwise than by reason only of being its employee) at the time the preference was given is presumed, unless the contrary is shown, to have been influenced in deciding to give it by such a desire as is mentioned in subsection (5).

(7) The fact that something has been done in pursuance of the order of a court does not, without more, prevent the doing or suffering of that thing from constituting the giving of a preference.

240 'Relevant time' under ss. 238, 239 (1) Subject to the next subsection, the time at which a company enters into a transaction at an undervalue or gives a preference is a relevant time if the transaction is entered into, or the preference given –

(a) in the case of a transaction at an undervalue or of a preference which is given to a person who is connected with the company (otherwise than by reason only of being its employee), at a time in the period of 2 years ending with the onset of insolvency (which expression is defined below),
(b) in the case of a preference which is not such a transaction and is not so given, at a time in the period of 6 months ending with the onset of insolvency, and
(c) in either case, at a time between the presentation of a petition

for the making of an administration order in relation to the company and the making of such an order on that petition.

(2) Where a company enters into a transaction at an undervalue or gives a preference at a time mentioned in subsection (1)(a) or (b), that time is not a relevant time for the purposes of section 238 or 239 unless the company –

(a) is at that time unable to pay its debts within the meaning of section 123 in Chapter VI of Part IV, or
(b) becomes unable to pay its debts within the meaning of that section in consequence of the transaction or preference,

but the requirements of this subsection are presumed to be satisfied, unless the contrary is shown, in relation to any transaction at an undervalue which is entered into by a company with a person who is connected with the company.

(3) For the purposes of subsection (1), the onset of insolvency is –

(a) in a case where section 238 or 239 applies by reason of the making of an administration order or of a company going into liquidation immediately upon the discharge of an administration order, the date of the presentation of the petition on which the administration order was made, and
(b) in a case where the section applies by reason of a company going into liquidation at any other time, the date of the commencement of the winding up.

245 Avoidance of certain floating charges (1) This section applies as does section 238, but applies to Scotland as well as to England and Wales.

(2) Subject as follows, a floating charge on the company's undertaking or property created at a relevant time is invalid except to the extent of the aggregate of –

(a) the value of so much of the consideration for the creation of the charge as consists of money paid, or goods or services supplied, to the company at the same time as, or after, the creation of the charge,
(b) the value of so much of that consideration as consists of the

discharge or reduction, at the same time as, or after, the creation of the charge, of any debt of the company, and

(c) the amount of such interest (if any) as is payable on the amount falling within paragraph (a) or (b) in pursuance of any agreement under which the money was so paid, the goods or services were so supplied or the debt was so discharged or reduced.

(3) Subject to the next subsection, the time at which a floating charge is created by a company is a relevant time for the purposes of this section if the charge is created –

(a) in the case of a charge which is created in favour of a person who is connected with the company, at a time in the period of 2 years ending with the onset of insolvency,

(b) in the case of a charge which is created in favour of any other person, at a time in the period of 12 months ending with the onset of insolvency, or

(c) in either case, at a time between the presentation of a petition for the making of an administration order in relation to the company and the making of such an order on that petition.

(4) Where a company creates a floating charge at a time mentioned in subsection (3)(b) and the person in favour of whom the charge is created is not connected with the company, that time is not a relevant time for the purposes of this section unless the company –

(a) is at that time unable to pay its debts within the meaning of section 123 in Chapter VI of Part IV, or

(b) becomes unable to pay its debts within the meaning of that section in consequence of the transaction under which the charge is created.

(5) For the purposes of subsection (3), the onset of insolvency is –

(a) in a case where this section applies by reason of the making of an administration order, the date of the presentation of the petition on which the order was made, and

(b) in a case where this section applies by reason of a company going into liquidation, the date of the commencement of the winding up.

(6) For the purposes of subsection (2)(a) the value of any goods or services supplied by way of consideration for a floating charge is the amount in money which at the time they were supplied could reasonably have been expected to be obtained for supplying the goods or services in the ordinary course of business and on the same terms (apart from the consideration) as those on which they were supplied to the company.

249 'Connected' with a company. For the purposes of any provision in this Group of Parts, a person is connected with a company if –

(a) he is a director or shadow director of the company or an associate of such a director or shadow director, or
(b) he is an associate of the company; and 'associate' has the meaning given by section 435 in Part XVIII of this Act.

251 Expressions used generally. In this Group of Parts, except in so far as the context otherwise requires –

... 'shadow director', in relation to a company, means a person in accordance with whose directions or instructions the directors of the company are accustomed to act (but so that a person is not deemed a shadow director by reason only that the directors act on advice given by him in a professional capacity).

284 Restrictions on dispositions of property (1) Where a person is adjudged bankrupt, any disposition of property made by that person in the period to which this section applies is void except to the extent that it is or was made with the consent of the court, or is or was subsequently ratified by the court.

(2) Subsection (1) applies to a payment (whether in cash or otherwise) as it applies to a disposition of property and, accordingly, where any payment is void by virtue of that subsection, the person paid shall hold the sum paid for the bankrupt as part of his estate.

(3) This section applies to the period beginning with the day of the presentation of the petition for the bankruptcy order and ending with the vesting, under Chapter IV of this Part, of the bankrupt's estate in a trustee.

(4) The preceding provisions of this section do not give a remedy against any person –

(a) in respect of any property or payment which he received before the commencement of the bankruptcy in good faith, for value and without notice that the petition had been presented, or
(b) in respect of any interest in property which derives from an interest in respect of which there is, by virtue of this subsection, no remedy.

(5) Where after the commencement of his bankruptcy the bankrupt has incurred a debt to a banker or other person by reason of the making of a payment which is void under this section, that debt is deemed for the purposes of any of this Group of Parts to have been incurred before the commencement of the bankruptcy unless –

(a) that banker or person had notice of the bankruptcy before the debt was incurred, or
(b) it is not reasonably practicable for the amount of the payment to be recovered from the person to whom it was made.

(6) A disposition of property is void under this section notwithstanding that the property is not or, as the case may be, would not be comprised in the bankrupt's estate; but nothing in this section affects any disposition made by a person of property held by him on trust for any other person.

323 Mutual credit and set-off (1) This section applies where before the commencement of the bankruptcy there have been mutual credits, mutual debts or other mutual dealings between the bankrupt and any creditor of the bankrupt proving or claiming to prove for a bankruptcy debt.

(2) An account shall be taken of what is due from each party to the other in respect of the mutual dealings and the sums due from one party shall be set off against the sums due from the other.

(3) Sums due from the bankrupt to another party shall not be included in the account taken under subsection (2) if that other party had notice at the time they became due that a bankruptcy petition relating to the bankrupt was pending.

(4) Only the balance (if any) of the account taken under subsection

(2) is provable as a bankruptcy debt or, as the case may be, to be paid to the trustee as part of the bankrupt's estate.

CONSUMER CREDIT ACT 1974

8 Consumer credit agreements (1) A personal credit agreement is an agreement between an individual ('the debtor') and any other person ('the creditor') by which the creditor provides the debtor with credit of any amount.

(2) A consumer credit agreement is a personal credit agreement by which the creditor provides the debtor with credit not exceeding £25,000.

(3) A consumer credit agreement is a regulated agreement within the meaning of this Act if it is not an agreement (an 'exempt agreement') specified in or under section 16.

9 Meaning of credit (1) In this Act 'credit' includes a cash loan, and any other form of financial accommodation.

(2) Where credit is provided otherwise than in sterling it shall be treated for the purposes of this Act as provided in sterling of an equivalent amount.

(3) Without prejudice to the generality of subsection (1), the person by whom goods are bailed or (in Scotland) hired to an individual under a hire-purchase agreement shall be taken to provide him with fixed-sum credit to finance the transaction of an amount equal to the total price of the goods less the aggregate of the deposit (if any) and the total charge for credit.

(4) For the purposes of this Act, an item entering into the total charge for credit shall not be treated as credit even though time is allowed for its payment.

10 Running-account credit and fixed-sum credit (1) For the purposes of this Act –

(a) running-account credit is a facility under a personal credit agreement whereby the debtor is enabled to receive from time to time (whether in his own person, or by another person) from the creditor or a third party cash, goods and services (or any of them) to an amount or value such that, taking into account payments made by or to the credit of the debtor, the credit limit (if any) is not at any time exceeded, and

(b) fixed-sum credit is any other facility under a personal credit agreement whereby the debtor is enabled to receive credit (whether in one amount or by instalments).

(2) In relation to running-account credit, 'credit limit' means, as respects any period, the maximum debit balance which, under the credit agreement, is allowed to stand on the account during that period, disregarding any term of the agreement allowing that maximum to be exceeded merely temporarily.

(3) For the purposes of section 8(2), running-account credit shall be taken not to exceed the amount specified in that subsection ('the specified amount') if –

(a) the credit limit does not exceed the specified amount, or

(b) whether or not there is a credit limit, and if there is, notwithstanding that it exceeds the specified amount –

(i)   the debtor is not enabled to draw at any one time an amount which, so far as (having regard to section 9(4)) it represents credit, exceeds the specified amount, or

(ii)   the agreement provides that, if the debit balance rises above a given amount (not exceeding the specified amount), the rate of the total charge for credit increases or any other condition favouring the creditor or his associate comes into operation, or

(iii)   at the time the agreement is made it is probable, having regard to the terms of the agreement and any other relevant considerations, that the debit balance will not at any time rise above the specified amount–

11 Restricted-use credit and unrestricted-use credit (1) A restricted-use credit agreement is a regulated consumer credit agreement –

(a) to finance a transaction between the debtor and the creditor, whether forming part of that agreement or not, or

(b) to finance a transaction between the debtor and a person (the 'supplier') other than the creditor, or

(c) to refinance any existing indebtedness of the debtor's, whether to the creditor or another person,
and 'restricted-use credit' shall be construed accordingly.

(2) An unrestricted-use credit agreement is a regulated consumer credit agreement not falling within subsection (1), and 'unrestricted-use credit' shall be construed accordingly.

(3) An agreement does not fall within subsection (1) if the credit is in fact provided in such a way as to leave the debtor free to use it as he chooses, even though certain uses would contravene that or any other agreement.

(4) An agreement may fall within subsection (1)(b) although the identity of the supplier is unknown at the time the agreement is made.

12 Debtor-creditor-supplier agreements. A debtor-creditor-supplier agreement is a regulated consumer credit agreement being –

(a) a restricted-use credit agreement which falls within section 11(1)(a), or

(b) a restricted-use credit agreement which falls within section 11(1)(b) and is made by the creditor under pre-existing arrangements, or in contemplation of future arrangements, between himself and the supplier, or

(c) an unrestricted-use credit agreement which is made by the creditor under pre-existing arrangements between himself and a person (the 'supplier') other than the debtor in the knowledge that the credit is to be used to finance a transaction between the debtor and the supplier.

13 Debtor-creditor agreements. A debtor creditor agreement is a regulated consumer credit agreement being –

(a) a restricted-use credit agreement which falls within section 11(1)(b) but is not made by the creditor under pre-existing arrangements, or in contemplation of future arrangements, between himself and the supplier, or

(b) a restricted-use credit agreement which falls within section 11(1)(c), or

(c) an unrestricted-use credit agreement which is not made by the creditor under pre-existing arrangements between himself and a person (the 'supplier') other than the debtor in the knowledge that the credit is to be used to finance a transaction between the debtor and the supplier.

14 Credit-token agreements (1) A credit-token is a card, cheque, voucher, coupon, stamp, form, booklet or other document or thing given to an individual by a person carrying on a consumer credit business, who undertakes –

(a) that on the production of it (whether or not some other action is also required) he will supply cash, goods and services (or any of them) on credit, or

(b) that where, on the production of it to a third party (whether or not any other action is also required), the third party supplies cash, goods and services (or any of them), he will pay the third party for them (whether or not deducting any discount or commission), in return for payment to him by the individual.

(2) A credit-token agreement is a regulated agreement for the provision of credit in connection with the use of a credit-token.

(3) Without prejudice to the generality of section 9(1), the person who gives to an individual an undertaking falling within subsection (1)(b) shall be taken to provide him with credit drawn on whenever a third party supplies him with cash, goods or services.

(4) For the purposes of subsection (1), use of an object to operate a machine provided by the person giving the object or a third party shall be treated as the production of the object to him.

48 Definition of canvassing off trade premises (regulated agreements) (1) An individual (the 'canvasser') canvasses a regulated agreement off trade premises if he solicits the entry (as debtor or hirer) of another individual (the 'consumer') into the agreement by making oral representations to the consumer, or any other individual, during a visit by the canvasser to any place (not excluded by subsection (2)) where the consumer, or that other individual, as the case may be, is, being a visit –

(a) carried out for the purpose of making such oral representations to individuals who are at that place, but

(b) not carried out in response to a request made on a previous occasion.

(2) A place is excluded from subsection (1) if it is a place where a business is carried on (whether on a permanent or temporary basis) by –

(a) the creditor or owner, or
(b) a supplier, or
(c) the canvasser, or the person whose employee or agent the canvasser is, or
(d) the consumer.

49 Prohibition of canvassing debtor-creditor agreements off trade premises (1) It is an offence to canvass debtor-creditor agreement off trade premises.

(2) It is also an offence to solicit the entry of an individual (as debtor) into a debtor-creditor agreement during a visit carried out in response to a request made on a previous occasion, where –

(a) the request was not in writing signed by or on behalf of the person making it, and
(b) if no request for the visit had been made, the soliciting would have constituted the canvassing of a debtor-creditor agreement off trade premises.

(3) Subsections (1) and (2) do not apply to any soliciting for an agreement enabling the debtor to overdraw on a current account of any description kept with the creditor, where –

(a) the Director has determined that current accounts of that description kept with the creditor are excluded from subsections (1) and (2), and
(b) the debtor already keeps an account with the creditor (whether a current account or not).

(4) A determination under subsection (3)(a) –

(a) may be made subject to such conditions as the Director thinks fit, and
(b) shall be made only where the Director is of opinion that it is not against the interests of debtors.

(5) If soliciting is done in breach of a condition imposed under subsection (4)(a) the determination under subsection (3)(a) does not apply to it.

50 Circulars to minors (1) A person commits an offence who, with a view to financial gain, sends to a minor any document inviting him to –

(a) borrow money, or
(b) obtain goods on credit or hire, or
(c) obtain services on credit, or
(d) apply for information or advice on borrowing money or otherwise obtaining credit, or hiring goods.

(2) In proceedings under subsection (1) in respect of the sending of a document to a minor, it is a defence for the person charged to prove that he did not know and had no reasonable cause to suspect, that he was a minor.

(3) Where a document is received by a minor at any school or educational establishment for minors, a person sending it to him at that establishment knowing or suspecting it to be such an establishment shall be taken to have reasonable cause to suspect that he is a minor.

51 Prohibition of unsolicited credit-tokens (1) It is an offence to give a person a credit-token if he has not asked for it.

(2) To comply with subsection (1) a request must be contained in a document signed by the person making the request, unless the credit-token agreement is a small debtor-creditor-supplier agreement.

(3) Subsection (1) does not apply to the giving of a credit-token to a person –

(a) for use under a credit-token agreement already made, or
(b) in renewal or replacement of a credit-token previously accepted by him under a credit-token agreement which continues in force, whether or not varied.

60 Form and content of agreements (1) The Secretary of State shall make regulations as to the form and content of documents embodying regulated agreements, and the regulations shall contain such provisions as appear to him appropriate with a view to ensuring that the debtor or hirer is made aware of –

(a) the right and duties conferred or imposed on him by the agreement,

(b) the amount and rate of the total charge for credit (in the case of a consumer credit agreement),

(c) the protection and remedies available to him under this Act, and

(d) any other matters which, in the opinion of the Secretary of State, it is desirable for him to know about in connection with the agreement.

(2) Regulations under subsection (1) may in particular –

(a) require specified information to be included in the prescribed manner in documents, and other specified material to be excluded,

(b) contain requirements to ensure that specified information is clearly brought to the attention of the debtor or hirer, and that one part of a document is not given insufficient or excessive prominence compared with another.

(3) If, on an application made to the Director by a person carrying on a consumer credit business or a consumer hire business, it appears to the Director impracticable for the applicant to comply with any requirement of regulations under subsection (1) in a particular case, he may, by notice to the applicant, direct that the requirement be waived or varied in relation to such agreements, and subject to such conditions (if any), as he may specify, and this Act and the regulations shall have effect accordingly.

(4) The Director shall give a notice under subsection (3) only if he is satisfied that to do so would not prejudice the interests of debtors or hirers.

61 Signing of agreement (1) A regulated agreement is not properly executed unless –

(a) a document in the prescribed form itself containing all the prescribed terms and conforming to regulations under section 60(1) is signed in the prescribed manner both by the debtor or hirer and by or on behalf of the creditor or owner, and

(b) the document embodies all the terms of the agreement, other than implied terms, and

(c) the document is, when presented or sent to the debtor or hirer for signature, in such a state that all its terms are readily legible.

(2) In addition, where the agreement is one to which section 58(1) applies, it is not properly executed unless –

(a) the requirements of section 58(1) were complied with, and

(b) the unexecuted agreement was sent, for his signature, to the debtor or hirer by post not less than seven days after a copy of it was given to him under section 58(1), and

(c) during the consideration period, the creditor or owner refrained from approaching the debtor or hirer (whether in person, by telephone or letter, or in any other way) except in response to a specific request made by the debtor or hirer after the beginning of the consideration period, and

(d) no notice of withdrawal by the debtor or hirer was received by the creditor or owner before the sending of the unexecuted agreement.

(3) In subsection (2) (c), 'the consideration period' means the period beginning with the giving of the copy under section 58(1) and ending –

(a) at the expiry of seven days after the day on which the unexecuted agreement is sent, for his signature, to the debtor or hirer, or

(b) on its return by the debtor or hirer after signature by him, whichever first occurs.

(4) Where the debtor or hirer is a partnership or an unincorporated body of persons, subsection (1)(a) shall apply with the substitution for 'by the debtor or hirer' of 'by or on behalf of the debtor or hirer'.

65 Consequences of improper execution (1) An improperly executed regular agreement is enforceable against the debtor or hirer on an order of the court only.

(2) A retaking of goods or land to which a regulated agreement relates is an enforcement of the agreement.

75 Liability of creditor for breaches by supplier (1) If the debtor under a debtor-creditor-supplier agreement falling within section 12(b) or (c) has, in relation to a transaction financed by the agreement, any claim against the supplier in respect of a misrepresentation or breach of contract, he shall have a like claim against the creditor, who, with the supplier, shall accordingly be jointly and severally liable to the debtor.

(2) Subject to any agreement between them, the creditor shall be entitled to be indemnified by the supplier for loss suffered by the creditor in satisfying his liability under subsection (1), including costs reasonably incurred by him in defending proceedings instituted by the debtor.

(3) Subsection (1) does not apply to a claim –

(a) under a non-commercial agreement, or

(b) so far as the claim relates to any single item to which the supplier attached a cash price not exceeding [£100] or more than [£30,000].

(4) This section applies notwithstanding that the debtor, in entering into transaction, exceeded the credit limit or otherwise contravened any term of the agreement.

(5) In an action brought against the creditor under subsection (1) he shall be entitled, in accordance with rules of court, to have the supplier made a party to the proceedings.

83 Liability for misuse of credit facilities (1) The debtor under a regulated consumer credit agreement shall not be liable to the creditor for any loss arising from use of the credit facility by another person not acting, or to be treated as acting, as the debtor's agent.

(2) This section does not apply to a non-commercial agreement or to any loss in so far as it arises from misuse of an instrument to which section 4 of the Cheques Act 1957 applies.

84 Misuse of credit-tokens (1) Section 83 does not prevent the debtor under a credit-token agreement from being made liable to the extent of [£50] (or the credit limit if lower) for loss to the creditor arising from use of the credit-token by other persons during a period beginning when the credit-token ceases to be in the possession of any authorised person and ending when the credit-token is once more in the possession of an authorised person.

(2) Section 83 does not prevent the debtor under a credit-token agreement from being made liable to any extent for loss to the creditor from use of the credit token by a person who acquired possession of it with the debtor's consent.

(3) Subsections (1) and (2) shall not apply to any use of the credit-token after the creditor has been given oral or written notice that it is lost or stolen, or is for any other reason liable to misuse.

(4) Subsections (1) and (2) shall not apply unless there are contained in the credit-token agreement in the prescribed manner particulars of the name address and telephone number of a person stated to be the person to whom notice is to be given under subsection (3).

(5) Notice under subsection (3) takes effect when received, but where it is given orally, and all the agreement so requires, it shall be treated as not taking effect if not confirmed in writing within seven days.

(6) Any sum paid by the debtor for the issue of the credit-token, to the extent (if any) that it had not been previously offset by use made of the credit-token, shall be treated as paid towards satisfaction of any liability under subsection (1) or (2).

(7) The debtor, the creditor, and any person authorised by the debtor to use the credit-token shall be authorised persons for the purposes of subsection (1).

(8) Where two or more credit-tokens are given under one credit-token agreement, the preceding provisions of this section apply to each credit-token separately.

126 Enforcement of land mortgages. A land mortgage securing a regulated agreement is enforceable (so far as provided in relation to the agreement) on an order of the court only.

127 Enforcement orders in cases of infringement (1) In the case of an application for an enforcement order under –

(a) section 65(1) (improperly executed agreements), or
(b) section 105(7)(a) or (b) (improperly executed security instruments), or

(c) section 111(2) (failure to serve copy of notice on surety), or

(d) section 124(1) or (2) (taking of negotiable instrument in contravention of section 123)

the court shall dismiss the application if, but (subject to subsections (3) and (4)) only if, it considers it just to do so having regard to –

(i)   prejudice caused to any person by the contravention in question, and the degree of culpability for it, and

(ii) the powers conferred on the court by subsection (2) and sections 135 and 136.

(2) If it appears to the court just to do so, it may in an enforcement order reduce or discharge any sum payable by the debtor or hirer, or any surety, so as to compensate him for prejudice suffered as a result of the contravention in question.

(3) The court shall not make an enforcement order under section 65(1) if section 61(1)(a) (signing of agreements) was not complied with unless a document (whether or not in the prescribed form and complying with regulations under section 60(1)) itself containing all the prescribed terms of the agreement was signed by the debtor or hirer (whether or not in the prescribed manner).

(4) The court shall not make an enforcement order under section 65(1) in the case of a cancellable agreement if –

(a) a provision of section 62 or 63 was not complied with, and the creditor or owner did not give a copy of the executed agreement, and of any other document referred to in it, to the debtor or hirer before the commencement of the proceedings in which the order is sought, or

(b) section 64(1) was not complied with.

(5) Where an enforcement order is made in a case to which subsection (3) applies, the order may direct that the regulated agreement is to have effect as if it did not include a term omitted from the document signed by the debtor or hirer.

Appendix 2
The Mortgage Code

THE CODE OF MORTGAGE LENDING PRACTICE

This is a voluntary code followed by lenders and mortgage inter-mediaries in their relations with personal customers in the United Kingdom. It sets standards of good mortgage lending practice which are followed as a minimum by those subscribing to it. As a voluntary code, it allows competition and market forces to operate to encourage higher standards for the benefit of customers.

The standards of the Code are encompassed in the 10 key commit-ments found at the beginning. These commitments apply to the conduct of business for all mortgage products and services provided to customers by lenders and mortgage intermediaries.

Banking practice is covered in more detail in the Banking Code issued by the British Bankers' Association, The Building Societies Association and the Association for Payment Clearing Services. Not all lenders subscribing to the Mortgage Code are members of the BBA, BSA and APACS.

The Code provides valuable safeguards for customers. It should help them understand how lenders and mortgage intermediaries are expected to deal with them. Customers should check which lenders subscribe to it by contacting the Council of Mortgage Lenders, and for mortgage intermediaries they should contact the Mortgage Code Register of Intermediaries. [Addresses for both of these organis-ations are shown on the inside front cover of this booklet.]

An Independent Review Body for the Banking and Mortgage Codes monitors compliance by lenders with the Code and also over-sees its review from time to time. Responsibility for monitoring mortgage intermediaries has been delegated by the Independent Review Body to the Mortgage Code Register of Intermediaries.

Within the Code, 'you' means the customer and 'we' means–

In Part 1 (Sections 1–3) – both lenders and mortgage intermediaries

In Part 2 (Sections 4–10) – lenders only

In Part 3 (Sections 11–16) – mortgage intermediaries only.

This Code was effective for lenders from 1 July 1997 and from April 1998 for mortgage intermediaries, except in relation to section 3.1(a) where the relevant dates are 31 March 1998 and 31 July 1998 respectively.

PART 1: BOTH LENDERS AND MORTGAGE INTERMEDIARIES

1.   KEY COMMITMENTS

1.1   We, the subscribers to this Code, promise that we will:

- act fairly and reasonably in all our dealings with you;
- ensure that all services and products comply with this Code, even if they have their own terms and conditions;
- give you information on our services and products in plain language, and offer help if there is any aspect which you do not understand;
- unless you have already decided on your mortgage, help you to choose a mortgage to fit your needs;
- help you to understand the financial implications of a mortgage;
- help you to understand how your mortgage account works;
- ensure that the procedures our staff follow reflect the commitments set out in this Code;
- correct errors and handle complaints speedily;
- consider cases of financial difficulty and mortgage arrears sympathetically and positively;
- ensure that all services and products comply with relevant laws and regulations.

2.   MARKETING OF MORTGAGES

Marketing loans to minors

2.1   We will not send marketing material indiscriminately and, in particular, we will be selective and careful if you are under eighteen years old and where material relates to loans.

Advertising

2.2   We will ensure that all our advertising and promotional material is clear, fair, reasonable and not misleading.

3.   HELPING YOU TO CHOOSE A MORTGAGE

Levels of service

3.1   Choosing a mortgage may be your most financial commitment. There are three levels of service which may be provided and we will tell you which we offer at the outset. These are:

(a) advice and a recommendation as to which mortgage is most suitable for you. When giving advice, we will take care to help you to select a mortgage to fit your needs by asking for relevant information about your circumstances and objectives. Our advice will also depend on your particular requirements and on the market conditions at the time. The reasons for the recommendation will be given to you in writing before you complete your mortgage. Where mortgage intermediaries plan to offer an advice and written recommendation service, they will do so by 31 July 1998.
(b) information on the different types of mortgage product we offer so that you can make an informed choice of which to take;
(c) information on a single mortgage product only, if we only offer one mortgage product or if you have already made up your mind.

Confirmation of service

Before you take out your mortgage, we will confirm, in writing, the level of service given.

Alternative repayment methods; Interest only mortgages; Early repayment; Interest rate alternatives; Future repayments; Insurance; Charges payable; Transfer of terms; Information to credit reference agencies; MIRAS; High percentage loans

3.2   When providing information to help you to choose a mortgage, for the purposes of (a), (b) and, for single product companies, (c), above, we will give you the following –

- an explanation of the main repayment methods we offer (for example, repayment or interest only) and the repayment periods available;
- for interest only mortgages:
- a general description of the types of investment (for example, endowment policy, personal equity plan, pension plan) or other means which may be used to repay the mortgage;
- an explanation of the effect of failing to make suitable arrangements to repay the mortgage;
- information on whose responsibility it is to ensure that an adequate repayment method is in place. Your lender will remind you annually of the need to make sure that an adequate repayment method is in place;
- an explanation that early repayment of a mortgage, early surrender of an investment, or changes in personal circumstances (for example, long-term sickness or relationship breakdown) can have adverse financial consequences, depending on the particular type of mortgage or investment;
- a description of the types of interest rates available (for example variable, fixed, discounted and capped rates);
- an explanation and illustration of future potential repayments at the end of any fixed, discounted or capped interest rate period, based on the current variable mortgage interest rate;
- a description of any insurance services which we can arrange (for example, buildings, contents, mortgage payment protection and life insurance);

- whether it is a condition of the mortgage that such insurance be taken out and whose responsibility it is to ensure that it is taken out;
- whether it is a condition of the mortgage that such insurance must be arranged by us;
- a general description of any costs, fees or other charges in connection with the mortgage which may be payable by you (for example, mortgage valuation fees, arrangement fees, early repayment charges, legal fees and insurance premiums);
- an explanation of whether your selected mortgage terms (for example, a fixed interest rate) can be continued if you move house;
- a description of when your account details may be passed to credit reference agencies;
- information on mortgage interest tax relief;
- if your mortgage represents a high percentage of the price or valuation of your property (usually 75% or more), you may have to pay a high percentage lending fee. Some or all of this fee may be used by the lender, at its discretion, to obtain mortgage indemnity insurance to act as extra security for its sole benefit. If this is the case, the lender will give you a written explanation, stating that:
- such insurance will not protect you if your property is subsequently taken into possession and sold for less than the amount you owe;
- you will remain liable to pay all sums owing, including arrears, interest and your lender's legal fees;
- if a claim is paid to your lender under such insurance, the insurers generally have the right to recover this amount from you.

PART 2: LENDERS ONLY

4.   LENDING

Financial assessment of the loan

4.1   All lending will be subject to our assessment of your ability to repay. This assessment may include:

- taking into account your income and commitments;
- how you have handled your financial affairs in the past;
- information obtained from credit reference agencies and, with your consent, others (for example employers, other lenders and landlords);
- information supplied by you, including verification of your identity and the purpose of the borrowing;
- credit assessment techniques (for example, credit scoring);
- your age;
- any security provided, including the condition and value of the property.

Guarantees

4.2   If you want to accept a guarantee or other security from someone for your liabilities, you may be asked to consent to the disclosure, by us, of your confidential information to the person giving the guarantee or other security or their legal adviser. We will also:

- encourage them to take independent legal advice to make sure that they understand their commitment and the potential consequences of their decision. All the documents they will be asked to sign will contain this recommendation as a clear and prominent notice;
- advise them that by giving the guarantee or other security they may become liable instead of or as well as you;
- advise them what the limit of their liability will be. An unlimited guarantee will not be taken.

5.   TERMS AND CONDITIONS

Plain language

5.1   All written terms and conditions will be fair in substance and will set out your rights and responsibilities clearly and in plain language, with legal and technical language used only where necessary.

Changes to terms and conditions

5.2   Occasionally terms and conditions may have to be changed. We will tell you how you will be notified of these changes and will give you reasonable notice before any change takes effect. If there have been significant changes in any one year, we will give or send you a copy of the new terms and conditions or a summary of the changes.

Interest rates

5.3   Before you take out a mortgage and at any time you ask, we will:

• tell you the interest rates which apply to your account(s) and will explain when interest is charged (for example, on the outstanding mortgage balance at the beginning of each year);
• tell you whether the interest rate may be varied;
• tell you when any capital repayments you make will reduce the balance and the outstanding interest on your mortgage.

Interest rate changes

5.4   The interest rate which applies to your account may change from time to time. When we change the interest rate we will tell you about the changes at the earliest opportunity by either:

• letter/other personal notice; or
• notices/leaflets in branches and press advertisements. If this option is used, we will tell you the interest rate applicable to your account at least once a year.

6.   CHARGES

Tariff

6.1   Before you take out a mortgage and at any time you ask, we will give you a tariff covering the operation and repayment of your mortgage, including charges and additional interest costs payable should you fall into arrears.

Other charges

6.2   We will tell you the charges for any other service or product before or when its provided or at any time you ask.

Tariff charges

6.3   We will send you a mortgage tariff each year, if there have been changes to it.

7.   CONFIDENTIALITY

Duty of privacy

7.1   We will treat all your personal information as private and confidential (even when you are no longer a customer). Nothing about your accounts, nor your name and address, will be disclosed to anyone, including other companies in our group, other than in four exceptional cases permitted by law.

Qualifications

These are:

- where we are legally compelled to do so;
- where there is a duty to the public to disclose;
- where our interests require disclosure;

This will not be used as a reason for disclosing information about you or your accounts (including your name and address) to anyone else including other companies in our group for marketing purposes.

- where disclosure is made at your request or with your consent.

Information to credit reference agencies

7.2   Information about your mortgage debts owed to us may be disclosed to credit reference agencies where:

- you have fallen behind with your payments; and
- the amount owed is not in dispute; and

- you have not made proposals satisfactory to us for repayment of your debt following formal demand; and
- you have been given at least 28 days' notice of our intention to disclose.

Information on possession cases

7.3   If we intend to take possession of your property, we will tell you that this information may be disclosed to credit reference agencies and that your name may be passed to other lenders by being placed on the CML Possessions Register.

Consent for other disclosures

7.4   We will not give up any other information about you to credit reference agencies without your consent.

Data protection access

7.5   We will explain that you have a right of access under the Data Protection Act 1984 to your personal records held on our computer files.

Marketing restrictions

7.6   Occasionally, we will bring to your attention additional services and products which may be of benefit to you. However, when you become a customer, we will give you the opportunity to say that you do not wish to receive this information.

No marketing reminder

7.7   We will remind you, at least once every three years, that you can ask not to receive this information.

Your Consent To Marketing

7.8   Unless you specifically request it, or give your express consent in writing, we will not pass your name and address to any company, including other companies in our group, for marketing purposes.

Responding to other marketing

7.9   We may tell you about another company's services or products, and if you respond positively, you may be contacted directly by that company.

8.   FINANCIAL DIFFICULTIES

Considering cases

8.1   We will consider cases of financial difficulty and mortgage arrears sympathetically and positively. Our first step will be to try to contact you to discuss the matter.

How we can help

8.2   **If you find yourself in financial difficulties you should let us know as soon as possible. We will do all we can to help you to overcome your difficulties. The sooner we discuss your problems, the easier will be for both of us to find a solution. The more you tell us about your full financial circumstances the more we may be able to help.**

General principles

8.3   We will follow the general principles of the CML's Statement of Practice on Handling Arrears and Possessions, including:

- with your co-operation, develop a plan with you for dealing with your financial difficulties and clearing the arrears, consistent with both our interests and yours;
- possession of your property will be sought only as a last resort

when attempts to reach alternative arrangements with you have been unsuccessful.

Co-operating with recognised debt advice agencies

8.4   If you are in difficulties, you can also get help and advice from debt counselling organisations. At your request and with your consent, we will liaise, wherever possible, with debt counselling organisations that we recognise, for example:

- Citizens Advice Bureau; or
- Money advice centres; or
- The Consumer Credit Counselling Service.

9.   COMPLAINTS

Internal complaints procedure

9.1   We have internal procedures for handling complaints fairly and speedily and we will tell you what these are. These will include establishing a set time for an initial acknowledgement to your complaint. We will tell you how long it might take us to respond more fully.

Making complaints

9.2   If you wish to make a complaint, we will tell you how to do so and what to do if you are not happy about the outcome. Staff will help you with any queries.

Ombudsmen and arbitration

9.3   Lenders have separate independent Ombudsmen or arbitration schemes. The Ombudsmen or arbitrators are available to resolve certain complaints made by you if the matter remains unresolved through our internal complaints procedures.

9.4   Lenders subscribing to this Code belong to one or other of the following:

- The Banking Ombudsman Scheme;
- The Building Societies Ombudsman Scheme;
- The Mortgage Code Arbitration Scheme.

9.5   We will display a notice in a prominent position in all our branches stating which Ombudsman or arbitration scheme we belong to and that copies of the Code are available on request.

9.6   We will give you details about which Ombudsmen or arbitration scheme is available to you.   You can also get information by contacting the appropriate Ombudsman or arbitration scheme at the addresses listed below.

> The Office of the Banking Ombudsman
> 70 Gray's Inn Road
> London WCIX 8NB
> Tel: 0171 404 9944
> Enquiries only – LO-call Tel: 0345 660902

> The Office of the Building Societies Ombudsman
> Millbank Tower
> Millbank
> London SWIP 4XS
> Tel: 0171 931 0044

> The Mortgage Code Arbitration Scheme
> The Chartered Institute of Arbitrators
> 24 Angel Gate
> City Road
> London EC1V 2RS
> Tel: 0171 837 4483

10.   MONITORING AND COMPLIANCE

Complying with the law and other codes

10.1   We will comply with the law and relevant codes of practice or similar documents which are followed by members of the Council of Mortgage Lenders. The main codes include:

CML Statement of Practice on Handling Arrears and Possessions;

CML Statement of Practice on the Transfer of Mortgages;
BBA/BSA/APACS Banking Code;
Association of British Insurers General Business Code of Practice;
British Codes of Advertising and Sales Promotion;
Independent Television Commission Code of Advertising Practice;
Guide to Credit Scoring.
Compliance officer and internal audit

10.2   We have a 'Code Compliance Officer' and our internal auditing procedures monitor compliance with the Code.

Compliance by mortgage intermediaries

10.3   We will only accept business from mortgage intermediaries who are registered with the Mortgage Code Register of Intermediaries and have thereby given an undertaking to comply with the code. We are not responsible for mortgage intermediaries' actions or advice, unless they are our appointed agent for mortgage business. Your mortgage intermediary should tell you if this is the case. Your mortgage intermediary will disclose to you whether it will receive a fee for arranging your mortgage. Before you take out your mortgage, we will tell you if your mortgage intermediary will receive a fee for arranging your mortgage. On request, we will confirm to you the amount.

Independent Review Body

10.4   The Code is monitored by the Independent Review Body for the Banking and Mortgage Codes comprised of representatives from the banks and building societies and independent consumers. The address is:
Pinners Hall, 105–108 Old Broad Street, London EC2N 1EX.
Tel: 0171 216 8800.
Complaints concerning the general operation of the Code can be made to them.

Statement of compliance

10.5   We complete a 'Statement of Compliance' every year which is signed by our Chief Executive and sent to the Independent Review Body for the Banking and Mortgage Codes.

PART 3: MORTGAGE INTERMEDIARIES ONLY

11.   DISCLOSURE OF STATUS

Appointed agent status

11.1   At the outset, we will tell you if we are the appointed agent for a lender for mortgage business and therefore act on their behalf, in which case they are responsible for our actions and advice.   Alternatively at the outset, we will tell you that we act on your behalf.

Access to the market

11.2   We will explain whether we usually arrange mortgages from a selection of preferred lenders, based on our research of the market, or from the market as a whole. If a selection of lenders is used, we will give you details.

12.   FEES AND CHARGES

Disclosures Of Fees

12.1   At the outset, we will tell you if we will receive a fee for arranging your mortgage. Before you take out a mortgage, we will tell you the amount of the fee in writing. If the fee is less than £250, we will confirm that we will receive up to this amount.   If the fee is £250 or more, we will tell you the exact amount.

Other Services

12.2   We will tell you the charges for any other service or product before or when it is provided or at any time you ask.

13.   TERMS AND CONDITIONS

13.1   All written terms and conditions will be fair in substance and will set out your rights and responsibilities clearly and in plain language, with legal and technical language used only where necessary.

14.   CONFIDENTIALITY

Duty of privacy

14.1   We will treat all your personal information as private and confidential (even when you are no longer a customer), except where disclosure is made at your request or with your consent in relation to arranging your mortgage.

Data protection access

14.2   We will explain that you have a right of access under the Data Protection Act 1984 to your personal records held on our computer files.

15.   COMPLAINTS

Internal complaints procedure

15.1   We have internal procedures for handling complaints fairly and speedily and we will tell what these are. These will include establishing a set time for an initial acknowledgement to your complaint. We will tell you how long it might take us to respond more fully.

Making complaints

15.2 If you wish to make a complaint, we will tell you how to do so and what to do if you are not happy about the outcome. We will help you with any queries.

Arbitration

15.3 Where applicable, we will display a notice in a prominent position in all our branches stating that we belong to the Mortgage Code Arbitration Scheme and that copies of the Code are available on request. The arbitrators are available to resolve certain complaints made by you if the matter remains unresolved through our interest complaints procedure. The address of the Scheme is:

> The Mortgage Code Arbitration Scheme
> The Chartered Institute of Arbitrators
> 24 Angel Gate
> City Road
> London EC1V 2RS
> Tel: 0171 837 4483

16. MONITORING AND COMPLIANCE

Compliance officer and internal audit

16.1 We have a 'Code compliance officer' and our internal auditing procedures will include monitoring compliance with the Code.

Independent Review Body

16.2 The Code is monitored by the Independent Review Body for the Banking and Mortgage Codes comprised of representatives from the banks and building societies and independent consumers. The address is:

> Pinners Hall
> 105–108 Old Broad Street

London EC2N 1EX
Tel: **0171 216 8800**

Complaints concerning the general operation of the Code can be made to them.

Mortgage Code Register of Intermediaries

16.3   The Mortgage Code Register of Intermediaries keeps a list of mortgage intermediaries which have undertaken to comply with the Code. The address is:

> The Mortgage Code Register of Intermediaries
> Festival Way
> Festival Park
> Stoke-on-Trent
> Staffordshire ST1 5TA
> Tel: **01782 216300**

Complaints concerning the general operation of the Code by mortgage intermediaries can be made to them.

PART 4: HELP SECTION

What Loans does this Code apply to?

This Code applies to all loans (not overdrafts) secured on the home which you, as a personal customer, own and occupy, unless the loan is governed by the Consumer Credit Act 1974 (when the provisions and protection of that Act apply to your loan), The Code does not apply to the selling of investments which are covered by the Financial Services Act 1986.

Sponsoring Association

Enquiries about the Code and requests for copies of it can be addressed to the Council of Mortgage Lenders or the Mortgage Code Register of Intermediaries, [whose address and telephone numbers are shown on the inside front cover of this booklet.]

Copies of the Code

All subscribers of the Code will make copies of it available to customers. Copies of the Code of Banking Practice are available from the British Bankers Association, Pinners Hall, 105–108 Old Broad Street, London EC2N 1EX. Tel: 0171–216 8800.

Additional Information

Additional information on a variety of mortgage matters is available in the form of 'Factsheets' available from the Council of Mortgage Lenders. In addition the CML operates a recorded customer information line, [the number of which appears on the inside front cover of this booklet.]

USEFUL DEFINITIONS

These definitions explain the meaning of words and terms used in the Code. They are not precise legal or technical definitions.

Credit Reference Agencies

Organisations licensed under the Consumer Credit Act 1974, which hold information about individuals which is of relevance to lenders. Lenders may refer to these agencies to assist with various decisions, eg whether or not to provide a loan. Lenders may give information or seek information from the agencies.

Credit Scoring

This is a system which lenders use to assist in making decisions about granting consumer credit. Credit scoring uses statistical techniques to measure the likelihood that an application for credit will be a good credit risk.

Guarantee

An undertaking given by a person called the guarantor promising to pay the debts of another if that person fails to do so.

Mortgage Intermediary

An individual, firm or organisation which helps customers to choose a mortgage and introduces mortgage applications to lenders. Mortgage intermediaries include, for example, estate agents, mortgage brokers, independent financial advisers, solicitors, accountants and life assurance companies.

Personal Customer

A private individual who maintains an account (including a joint account with another private individual, but excluding the accounts of sole traders, partnerships, companies, clubs and societies) or who receives other services from a lender.

Security

A word used to describe items of value such as title deeds to houses, share certificates, life policies etc, which represent assets used as support for a loan. Under a secured loan the lender has the right to sell the security if the loan is not repaid.

Tariff

A list of charges for services provided by a lender.

Second edition: April 1998
Published by the Council of Mortgage Lenders

Appendix 3
The Banking Code

This is a voluntary Code followed by banks and building societies in their relations with personal customers in the United Kingdom. It sets standards of good banking practice which are followed as a minimum by banks and building societies subscribing to it. As a voluntary Code, it allows competition and market forces to operate to encourage higher standards for the benefit of customers. The standards of the Code are encompassed in the 11 key commitments found at the beginning. These commitments apply to the conduct of business for all products and services provided to customers.

Mortgages are covered in more detail in the Council of Mortgage Lenders' Code of Mortgage Lending Practice. Not all subscribers to the Banking Code are members of the Council of Mortgage Lenders.

The Code provides valuable safeguards for customers. It should help them understand how banks and building societies are expected to deal with them. Customers should check who subscribes to it by contacting the Associations shown opposite.

The Independent Banking Code Review Body for the Banking and Mortgage Codes monitors compliance by banks and building societies with the Code and also oversees its review from time to time.

Copies of the Code are available from banks and building societies and the Associations shown opposite.

Within the Code, 'you' means the customer and 'we' means the bank or building society the customer deals with.

It is effective from 1 July 1997 unless otherwise indicated.

1. KEY COMMITMENTS

1.1 We, the subscribers to this Code, promise that we will:

- act fairly and reasonably in all our dealings with you;

- ensure that all services and products comply with this Code, even if they have their own terms and conditions;

- give you information on our services and products in plain language, and offer help if there is any aspect which you do not understand;

- help you to choose a service or product to fit your needs;

- help you to understand the financial implications of:

- a mortgage;
  other borrowing;
  savings and investment products;
  card products.

- help you to understand how your accounts work;

- have safe, secure and reliable banking and payment systems;

- ensure that the procedures our staff follow reflect the commitments set out in this Code;

- correct errors and handle complaints speedily;

- consider cases of financial difficulty and mortgage arrears sympathetically and positively;

- ensure that all services and products comply with relevant laws and regulations.

2. INFORMATION

INFORMATION AVAILABLE

2.1 When you become a customer and at any time you ask, we will give you:

Key features

- Clear written information explaining the key features of our main services and products;

Your account

- information on how your account works, including:

  stopping a cheque or other types of payment;
  when funds can be withdrawn after a credit has been paid into your account and when funds begin to earn interest;
  unpaid cheques;
  when your account details may be passed to credit reference agencies;

Tariff

- a tariff, covering basic account services. This will also be available in branches;

Interest rates

- Information on the interest rates which apply to your account(s), when interest will be deducted or paid to you and the basis on which interest is calculated.

ATM charges

2.2 We will give you details of any charges we make for using Automated Teller Machines (ATMs) when we issue the card.

Overdrafts and fixed term products

2.3 We will tell you of any additional charges and interest you may have to pay if:

- your account becomes overdrawn without agreement;
- you exceed your overdraft limit;
- your loan falls into arrears;
- you change your mind about a fixed term product.

Mortgage tariff

2.4 Before you take out a mortgage and at any time you ask, we will give you a tariff covering the operation and repayment of your mortgage, including charges and additional interest costs payable should you fall into arrears.

Other charges

2.5 We will tell you the charges for any other service or product before or when it is provided or at any time you ask.

TERMS & CONDITIONS

Plain language

2.6 All written terms and conditions will be fair in substance and will set out your rights and responsibilities clearly and in plain language, with legal and technical language used only where necessary.

Joint accounts

2.7 If you have a joint account, we will give you additional information on your rights and responsibilities.

Closure

2.8 We will not close your account without giving you reasonable notice.

KEEPING YOU INFORMED OF CHANGES

Terms and conditions

2.9 Occasionally terms and conditions may have to be changed. We will tell you how you will be notified of these changes and will give you reasonable notice before any change takes effect. If there have been significant changes in any one year, we will give or send you a copy of the new terms and conditions or a summary of the changes.

Charges

2.10 If we increase a charge for basic account services, we will give you reasonable notice.

Interest rates

2.11 The interest rates which apply to your accounts may change from time to time. When we change the interest rates we will tell you about the changes at the earliest opportunity by either:
letter/other personal notice; or
notices/leaflets in branches and press advertisements. If this option is used, we will tell you the interest rate applicable to your account at least once a year, unless you have a type of account which has a passbook. If this is the case, you can collect this information from us whenever you update your passbook (which you are encouraged to do at least once a year).

Superseded accounts

2.12 If you have a type of savings or investment account, other than a fixed rate account, which is no longer available to customers, we will send you, once a year, a summary of all our interest rates. To help you compare interest rates and to consider whether or not to switch your money into another account, those accounts no longer available to customers will be clearly marked.

MARKETING OF SERVICES

2.13 Occasionally we will bring to your attention additional services and products which may be of benefit to you. However, when you become a customer, we will give you the opportunity to say that you do not wish to receive this information.
2.14 We will remind you, at least once every three years, that you can ask not to receive this information.

Consent to marketing

2.15 Unless you specifically request it, or give your express consent in writing, we will not pass your name and address to any company, including other companies in our group, for marketing purposes. You will not be asked to give your permission in return for basic banking services.

Host mailing

2.16 We may tell you about another company's services or products and, if you respond positively, you may be contacted directly by that company.

Minors

2.17 We will not send marketing material indiscriminately and, in particular, we will be selective and careful if you are under eighteen years old or where material relates to loans and overdrafts.

Advertising

2.18 We will ensure that all advertising and promotional material is clear, fair, reasonable and not misleading.

HELPING YOU TO CHOOSE A MORTGAGE

2.19 Choosing a mortgage may be your most important financial commitment. There are three levels of service which may be provided and we will tell you which we offer at the outset. These are:

(a) advice and a recommendation as to which of our mortgages is most suitable for you. When giving advice, we will take care to help you to select a mortgage to fit your needs by asking for relevant information about your circumstances and objectives. Our advice will also depend on your particular needs and requirements and on the market conditions at the time. The reasons for the recommendation will be given to you in writing before you complete your mortgage. If we plan to offer this service we will do so by 31 March 1998;

(b) information on the different types of mortgage products we offer so that you can make an informed choice of which to take;

(c) information on a single mortgage product only, if we offer only one mortgage product or if you have already made up your mind.

Before you take out your mortgage, we will confirm, in writing, the level of service given.

2.20 Mortgages are covered in more detail in the Council of Mortgage Lenders' Code of Mortgage Lending Practice.

HELPING YOU TO CHOOSE SAVINGS & INVESTMENT ACCOUNTS

2.21 We will take care to give you clear and appropriate information on the different types of savings and investment accounts available from us to help you to make an informed choice on the product to fit your needs. We will help you understand how your savings and investment accounts work, including any additional charges or loss of interest for withdrawal or cancellation.

2.22 We will give you information on a single savings or investment account if you have already made up your mind.

3. ACCOUNT OPERATIONS

RUNNING YOUR ACCOUNT

Statements

3.1 To help you manage your account and check entries on it, we will give you regular account statements.

These are normally provided monthly, quarterly or as a minimum annually, unless this is not appropriate for the type of account (for example on a passbook account). You may ask for account statements to be sent more frequently than normally available on your type of account.

3.2 If you have a type of account which is accessible by card, and you have a card, we will introduce systems by I July 1999 to send you account statements at least quarterly if there have been any card transactions on that account. This does not apply to passbook accounts.

3.3 If your statement or passbook has an entry which seems to be wrong, you should tell us as soon as possible so that we can resolve matters.

Pre-notification

3.4 If charges and/or debit interest accumulate to your current or savings account during a charging period, you will be given at least 14 days' notice of the amount before it is deducted from your account. The 14 days start from the date of posting the notification.

Cheques

3.5 We will keep original cheques paid from your account or copies for at least six years except where these have already been returned to you.

3.6 If, within a reasonable period after the entry has been made, there is a dispute with us about a cheque paid from your account, we will give you the cheque or a copy as evidence (except where the cheque has already been returned to you). If there is an unreasonable delay we will recredit your account until the matter is resolved.

3.7 If you already have your paid cheques returned, we will continue to return your cheques or copies to you and we will tell you our charges for this service.

3.8 When we need to tell you that one of your cheques or other items has been returned unpaid, we will do this either by letter or by other private and confidential means.

CARDS & PINS

3.9 We will send you a card only if you request it or to replace one which has already been issued.

3.10 Your PIN (Personal Identification Number) will be advised only to you and will be issued separately from your card.

PIN self selection

3.11 We will tell you if you can select your own PIN and, if so, you will be encouraged to do so carefully. This should make it easier for you to remember your PIN.
We will have systems in place to allow you to select your own PIN by 1 July 2000.
3.12 You can ask not to be issued with a PIN.

LENDING

Financial assessment

3.13 All lending will be subject to our assessment of your ability to repay. This assessment may include:
taking into account your income and commitments;
how you have handled your financial affairs in the past;
information obtained from credit reference agencies and, with your consent, others, for example employers, other lenders and landlords;
information supplied by you, including verification of your identity and the purpose of the borrowing;
credit assessment techniques, for example credit scoring;
your age;
any security provided.

Guarantees

3.14 If you want us to accept a guarantee or other security from someone for your liabilities, you may be asked to consent to the disclosure, by us, of your confidential financial information to the person giving the guarantee or other security or to their legal adviser. We will also:
encourage them to take independent legal advice to make sure that they understand their commitment and the potential consequences of their decision. All the documents they will be asked to sign will contain this recommendation as a clear and prominent notice;
advise them that by giving the guarantee or other security they may become liable instead of or as well as you;

advise them of what the limit of their liability will be. An unlimited guarantee will not be taken.

FOREIGN EXCHANGE SERVICES

3.15 We will give you an explanation of the service, details of the exchange rate and an explanation of the charges which apply to any foreign exchange transactions which you are about to make. Where this is not possible, we will tell you the basis on which these will be worked out.

3.16 If you wish to transfer money abroad, we will tell you how this is done and will give you, at least, the following information:

a description of the services and how to use them;

an explanation of when the money you have sent abroad should get there and any reason for potential delays;

any commission or charges which you will have to pay, including a warning where a foreign bank's charges may also have to be paid by the recipient.

4. PROTECTION

CONFIDENTIALITY

4.1 We will treat all your personal information as private and confidential (even when you are no longer a customer). Nothing about your accounts nor your name and address will be disclosed to anyone, including other companies in our group, other than in four exceptional cases permitted by law. These are:

where we are legally compelled to do so;
where there is a duty to the public to disclose;
where our interests require disclosure;

This will not be used as a reason for disclosing information about you or your accounts (including your name and address) to anyone else including other companies in our group for marketing purposes.

where disclosure is made at your request or with your consent;

Credit reference agencies

4.2 Information about your personal debts owed to us may be disclosed to credit reference agencies where:
you have fallen behind with your payments; and
the amount owed is not in dispute; and
you have not made proposals satisfactory to us for repayment of your debt following formal demand; and
you have been given at least 28 days' notice of our intention to disclose.
4.3 We will not give any other information about you to credit reference agencies without your consent.

Data protection

4.4 We will explain that you have a right of access under the Data Protection Act 1984 to your personal records held on our computer files.

Bankers' references

4.5 We will tell you if we provide bankers' references. If a banker's reference about you is requested, we will require your written consent before it is given.

PROTECTING YOUR ACCOUNTS

Identification

4.6 When you first apply to open an account, we will tell you what identification we need to prove identity. This is important for your security and is required by law. We will also tell you what checks we may make with credit reference agencies.
4.7 If we record telephone conversations, our terms and conditions will explain this.

Taking care

4.8 The care of your cheque book, passbook, cards, electronic purse, PINs, passwords and selected personal information is essential to help prevent fraud and protect your accounts. Please ensure that you:

do not keep your cheque book and cards together;

do not allow anyone else to use your card, PIN and/or password;

always take reasonable steps to keep your card safe and your PIN, password and selected personal information secret at all times;

never write down or record your PIN on the card or on anything kept with or near it;

never write down or record your PIN, password or selected personal information without disguising it, for example, never write down or record your PIN using the numbers in the correct order;

destroy the notification of your PIN and/or password as soon as you receive it.

4.9 It is essential that you tell us as soon as you can if you suspect or discover that:

your cheque book, passbook, card and/or electronic purse has been lost or stolen;

someone else knows your PIN, password or your selected personal information.

Loss – what to do

4.10 The fastest method of notifying us is by telephone, using the numbers previously advised or in telephone directories.

4.11 Once you have told us that a cheque book, passbook, card or lectronic purse has been lost or stolen or that someone else knows your PIN, password or selected personal information, we will take immediate steps to prevent these from being used to access your accounts.

4.12 We will refund you the amount of any transaction together with any interest and charges:

where you have not received your card and it is misused by someone else;

for all transactions not authorised by you after you have told us that someone else knows your PIN, password or selected personal information;

if additional money is transferred from your account to your electronic purse after you have told us of its loss, theft or that someone else knows your PIN;

where faults have occurred in the ATMs, or associated systems used, which were not obvious or subject to a warning message or notice at the time of use.

Electronic purse

4.13 You should treat your electronic purse like cash in a wallet. You will lose any money left in the electronic purse at the time it is lost or stolen, in just the same way as if you lost your wallet. However, if your electronic purse is credited by unauthorised withdrawals from your account before you tell us of its loss, theft or misuse, your liability for such amounts will be limited to a maximum of £50, unless you have acted fraudulently or with gross negligence.

Cards

4.14 If your card is misused before you tell us of its loss or theft, or that someone else knows your PIN, your liability will be limited to a maximum of £50, unless you have acted fraudulently or with gross negligence.

4.15 Where a card transaction is disputed, we have the burden of proving fraud or gross negligence or that you have received your card. In such cases we would expect you to co-operate with us and with the police in any investigation.

Fraud and gross negligence

4.16 If you act fraudulently you will be liable for all losses. If you act with gross negligence which has caused losses you may be liable for them. This may apply if you fail to follow the safeguards set out in section 4.8.

5. DIFFICULTIES

FINANCIAL DIFFICULTIES

5.1 We will consider cases of financial difficulty sympathetically and positively. Our first step will be to try to contact you to discuss the matter.

How we can help

5.2 If you find yourself in financial difficulties, you should let us know as soon as possible. We will do all we can to help you to overcome your difficulties. The sooner we discuss your problems, the easier it will be for both of us to find a solution. The more you tell us about your full financial circumstances, the more we may be able to help.

5.3 With your cooperation, we will develop a plan with you for dealing with your financial difficulties, consistent with both our interests and yours.

5.4 If you are in difficulties you can also get help and advice from debt counselling organisations. At your request and with your consent, we will liaise, wherever possible, with debt counselling organisations that we recognise, for example:

Citizens Advice Bureaux; or

Money advice centres: or

The Consumer Credit Counselling Service.

COMPLAINTS

Internal procedures

5.5 We have internal procedures for handling complaints fairly and speedily and we will tell you what these are. These will include establishing a set time for an initial acknowledgement to your complaint. We will tell you how long it might take us to respond more fully.

5.6 If you wish to make a complaint, we will tell you how to do so and what to do if you are not happy about the outcome. Staff will help you with any queries.

Ombudsmen

5.7 Banks and building societies have separate independent ombudsmen or arbitration schemes. The ombudsmen or arbitrators are available to resolve certain complaints made by you if the matter remains unresolved through our internal complaints procedures.

5.8 All building societies must belong to the Building Societies Ombudsman Scheme.

5.9 All banks subscribing to this Code must belong to the Banking Ombudsman Scheme or, where appropriate, to one of the arbitration chemes listed overleaf.

5.10 We will display a notice in a prominent position in all our branches stating which Ombudsman or arbitration scheme we belong to and that copies of the Code are available on request.

5.11 We will give you details about which Ombudsman or arbitration scheme is available to you. You can also get information by contacting the appropriate Ombudsman or arbitration scheme at the addresses listed below.

> The Office of the Banking Ombudsman
> 70 Gray's Inn Road
> London WC1X 8NB
> Tel: 0171 404 9944
> Enquiries only –
> LO-call Tel: 0345 660902

> The Office of the Building Societies Ombudsman
> Millbank Tower
> Millbank
> London SW1P 4XS
> Tel: 0171 931 0044

> The Finance and Leasing Association Arbitration Scheme
> 18 Upper Grosvenor Street
> London W1X 9PB
> Tel: 0171 491 2783

The Consumer Credit Trade Association Arbitration Scheme
Tennyson House
159 Great Portland Street
London W1N 5FD
Tel: 0171 636 7564

MONITORING & COMPLIANCE

5.12 We will comply with the law and follow relevant codes of practice or similar documents as members of the British Bankers' Association (BBA), The Building Societies Association (BSA) and the Association for Payment Clearing Services (APACS). The main codes include:

BBA, BSA, FLA Code of Practice on the Advertising of Interest Bearing Accounts;
BBA Guide to Bankers' References (Status Enquiries);
BSA Code of Practice on Linking of Services;
CML Code of Mortgage Lending Practice;
CML Statement of Practice on Handling Arrears and Possessions;
CML Statement of Practice on the Transfer of Mortgages;
Association of British Insurers (ABI) General Business Code of Practice;
British Codes of Advertising and Sales Promotion;
ITC (Independent Television Commission) Code of Advertising Practice;
Guide to Credit Scoring.

5.13 We have a 'Code Compliance Officer' and our internal auditing procedures monitor compliance with the Code.

Review body

5.14 The Code is monitored by the Independent Review Body for the Banking and Mortgage Codes comprised of representatives from the banks and building societies and independent consumers. The address is:

Pinners Hall
105–108 Old Broad Street
London EC2N 1EX
Tel: 0171 216 8800

Complaints concerning the general operation of the Code can be made to them.

5.15 We complete a 'Statement of Compliance' every year which is signed by our Chief Executive and sent to the Independent Review Body for the Banking and Mortgage Codes.

6. HELP SECTION

Sponsoring associations

Enquiries about the Code and requests for copies of it can be addressed to the British Bankers' Association, The Building Societies Association and the Association for Payment Clearing Services. The addresses and telephone numbers are shown at the front of this booklet.

Copies of the Code

All institutions subscribing to the Code will make copies of it available to customers. Copies of the CML Code of Mortgage Lending Practice are available from the Council of Mortgage Lenders (CML) 3 Savile Row, London W1X 1AF, recorded help line telephone number 0171 440 2255.

Additional information

Additional information on a variety of banking and mortgage matters is available in the form of 'Bank Facts' from the BBA, 'Fact Sheets' and information leaflets from the BSA and the CML and 'Pay Points' from APACS. In addition, the Associations operate customer information lines or 'help lines'.

USEFUL DEFINITIONS

These definitions explain the meaning of words and terms used in the Code. They are not precise legal or technical definitions.

ATM (Automated Teller Machine)

A cash machine or free standing device dispensing cash and providing other information or services to customers who have a card.

Banker's reference

A banker's reference is an opinion about a particular customer's ability to enter into or repay a financial commitment.

Basic banking service

The opening, maintenance and operation of accounts for money transmission by means of cheque and other debit instruments. This would normally be a current account.

Cards

A general term for any plastic card which may be used to pay for goods and services or to withdraw cash. For the purposes of this Code, it excludes electronic purses.

Credit reference agencies

Organisations, licensed under the Consumer Credit Act 1974, which hold information about individuals which is of relevance to lenders. Banks and building societies may refer to these agencies to assist with various decisions, e.g. whether or not to open an account or provide loans or grant credit. Banks and building societies may give information to or seek information from these agencies.

Credit scoring

A system which banks and building societies use to assist in making decisions about granting consumer credit. Credit scoring uses statistical techniques to measure the likelihood that an application for credit will be a good credit risk.

Electronic purses

Any card or function of a card which contains real value in the form of electronic money which someone has paid for in advance, some of which can be reloaded with further funds and which can be used for a range of purposes.

Guarantee

An undertaking given by a person called the guarantor promising to pay the debts of another if that other person fails to do so.

Out of date cheque

A cheque which has not been paid because its date is too old, normally more than six months.

Password

A word or an access code which the customer has selected to permit them access to a telephone or home banking service and which is also used for identification.

Personal customer

A private individual who maintains an account (including a joint account with another private individual or an account held as an executor or trustee, but excluding the accounts of sole traders, partnerships, companies, clubs and societies) or who receives other services from a bank or building society.

PIN (Personal Identification Number)

A number provided on a strictly confidential basis by a bank or building society to a card holder. Use of this number by the customer will allow the card to be used to withdraw cash and access other services from an Automated Teller Machine (ATM).

Security

A word used to describe items of value such as title deeds to houses, share certificates, life policies etc, which represent assets used as support for a loan. Under a secured loan the lender has the right to sell the security if the loan is not repaid.

Selected personal information

A selection of memorable facts and information of a private and personal nature chosen by the customer (the sequence of which is known only to the customer) which can be used for identification and to verify identification when accessing accounts.

Tariff

A list of charges for services provided by a bank or building society.

Unpaid cheque

This is a term for a cheque which, after being paid into the account of a person to whom it is payable, is subsequently returned 'unpaid' ('bounced') by the bank or building society whose customer issued the cheque. This leaves the person to whom the cheque is payable without the money in his/her account.

Third Edition March 1997

Subject Index